Revolution of Innovation Management

Acknowledgements

We would like to express our gratitude to Madeleine Holder and Liz Barlow at Palgrave Macmillan. We also thank the authors for their patience in going through several revisions, as well as Kari Kleine for his engagement.

Contents

Notes on Contributors

Alexander Brem is Professor of Technology and Innovation Management at the Mads Clausen Institute (MCI), University of Southern Denmark. He is also Head of SDU Innovation and Design Engineering, an interdisciplinary department in the Faculty of Engineering. His research interest focuses on technology and innovation management, with a special focus on boundaries to psychology, marketing, and entrepreneurship.

Uwe Cantner is currently Full Professor and Chair of Economics/Microeconomics at the Department of Economics and Business Administration at the Friedrich Schiller University Jena (FSU) and Temporary Professor at the Department of Marketing and Management, I2M Group at the University of Southern Denmark. Besides that, he is among others member of the *Expertenkommission Forschung und Innovation* (expert commission on research and innovation) at the German Federal Government and holds the position of Vice-President for Young Researchers and Diversity Management at the Friedrich Schiller University Jena. Recent research fields comprise entrepreneurial success and failure, team structure and performance, firm strategies and open innovation, the dynamics of knowledge exchange in invention and innovation collaboration, innovation dynamics related to systems transitions, and industrial dynamics in relation to General Purpose Technologies as well as policy programs. Research has been published among others in *Applied Economics, Economica, Empirica, European Planning Studies, Homo Oeconomicus, Industrial and Corporate Change, Industry* *and Innovation, International Business Review, Journal of Business and Psychology, Journal of Common Market Studies, Journal of Economic Coordination and Inter-action, Journal of Economic Psychology, Journal of Evolutionary Economics, Journal of Innovation Economics, Journal of Knowledge Management, Journal of Vocational Behaviour, Metroeconomica, Papers in Regional Science, Regional Studies, Research Policy, Small Business Economics, Social Indicators Research,* and *Technovation.*

Jin Chen is a professor in the Department of Innovation, Entrepreneurship and Strategy at Tsinghua SEM. He received his Bachelor's degree in chemical process control in the Department of Chemical Engineering from Zhejiang University in 1989; and his PhD in Management Engineering in the Department of Management also from Zhejiang University in 1994. Dr Chen went to MIT Sloan School of Management in 1998 as a visiting scholar. In 2000, he went to SPRU of Sussex University as a visiting fellow. Dr Chen has been awarded a Special Government Allowance from the State Council of China, the Huo Yingdong Youth Teacher Prize, and the Third "Young university teachers award" from the Ministry of Education of China. He was awarded the Outstanding Youth Fund in 2002 by the National Science Foundation of China. In 2009, he was selected for the China's National Talents Project. In 2014, Professor Chen was honored as a distinguished professor of Chang Jiang scholars, and he is the first Chang Jiang scholar in the field of China's technological innovation management. Dr Chen worked as the Executive Vice Dean of the Undergraduate School and the Chu Kechen Honors College before joining Tsinghua SEM. His research and teaching mainly focuses on management of technological innovation.

Robin Chu is Manager at Simon-Kucher & Partners—a globally renowned strategy consulting firm focused on strategy, marketing, pricing, and sales, with 860 employees in 29 offices worldwide. Prior to Simon-Kucher & Partners, Robin worked as Senior Strategy & Innovation Consultant at Capgemini Consulting. He holds Master's degrees in Strategic Management and Supply Chain Management. Robin specializes in commercial and innovation growth strategy and is particularly passionate about new proposition strategies. He specifically focuses on business and monetization model innovation, reinvention, and optimization to enable maximum value capture and commercial growth.

Simone Franzò is a PhD Candidate in Management, Economics and Industrial Engineering at the School of Management of Politecnico di Milano (Italy). His research area is innovation management, with a particular focus on open innovation. Simone has long experience in consulting energy firms on topics such as strategy, innovation, business planning, and marketing. He also teaches Strategy in MBA and Executive MBA courses at MIP, the Graduate School of Business of Politecnico di Milano.

Federico Frattini is an associate professor at the School of Management of Politecnico di Milano (Italy). He is the Director of the MBA & Executive MBA programs at MIP, the Graduate School of Business of Politecnico di Milano. His research area is innovation and technology management. He has published more than 160 articles in edited books, conference proceedings, and leading journals such as *Academy of Management Perspectives* and *California Management Review*. In 2013, Federico was nominated among the Top 50 Authors of Innovation and Technology Management Worldwide by IAMOT, the International Association for Management of Technology.

Mette Præst Knudsen is Professor of Innovation Management and Director of the Centre for Integrative Innovation Management in the Department of Marketing & Management at the University of Southern Denmark. Her research focuses on open innovation and ways to operationalize openness in firms' innovation activities. As part of this research, she is also concerned with the internal coordinating competencies of firms required for successful adoption of open innovation. Also, she has investigated the links between creativity, organizing for creativity, and the effects on innovation performance. Finally, her research is concerned with eco-innovation, measurement of eco-innovation and the relationships with "ordinary" innovation, and innovation performance. Her research has been published in journals such as *Journal of Product Innovation Management, Technovation, Journal of Engineering and Technology Management,* and *International Journal of Operations & Production Management*.

Fiona Lettice is Professor of Innovation Management at Norwich Business School. She has co-authored over 100 refereed journal and conference papers in academic journals including *Research Policy, International Journal of Production Economics, Entrepreneurship and Regional Development, Transportation Research Part E: Logistics and Transportation Review, Human Resource Management Journal, International Journal of Technology Management,* and *Journal of Knowledge Management*. She is a Fellow of the Higher Education Academy and a Fellow of the Royal Society for the encouragement of Arts, Manufactures and Commerce (RSA). Her areas of research interest and expertise are: innovation management and new product development—including disruptive, green, open, social, and responsible innovation; diversity management; buyer-supplier relationships; and social media and branding. She has successfully raised external research funding from the European Commission, the Engineering and Physical Sciences Research

Council (EPSRC), and the Economic and Social Sciences Research Council (ESRC) worth over £1m. She was Editor-in-Chief for the *Team Performance Management* journal (2007–2013), and is currently on the Editorial Advisory Boards for the *British Journal of Management* and the *Team Performance Management* journal.

Rebecca Wenjing Lyu works in the Research Center for Technological Innovation, Tsinghua University, Beijing, China.

Alfredo De Massis is Professor of Entrepreneurship & Family Business at the Free University of Bozen-Bolzano (Italy) and Lancaster University Management School. He serves as Associate Editor of Family Business Review and on the Editorial Boards of *Entrepreneurship Theory & Practice, Strategic Entrepreneurship Journal and Journal of Family Business Strategy*, and as Chair of the Family Business Research SIG at the European Academy of Management. In September 2015, Family Capital ranked him among the world's top 25 star professors for family business. Alfredo is the former Chairman of the European Leadership Council and Global Board Member of the Global STEP Project for Family Enterprising at Babson College, USA.

Ingyu Oh is Professor of Hallyu Studies at the Research Institute of Korean Studies, Korea University, Seoul (Korea). Previously, he taught at Bristol Business School, UC Berkeley, Waikato University, and Ritsumeikan Asia Pacific University. His main research interests are innovation and technology management, East Asian business, and cultural industries.

Kulwant Pawar is the Director of CCE and Professor of Operations Management at Nottingham University Business School (UK). His research interests include managing new product design, linkages between product development and supply chain, managing design teams in extended enterprises, and comparative analysis of supply chain networks and configurations between Europe, China, and India. He has published almost 300 papers, including articles in leading international journals such as the *International Journal of Operations and Production Management, International Journal of Production Economics, Production Planning & Control, R&D Management, Technovation, Concurrent Engineering*, and *Manufacturing Technology Management*. He was Editor-in-Chief of the *International Journal of Logistics: Research & Applications* and sits on the editorial board of several international journals and conferences. He is Founder and Chairman of the International Symposium on Logistics (www.ISL21.org), and co-organizer of the International Conference on Concurrent Enterprising (ICE). He is also an expert reviewer, evaluator, and consultant to the European Commission.

Dr. Ing. Nicole Pfeffermann is an experienced management consultant, senior lecturer, and author specialized in innovation communication. Since 1999, she has been working as a management consultant in strategic marketing and innovation projects for companies and institutions (Vorwerk Group, Switzerland; Deutsche Post, DHL; University of Bremen). Nicole is a senior researcher and co-editor of the 2nd edition of the international contributed volume *Strategy and Communication for Innovation* (2016, in progress), Springer Publishing, in collaboration with researchers from the University of Cambridge. She teaches, reviews, and coaches students, PhDs, and start-ups on state-of-the-art topics in digital business and was visiting scholar at UCLA Anderson and associate researcher at ESCP Europe Paris, Chair Entrepreneurship. She received a PhD in Engineering in an international PhD program at the University of Bremen.

Helen Rogers is Professor of International Business at Nuremberg Institute of Technology (Germany) and a Research Fellow at Nottingham University (UK). Her current research interests include developing business models for additive manufacturing technologies and understanding the effects on global supply chains; negotiating procurement contracts; and the cultural challenges of global sourcing. She has co-authored international journal papers, conference papers and book chapters (including *International Business Review, International Journal of Production Economics, Production Planning & Control,* and *Supply Chain Management: An International Journal*); primarily on international business and global supply chain-related topics. She is Associate Editor of *Team Performance Management* journal, an Editorial Board Member of the *International Journal of Physical Distribution and Logistics Management*, and co-organizer of the International Symposium on Logistics.

Arvind Sahay joined IIMA in June 2004 from London Business School where he had been teaching since his PhD in 1996 from the University of Texas at Austin. His research has been in the areas of behavioral pricing, brand relationships, the role of the organization customer interface in creating competitive advantage, life cycles in marketing, finding the balance between being market-driven and market-driving, customer responses to dynamic pricing and how and when to implement dynamic pricing, and neuroscience and decision making. He has authored more than 50 cases and published in leading international journals such as the *Journal of Marketing, Journal of Product Innovation Management, Journal of International Business Studies, Sloan Management Review, Vikalpa, Journal of Indian Business Research,* and the *Journal of Academy of Marketing Science*. His paper in the *Journal of Academy of Marketing Science* is one of the most widely cited papers in marketing. Arvind has been a visiting faculty at the Mason School at the College of William and Mary (USA), University of Texas at Austin (USA), IIM Lucknow, Asian Institute of Technology (Vietnam), Gordon Institute of Business Science, University of Pretoria (South Africa), SP Jain Institute of Management Research (Singapore, Dubai), Retail Alliance (Dubai), EADA (Spain) and the Indian School of Business, Hyderabad.

Arunaditya Sahay is Professor of Strategy at the Birla Institute of Management Technology, Greater Noida (India). He was previously Professor of Strategy at Management Development Institute, Gurgaon (India). Previous to that, he was Chairman and Managing Director of Scooters India Ltd, a miniratna public sector company that he turned around and made profitable before he moved into academia. Arun has a PhD in Foundry from Brno Technological University in what was then Czechoslovakia and an MBA.

Tina Lundø Tranekjer is Assistant Professor of Innovation Management in the Integrative Innovation Management Unit at the University of Southern Denmark. Her research focuses on NPD and inter-organizational innovation, in particular in the specific roles as providers to NPD process, and abandoned and failed innovation projects. Her research has been published in *Journal of Product Innovation Management* and *International Journal of Technology Management.*

Andrea Urbinati is a PhD Candidate in Management, Economics and Industrial Engineering at the School of Management of Politecnico di Milano (Italy). His research area is innovation management, with a particular focus on disruptive innovation and digital technologies. Andrea teaches Strategy and Innovation in MBA and Executive MBA courses at MIP, the Graduate School of Business of Politecnico di Milano.

Eric Viardot is Professor of Strategy and Marketing and Director of The Global Innovation Management Centre at EADA Business School, Barcelona, Spain. Before joining academia, Eric worked in different management positions for Hewlett-Packard, MSF, and Bain & Company in Europe, Asia, and North America. Eric has written various books and articles on strategic management and marketing with a strong focus on technology and innovation management.

Emad Yaghmaei is a Research Fellow and Doctoral Candidate at the Mads Clausen Institute (MCI) at the University of Southern Denmark. Emad holds a MBA&E degree from HTW Berlin and was a Research Affiliate at Idee-Innovation Center of FAU Erlangen-Nürnberg (Germany). His research interests cover innovation management issues arising from the intersections of science, technology, and society. This includes corporate social responsibility (CSR) and responsible research and innovation (RRI). He focuses on RRI principles in an industrial context to demonstrate how industry can work together productively with societal actors and integrate methodologies of RRI into research and innovation processes. The research has a strong empirical focus, including cooperation with major companies, and applying empirical methods such as case studies, controlled experiments, and surveys.

List of Figures

List of Tables

1

Revolution of Innovation Management: Internationalization and Business Models

Alexander Brem and Eric Viardot

1.1 Motivation

What a change in the last three years in the realm of innovation Management! Three years ago, we concluded our book about "Evolution of Innovation Management" (Brem and Viardot 2013) by underlining some essential trends in the management of innovation. Most specifically, we stressed the importance of ambidexterity, which we defined as the ability of companies to realize exploration and exploitation simultaneously in their innovation management process. Some contributions in the book also emphasized the necessity to adopt a more collaborative process with external stakeholders and to move to more "open innovation" (Brau et al. 2013). Other authors underscored the burgeoning importance of platforms (Gawer 2014) and the nurturing of an innovation ecosystem (Thomas and Wind 2013) that federates and coordinates constitutive agents who can innovate and compete. The book had also singled out some key capabilities that innovative companies had to develop in order to

A. Brem (⊠) • E. Viardot
EADA, Barcelona, Spain

© The Author(s) 2017
A. Brem, E. Viardot (eds.), *Revolution of Innovation Management*,
DOI 10.1057/978-1-349-95123-9_1

1

be more successful, including the role of communication, culture, leadership, structure, and key performance indicators.

But the trends we identified at that time have now become common practice. Open innovation and collaborative processes have become the rule more than the exception. Platforms are well known and tend to be the basic norm for companies that are innovating. Building ecosystems around the development of new products and services is also converted into a fundamental principle of innovation strategies. As a consequence, we need to go beyond the functional/competency approach of innovation management that we had highlighted previously. That calls for a more integrated perspective about innovation management because the pace and the scope of innovation has increased so dramatically that it is not exaggerated to talk about a revolution of innovation management today.

Never has innovation been faster, wider, and with more tremendous sectorial consequences! Like with any revolutions, some heads are falling off while new leaders are emerging. The two largest companies in terms of stock value in 2015 were Apple and Google, while Microsoft ranks number five behind two financial companies (PWC 2015). In less than five years, they have managed to dislodge large traditional companies that had been at the top of the class for decades. In their race to reach the top, they have also caused much collateral damage and ruined many traditional or slower competitors such as Nokia, Blackberry, or Siemens, and a score of lesser known companies in the retail, travel, and media industries.

As illustrated in Fig. 1.1, there are three driving forces behind the revolution of innovation management: first, the creation of value for the market is moving from the material world to the digital world. Second, innovation is more and more scaling up from a national scope to global markets. Finally, innovation is no longer based only on new products and services but increasingly on drastic changes in the way of making business, i.e., the business model.

In the first volume of this collection dedicated to "Revolution of Innovation Management: The digital breakthrough", we have analyzed in detail the first driving force, namely the role of digitalization in innovation (Brem and Viardot 2016). The first part of that book explores the quest for innovative users in firm and community collaboration, the role of crowdsourcing and crowdfunding, and how to leverage the use of

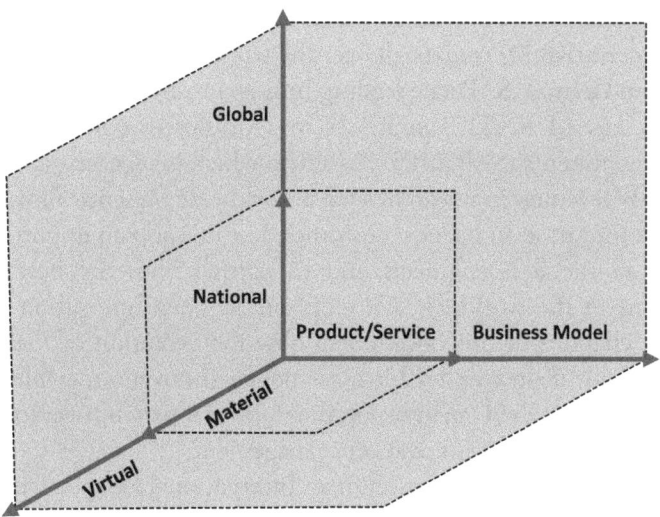

Fig. 1.1 The three drivers for the revolution of innovation management

social media. The second part sheds light on information technologies and corporate value creation, the role that governments can play in helping companies to embrace the digital revolution, and the importance of creativity in the use of social media. Finally, the special situation of legacy firms in keeping innovation alive and in dealing with the digital innovation that is going to strike them is discussed.

This second volume covers the two other fundamental forces that are behind the current revolution in innovation management: the increased globalization of innovation and the rise of business model innovation.

First, there is no doubt that the recent *acceleration of globalization* has significantly contributed to revolutionizing innovation management. This comes from both the demand and the supply. In recent years, it is estimated that the global middle class has grown from 1.3 billion consumers in 2010 to 2 billion in 2015 and it could reach the 3 billion threshold by 2020 (Kharas 2010). That growth has created a massive appeal for new products and services, especially in Asian and South American countries in addition to Russia and some wealthy countries from the Middle East. This appetite for innovation, usually driven by the need to adapt to local needs and desires, has been matched on the supply side by international companies which have deployed their Research and Development (R&D) centers all over the world. For instance, a company such as the German SAP, the leading business-to-business software manufacturer, has 14 R&D laboratories in 13 different countries on three different continents (SAP 2015). As a firm which is spending almost 14% of its yearly revenues in research, such a worldwide presence allows SAP to adapt its innovation to its local customer; but it is also an opportunity for SAP to tap the best engineers and to partner with the best research institutions in the world as SAP relies on an open innovation strategy. Different chapters of this book detail how the evolution of Asian countries, especially Korea and China, is fueling innovation, while another chapter makes a vivid analysis of the role of open innovation in the globalization process of innovation management.

In Chap. 2, "Open Innovation in an International Perspective: How to Organize for (Radical) Product Innovation", Knudsen et al. investigate the organization of external relationships, access to external R&D, and the building of innovative partnerships in an open innovation context. The study is based on a consolidated dataset of approximately 500 Danish manufacturing firms and focuses especially on international external R&D compared to domestic external R&D and the effect on the degree of novelty in product innovation. The authors find that strategies directed at more openness and a higher degree of international R&D input are improving a company's ability to market both new and more radical products. This is attributed to the access to superior technology expertise that accompanies an international-oriented strategy. Interestingly enough, companies pursuing such a strategy are also more likely to abort innovative projects due to their generally higher R&D output. Strategies based on open innovation mechanisms are superior to those focusing on internal R&D. This is clearly an important implication to innovation management, as task complexity in terms of managing knowledge sourcing, external participation, and external sharing increases significantly in an open innovation context. Knudsen et al. state that future research should focus on strategies that utilize both external sources of innovation and a company's internal innovation potential. Although there are limitations to the study, this chapter emphasizes the benefits of internationally oriented strategies in pursuing successful R&D, which contributes to revolutionizing innovation management in theory and practice.

Chapter 3, "Chaebols' Innovation Management Without an Economic Miracle" by Ingyu Oh, focuses on the Korean *chaebols*, which are family-owned large corporations that operate on an inter-market level in intense competition over a small domestic market. Innovative chaebols have been elemental in the astonishing Korean economic development in the past decades, which the author explains in relation to other economies, especially Japan and China. Ingyu Oh goes on to describe chaebols' innovation management during years of extreme economic growth, which was primarily impacted by four elements of the Korean economic miracle. These elements are: (1) a "predatory state" that enforced class polarization and thus fostered gross domestic product (GDP) growth; (2) chaebols that depended on the predatory state for survival; (3) cultural factors in institutions that relied on credible threats and distrust in and between organizations; and (4) technological innovations based on parodying. In order to be successful in times of less intense economic growth, chaebols need to adapt a different innovation strategy. The author suggests that cultural aspects have to be taken into account when adapting modern innovation management principles, which is necessary to be successful in a recessive period. Cultural management is a highly important factor in times where internationalization of business models becomes standard practice.

In Chap. 4, "Innovation in China: The State of Art and Future Perspectives", Jin Chen and Rebecca Wenjing Lyu summarize innovation patterns in China during recent years in order to introduce current innovation practices. Four representative innovation theories in China are the 3-I pattern (imitation, improvement, innovation), indigenous innovation, integrated innovation, and total innovation management. These approaches have found relevance in practice and the companies Beijing Oriental Electronics (BOE), Huawei, CRRC Zhuzhou Institute, and Haier are described as case examples, one for each approach. Based on the innovation development in China, the authors point at a gap between innovation literature and practice, and propose an innovation best practice for enterprises in today's world. The key sources for innovation are twofold: an open ecosystem on the one hand and core technology competitiveness on the other. The authors label this framework "dual source innovation" and claim it can be beneficial to innovation in Chinese enterprises as they observed positive effects in two case companies (Letv and Midea) in comparison to enterprises focusing on different innovation frameworks. This study certainly has implications for innovation management and its development in today's rapidly changing markets.

Unquestionably, the present revolution of innovation management has also been fueled by the surge of business model innovation. They are various definitions of what is a *business model* but a generic characterization is "how an organization manages incomes and costs through the structural arrangement of its activities to deliver a value proposition in order to generate profit" (Johnson et al. 2013). Innovating with a different way of doing business has always been one way to proceed: in their time, companies such as Ikea, Carrefour, Starbucks, and a score of other firms have managed to achieve a sustainable competitive advantage with a groundbreaking business model. But what was an exception some years ago seems to become a more typical and radical way to innovate for companies which prefer to break the common practice than just to offer a new product or to apply original processes.

In Chap. 5, "Looking at Business Model Innovation and Innovation Ecosystems and How They Are Evolving", Sahay and Sahay investigate the effect of business model innovation on the overall innovation performance of firms. They state that business model changes are a significant source of innovation and that business model innovators gain competitive advantage over other less innovative market actors. In business models, clear thinking, design, execution and flexibility are critical for success. Today, technological change and changes in customer behavior are the main drivers of business model innovation, accompanied by infrastructure characteristics and strategic planning of firms. Based on this, the authors develop a framework for business model innovation and extend the topic to innovation ecosystems, which can contribute significantly to innovating business models. Applying the framework to existing business models can increase the innovativeness thereof and thereby also the innovative performance of firms, both by internal means and in interaction with the respective innovation ecosystem. Thus, this chapter contains important implications for innovation management in practice.

The title of Chap. 6, "Business Model Revolution: Four Cases of the Fastest-Growing, Disruptive Companies of the Twenty-First Century", is quite explicit about its aim. The author, Robin Chu, uses four exemplary cases of fast-growing, market-disrupting companies to conceptualize some catalysts for business model innovation. The four cases in this article are Uber (the world's largest taxi company without owning vehicles), Spotify (the fastest-growing music provider), Alibaba (the most valuable retailer without having any inventory), and Airbnb (the world's largest accommodation provider without owning any real estate). Chu argues that change and innovation are unalterably interrelated; this fact points to a significant challenge as innovation is something to which most companies aspire while change is something uncomfortable not only to the human nature but also to corporations in general. Through modern technology and an accompanying abundance of information, the pace of innovation quickens, which creates pressure not only on individual companies, but on entire industries. Based on the four cases, Chu concludes that business model innovation as a means to develop new value propositions is essential for survival. The fast-changing environment of modern markets through newcomers and their threat of potentially disrupting whatever is perceived to be advantageous in competition calls for a different attitude toward change, namely not to avoid it but to utilize it as a source of innovation.

In Chap. 7, "The Role of Communication as a Dynamic Capability in Business Model Innovation", Nicole Pfeffermann yields information on the interface between business model innovation and strategic innovation communication. She argues that innovation depends on information itself and on success in turning it into value-creating knowledge. In dynamic environments, companies need to be able to adapt and reinvent on a continuous basis in order to be innovative, which is essential for business success in this age where information is abundantly available. Communication for innovation includes the absorbing of information on disruptive technologies and changes in consumer demands, which builds the basis for new value creation suited to a fast-changing market environment. Through a qualitative study with international new ventures on the management of innovation communication activities in relation to business models, the author attempts to describe the role of communications in the context of business model innovation. She concludes that integrated innovation communication contributes effectively to building new capabilities. As not many new ventures do this currently, communication for innovation as part of business models can create competitive advantages and helps companies to flourish in times of highly dynamic and fluctuating markets.

Actually, it would be an error to consider that the current revolution of innovation management is limited to large multinational companies, public or private. This revolution also has major impacts on smaller family businesses that are neither immune to digitalization nor to globalization and business creativity. We also believe that the revolution of innovation management is not limited to business issues but also includes societal and environmental issues, with the keyword sustainable innovation. Hence, we conclude this book with two general but fundamental contributions: one is about family businesses and the other relates to sustainable innovation.

In Chap. 8, "Innovation in Family Firms: A Review of Prior Studies and a Framework for Future Research", Urbinati et al. provide insights into existing research on family firms, which are present all around the world and are therefore of considerable importance in relation to innovation management. Additionally, there seems to have been a lack of research on different corporate government systems in family businesses, which explains a now growing body of literature on this topic and on the impact corporate governance has on innovation. As family firms contribute significantly to innovation in all parts of the world and as research on innovation in family firms is limited, the authors aim at defining implications for future research. They state that there is a gap of knowledge on the management models that ought to be applied in family firms and that there is a need to identify dynamic capabilities and their origin. Dynamic capabilities allow family firms to utilize knowledge from different sources, namely internal R&D, tradition and past history, clients/suppliers/competitors, and universities/research centers. Urbinati et al. conclude that empirical studies will test their framework on dynamic capabilities and will subsequently introduce best-practice advice and feasible approaches to foster innovation in family firms.

Finally in Chap. 9, "Responsible Research and Innovation Revisited: Aligning Product Development Processes with the Corporate Responsibility Agenda", Lettice et al. explore the meaning and the implication of responsible research and innovation (RRI) in regard to corporate responsibility. The authors argue that industry has to collaborate with societal actors during the entire research and development process in order to create products and technologies that are in accord with society's values, needs, and expectations. This might not only result in more innovative products and services, but also in more socially desirable solutions. Besides introducing the general RRI framework and its previous use, Lettice et al. outline RRI tools and techniques usable in new product development and propose a future agenda for RRI in research and practice. They emphasize awareness, implementation, and assessment of RRI in innovation management practices and propose the following agenda for extending corporate social responsibility through implementing RRI principles: (1) review RRI developments in relation to new product development (NPD); (2) generate practical insight through primary research; (3) develop a maturity assessment tool for RRI in NPD; (4) develop future-oriented planning and implementation strategies. This chapter underlines the importance of responsible research and innovation and implies that innovation management needs to take RRI principles into account in order to be sustainable and effective.

1.2   Conclusion

In our book on the adoption of innovation (Brem and Viardot 2015), we aimed to link our research results with an overall conceptual framework. This was driven by the idea of having a starting point for future researchers (including ourselves) to integrate new research insights. This approach resulted in the extension of the model from West and Bogers (2014), which is shown in Fig. 1.2.

Our aim for this conclusion is to link the key innovation activities from the shown innovation process model—namely *obtaining, integrating, and commercializing ideas*—with future research potential. The rationale for this is the fact that we see specific influences of all three revolutionary topics with the management of ideas. The first one, digitalization, may

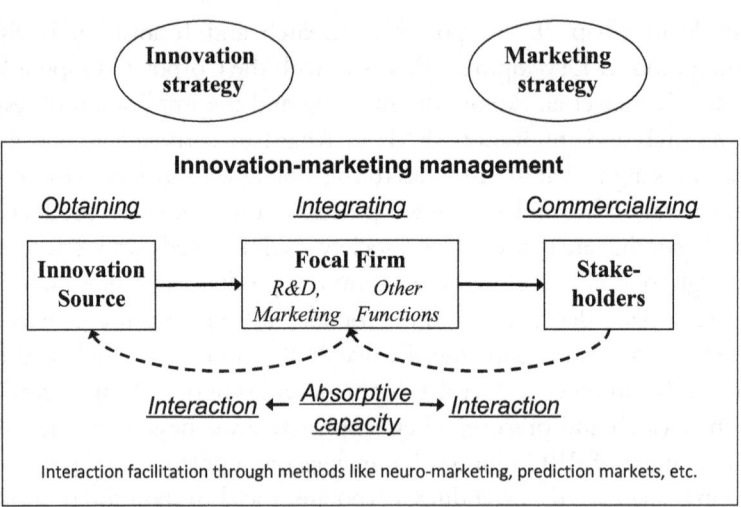

Fig. 1.2 Innovation process model (Brem and Viardot 2015: 8)

lead to changing customer and supplier behavior in obtaining ideas, to an adopted employer behavior for integrating them, and to different customer behaviors in the commercialization phase. Globalization might have an impact on the obtaining phase as ideas must be identified and adopted globally. Integrating them becomes even more complex as the setup of internal resources has to be adopted. Commercialization implicates a global view on approaching customers in different cultural setups, which might also entail a new approach to marketing and sales activities. Last but not least, the awareness of business model innovation is also important for all three phases. While obtaining ideas, a strategic integration of customers and suppliers from the beginning will be necessary. A successful integration calls then for a comprehensive view on innovation including marketing, sales, controlling, and production. The criterion of high flexibility to adapt to market changes becomes even more critical in the adoption phase.

We see these developments as key drivers for future research, leading to new research approaches and research questions. Although there are many established academic fields like marketing, digitalization, and globalization, business model innovation will also have a high impact on completely new theories in such fields.

Table 1.1 below shows some examples of topics we think might become relevant in the future. The idea is not to show a complete list, rather to inspire for even more topics. Furthermore, we do not explicitly link it to different company characteristics like company size, industry, etc., as we see these topics as relevant overall.

Table 1.1 Key drivers for future research

	Obtaining	Integrating	Commercializing
Digitalization	– Virtual customer and supplier integration – User innovation with social media – Supplier innovation in networks	– New tools for integration management – Automatization of processes – Digital manufacturing	– Marketing in real-time – Product information available 24/7 – Full market transparency
Globalization	– Need for the integration of distributed needs – Integration of customers and users through crowdsourcing – Management of complex supplier relationships	– Worldwide and parallel product development and production – Motivation of people in different work environments – "Glocalized" production	– Cultural branding of products – Flexibility in new market adoption – Use of customer engagement through crowdfunding
Business model innovation	– Planning of key business model elements beforehand – New market areas through identification of niches – Value propositions already in the idea obtaining phase	– New way of an overall product management – Structured and systematic idea evaluation – Focus on key partners, activities and channels	– Revenue streams are linked with customer relationships and segments – Channels become visible and optional – Established players can be challenged by new market entrants

To conclude, we hope to offer all readers of both books—students, academics, and practitioners alike—an interesting and especially inspiring read. We are very open to any kind of feedback and to get in touch with future contributors to projects like this one.

We are looking forward to your feedback!

Alexander Brem & Eric Viardot

Acknowledgements Finally, we would like to express our gratitude to Madeleine Holder and Liz Barlow at Palgrave Macmillan. We also thank the authors for their patience in going through several revisions, as well as Kari Kleine for his engagement.

References

Brem, A., and E. Viardot. 2013. *Preface/Conclusion, Evolution of Innovation Management: Trends in an International Context*. London, UK: Palgrave Macmillan.

Brem, A., and É. Viardot. 2015. *Adoption of Innovation: Balancing Internal and External Stakeholders in the Marketing of Innovation*. Berlin, Germany: Springer International Publishing.

Brem, A., and E. Viardot. 2016. *Revolution of Innovation Management. The Digital Breakthrough Volume 1*. London, UK: Palgrave Macmillan.

Brau, E., R. Reinhardt, and S. Gurtner. 2013. Measuring the Success of Open Innovation. In *Evolution of Innovation Management*, ed. Alexander Brem and Eric Viardot, 52–74. London: Palgrave Macmillan.

Gawer, A. 2014. Bridging Differing Perspectives on Technological Platforms: Toward an Integrative Framework. *Research Policy* 43(7): 1239–1249.

Johnson, G., R. Whittington, K. Scholes, D. Angwin, and P. Regnér. 2013. *Exploring Strategy*. Harlow, England: Pearson.

Kharas, H. 2010. The Emerging Middle Class in Developing Countries. *OECD Development Centre Working Paper 285*. http://www.livemint.com/Opinion/Y7pUto4hf2Z2HS7TyFWfOP/Revisiting-innovation-at-the-bottom-of-the-pyramid.html

PWC. 2015. Global Top 100 Companies by Market Capitalisation. Accessed June 3, 2016. https://www.pwc.com/gx/en/audit-services/capital-market/publications/assets/document/pwc-global-top-100-march-update.pdf

SAP. 2015. Reimagine Your Business. Accessed June 3, 2016. go.sap.com/docs/download/investors/2015/sap-2015-annual-report.pdf

Thomas, R. J., and Y. J. Wind. 2013. Symbiotic Innovation: Getting the Most Out of Collaboration. In *Evolution of Innovation Management*, ed. Alexander Brem and Eric Viardot, 1–31. London: Palgrave Macmillan.

West, J., and M. Bogers. 2014. Leveraging External Sources of Innovation: A Review of Research on Open Innovation (with Joel West). *Journal of Product Innovation Management* 31(4): 814–831.

2

Open Innovation in an International Perspective: How to Organize for (Radical) Product Innovation

Mette Præst Knudsen, Tina Lundø Tranekjer, and Uwe Cantner

2.1 Introduction

In a world of increasing global knowledge flows with better potential access to domestic as well as international external R&D providers and collaboration partners, innovation management is increasingly challenged to access and relate to the right sources, for the right knowledge at the right time, to ensure long-term innovative performance. Identifying providers and collaborating with appropriate partners that possess heterogeneous and tacit knowledge are truly challenging tasks for even the most experienced innovation managers.

M.P. Knudsen (✉) • T.L. Tranekjer
Department of Marketing & Management, Centre for Integrative Innovation Management, University of Southern Denmark, Odense, Denmark

U. Cantner
Department of Economics and Business Administration, Friedrich Schiller University Jena and Marketing & Management, Centre for Integrative Innovation Management, University of Southern Denmark, Odense, Denmark

© The Author(s) 2017   **15**
A. Brem, E. Viardot (eds.), *Revolution of Innovation Management*,
DOI 10.1057/978-1-349-95123-9_2

This chapter offers a comparative perspective on the access and use of domestic versus international sources of knowledge for innovation performance. These dimensions are revolutionizing the tasks and challenges of innovation managers where the question is how to organize the external relationships for innovation while matching the diverse knowledge sourcing opportunities with the innovative efforts, abilities, and problems in-house. The chapter additionally addresses and investigates the separation of R&D-relevant knowledge coming predominantly from transfer relationships with R&D providers or from collaborative partnerships (Grimpe and Kaiser 2010; Tranekjer and Knudsen 2012). The opportunities to access inter-organizational relationships, and to acquire knowledge through contracts with external R&D providers, whether domestic or international, are all part of a wide array of organizing opportunities for a firm to conduct the sourcing, creation, and application of knowledge for product innovation activities.

The concept of open innovation was coined by Chesbrough (2003) to explain and understand various (combinations of) knowledge sourcing strategies. Researchers developed the open innovation concept by extending existing literature to include alliances and inter-organizational relationships (see e.g., Knudsen 2007; Pisano and Verganti 2008). In particular, studies focusing on the structural organization of open innovation partnerships have been frequently conducted (Fey and Birkinshaw 2005; Henttonen and Ritala 2013; Henttonen et al. 2011; Inauen and Schenker-Wicki 2011; Knudsen and Mortensen 2011; Laursen and Salter 2006). In this context, Enkel et al. (2009: 312–313) have named three organizing processes related to whether knowledge flows from outside-in, inside-out, or is coupled. The outside-in processes are typically associated with the utilization of external relations like partnerships and alliances, whereas inside-out processes address the search for other and new applications of the firm's own technology and the provision of knowledge to other firms' innovative activities (Tranekjer and Knudsen 2012). The coupled processes "combine the outside-in process (to gain external knowledge) with the inside-out process (to bring ideas to market) and, in doing so, jointly develop and commercialize innovation" (Enkel et al. 2009: 313). Within outside-in processes, a number of choices are available and the literature particularly differentiates between two general outside-in strategies: the acquisition of external R&D through licences or contracts with R&D suppliers on the one hand, and the joint development of innovation with collaboration partners on the other. The first strategy implies the acquisition of a research outcome from external contracting partners, whereas the latter strategy refers to a joint effort of the partner firms to develop valuable (knowledge) assets that they may not have been able or willing to develop alone through their internal R&D efforts.

Open innovation strategies are characterized by different *types* of openness (diversity) (Barge-Gil 2010; Knudsen 2007) and by different *intensities* of openness (Laursen and Salter 2006). Diversity can refer to dimensions of domestic and international partnerships as well as to distinct types of openness such as external R&D contracting and collaboration. In our estimation, a better understanding of these different dimensions requires simultaneous investigation of five innovation strategies related to geographic aspects of the location of the knowledge sources: closed innovation (also known as internal R&D), domestic collaboration, international collaboration, domestic external R&D, and international external R&D. Our inclusive approach, which investigates the innovation strategies simultaneously, is particularly pertinent because the strategies have in previous research been examined separately.

This chapter therefore contributes to the literature by empirically identifying which open innovation strategies are comparatively more successful in contributing to innovation performance, while adding a specific geographic dimension of the location of the knowledge sources. Thus far, the literature is incomplete on the influence of the decision to source knowledge domestically or internationally (Arvanitis and Bolli 2013; Beers and Zand 2014). The limited literature on that dimension presents mixed results; some present a positive relationship between international collaboration and innovative performance (Lööf 2009; Miotti and Sachwald 2003; Arvanitis and Bolli 2013), while others find no effect (Jaklic et al. 2008). Furthermore, by taking an international collaboration (openness) perspective, a more fine-gained approach is contributed by investigating two different types: international external R&D and international innovation collaboration. This diversity of openness may be of relevance for a firm's capability to innovate radical, instead of only introducing incremental solutions. Thus, for firms to do radical innovation they need more diverse sources and partners, e.g., to be able to access new/complementary or even tacit knowledge (Beers and Zand 2014).

This chapter finds as the main result that firms sourcing knowledge internationally rather than from domestic sources appear to have greater success in bringing more radical products to the market. Based on this and other results, the chapter formulates specific recommendations for innovation managers seeking to develop their own abilities to navigate in the new and more revolutionary age of innovation management and organization.

2.2 Open Innovation, External Knowledge Sourcing and Innovation Performance

The organization of external knowledge sourcing in the form of acquiring external R&D on the one hand and forming innovation cooperation partnerships on the other and the combination with internal R&D have come to be an important managerial decision. Hence, firms may organize their activities with increasing degrees of openness by buying external R&D to source relevant external knowledge and/or establishing innovation collaboration while seeking to increase the speed or quality of innovation activities and to run them at a lower cost (Berchicci 2013; Chesbrough 2003; Grimpe and Kaiser 2010).

When firms buy knowledge from external R&D providers, they seek to enhance and fertilize their innovation activities through *acquisition*. Ideally, knowledge-based activities that give firms competitive advantages over their competitors should be organized internally and R&D activities that are less important for long-term competitiveness should be contracted out to external specialized suppliers (Quinn 1999, 2000). In this way, companies can reduce the cost and risk of non-core R&D activities, in which they lack internal competencies. Moreover, this division of R&D tasks enables firms to improve their efficiency and effectiveness in innovation through concentrating on the activities in which they have already accumulated valuable competencies.

The acquisition of external R&D may improve firms' innovation performance (Cassiman and Veugelers 2006; Gilley and Rasheed 2000; Grimpe and Kaiser 2010; Quinn 1999, 2000) in terms of new or qualitatively better products and/or cost-reducing process innovations. External R&D enables firms to overcome internal innovation constraints, such as a lack of suitable qualified personnel, a lack of technical expertise, and to minimize the cost and risk of R&D projects (Grimpe and Kaiser 2010; Quinn 1999, 2000). It may also allow firms to access better-quality resources than they can generate internally (Grimpe and Kaiser 2010). This is the case when firms lack expertise in certain innovation activities whereas an R&D supplier is specialized in just these activities. Moreover, external R&D may help firms to access complementary or heterogeneous knowledge assets (Cassiman and Veugelers 2006; Grimpe and Kaiser 2010), which are considered to be the primary source of innovation (Nelson and Winter 1982; Rosenkopf and Nerkar 2001). For these reasons, firms diversify their external knowledge sources and search for complementary resources (Bertrand and Mol 2013; Lewin et al. 2009; von Zedtwitz and Gassmann 2002; von Zedtwitz et al. 2004). Despite these advantages, the decision to outsource R&D activities has also the one or other downside: the uniqueness of research results acquired from an R&D provider is questionable, because competitors may have access to the expertise of the same R&D provider (Grimpe and Kaiser 2010); and, a client firm purchases research results from an R&D provider without being (or being only slightly) involved in the knowledge generation of external R&D. Hence, in the long run, relying heavily on external R&D may even exhaust firms' innovation potential—understood as the inherent ability of a firm to successfully create and economize on new knowledge—through not holding available or even reducing skilled employees, problem-solving activities, and respective infrastructures in internal R&D (Bettis et al. 1992; Weigelt 2009).

An alternative external way to source new knowledge for R&D activities is *innovation collaboration*. In the context of our analysis this concept is meant to comprise all collaboration activities along the innovation process (from invention to commercialization) and addresses partners such as following types: suppliers, customers, competitors, approved technological service institutes, consulting organizations, companies from other industries (excluding customers and suppliers), universities, public research institutions, public services, and other public institutions. Previous studies have shown that internal R&D and innovation collaboration are important drivers of product innovation (Becker and Dietz 2004; Deeds and Hill 1996; Nieto and Santamaria 2007; Vega-Jurado et al. 2008). To cope with the increased complexity of innovation, collaboration provides access to resources firms can generate neither internally (Powell et al. 1996) nor alone. This allows them to develop valuable (knowledge) assets through a joint effort with partner firms (Hagedoorn 1993). This strategy is characterized by intensive interaction, resource sharing, and mutual learning, which help firms to enhance their innovation activities (Becker and Dietz 2004; Belderbos et al. 2004; Hagedoorn 1993; Nieto and Santamaria 2007; Powell et al. 1996).

In contrast to sourcing new knowledge via external R&D providers, innovation collaboration allows the firm to keep some degree of control over jointly performed business processes in general and over the commonly induced knowledge-generating processes in particular through their mutual learning and knowledge-generating efforts. Collaboration is whereby firms commit their resources to a common project and interact intensively to induce and benefit from learning processes (Hillebrand and Biemans 2004; Mudambi and Tallman 2010). The frequent interaction between the employees coming from the partner firms is likely to build a trust-based relationship between them (Powell 1990) that is intended to share unwritten knowledge such as skills and know-how (Holste and Fields 2010). For these reasons, innovation collaboration may enable firms to monitor the behaviour of the partners for transferring as well as exchanging knowledge (Mudambi and Tallman 2010). Furthermore, innovation collaboration allows firms to reduce the costs and risks of R&D projects as well as to speed up new product development through pooling complementary resources (Hagedoorn 1993).

Open innovation does not stop at national borders, but rather opens global opportunities for accessing knowledge, although the issue has only rarely been addressed (Gassmann et al. 2010). Due to the increased access to and use of communication technologies, the internationalization of R&D activities has increased, which has enabled firms to access cheaper R&D inputs from low-cost countries and to draw on valuable knowledge abroad (Lewin et al. 2009; von Zedtwitz and Gassmann 2002; von Zedtwitz et al. 2004). If firms do not manage to identify appropriate knowledge partners in their own country, they may organize R&D on an international or even a global scale. Through these efforts of internationalizing their R&D activities, firms may further obtain more direct access to customers abroad, to align their needs with new product development, and thereby to meet the requirements of various foreign markets.

Given that scientific expertise is distributed worldwide, the acquisition of external R&D from these sources can be essential to keep pace in various fields of technological development especially in high-technology markets (Lewin et al. 2009; von Zedtwitz and Gassmann 2002; von Zedtwitz et al. 2004). In other words, firms outsource some R&D tasks outside their home country because international external R&D providers may possess superior technological expertise compared to domestic providers (Lewin et al. 2009; Nieto and Rodriguez 2011). For example, Lewin et al. (2009) find that the limited resources and shortages of highly skilled workers within the home market induce firms to outsource some R&D activities outside the national borders.

In view of the internationalization of knowledge sourcing, one may ask whether there is a difference between sourcing knowledge from respectively domestic and international providers. Despite the fact that the coordination of international partners increases transaction costs, firms organize R&D on a global scale to access resources that are unavailable within the domestic market. Moreover, the knowledge-based assets sourced from international marketplaces or by innovation collaboration might be more heterogeneous than those within the home country due to the different institutions and national innovation systems (Freeman 1995). In this sense, international, rather than domestic, external R&D as well as innovation collaboration can help firms to access more diverse knowledge inputs. Hence, the higher transaction costs appear to go hand in hand with a higher potential value of the externally addressed knowledge accessed. Looking at the empirical evidence, firms with external R&D from international marketplaces can have more opportunities for knowledge recombination and perform better in innovation than others relying only on domestic resources (Bertrand and Mol 2013).

2.3   Data and Variable Description

The empirical analysis of the paper is based on the Danish part of the Community Innovation Survey (CIS).[1] The CIS is conducted at the enterprise level, and it gives a broad variety of information on innovation activities such as internal R&D, domestic and international external R&D, domestic and international innovation collaboration, and different types of product innovations.

The aim of the Danish Community Innovation Survey is to get information on and examine innovation activities in the Danish economy. The methods and types of questions are described in the Oslo manual, and the data is therefore comparable with data from other Organization for Economic Co-operation and Development (OECD) countries. The total population in the two surveys are 22,215 firms in 2008 and 19,483 firms in 2010. The survey was sent to approximately 5000 firms in 2008 and 4800 in 2010, based on stratified simple random sampling. The number of responses was from 4438 firms in 2008 and 4322 firms in 2010. By this we are able to impose a time-lag between innovation input and output variables. The samples used for this article consists of Danish manufacturing firms with ten employees or more. The data in the two surveys consist of self-reported answers, and therefore there are the possibilities of subjective answers and of common source bias.

The analysis of the data for this paper is descriptive due to an explorative approach. As the literature suggests (Griliches and Mairesse 1984; Pakes and Griliches 1984), time is required to finalize an R&D project and to introduce a new product to a market before revenues from the new product sales can be reaped. Although the time-lag may vary across firms and depend on the type of R&D projects that they run, an average lag between innovation input and innovation output is about two years (Griliches and Mairesse 1984). Therefore, we combine the 2008 and 2010 CIS datasets, implying that innovation strategies are drawn from the 2008 CIS, whereas the innovation output (i.e., product innovation) is taken from the 2010 CIS. To some degree, this design also helps to avoid cross-sectional data-related problems in the empirical analysis, i.e., endogeneity and causality issues—however, we do not claim these issues to be resolved completely.

In the original 2008 and 2010 CIS datasets from Denmark, there were 939 and 1111 firms, respectively. After combining these two datasets and restricting the sample to manufacturing firms, the data set consists of 491 observations. For the analysis of innovative activities, it appears fruitful to distinguish between manufacturing industries by the level of technology applied and used; hence we look at low-technology, medium-technology and high-technology industries separately.

In Table 2.1, not surprisingly the majority of firms we consider are assigned to the *medium-technology* class, followed by *low-technology* and *high-technology* rather equally. Also from Table 2.1 we take that the share of firms that are product innovative is higher for high-technology industries as compared to medium and low-technology industries, which is what would be expected.

With respect to firm size, the data also shows that firms are distributed with the largest share for small firms with less than 250 employees (Table 2.2), which is as would be expected. Similarly, it is observable that the share of innovative firms increases with size, which is also aligned with the expectations. Therefore, the data sample follows existing empirical observations regarding innovativeness, size, and industry.

The core variables for a firm's open innovation strategy for sourcing external knowledge are domestic external R&D, international external R&D, domestic innovation collaboration, and international innovation collaboration. Obviously, firms may choose to stay "closed" and not to collaborate or to contract external R&D providers, and even further, firms may choose to engage in only internal R&D (Table 2.3). About two third of the firms are engaged in internal R&D whereas the degree of openness ranges from 16.3 % in international external R&D to 44.2 % in domestic innovation collaboration.

The CIS lists different types of innovation collaboration partners (i.e., suppliers, customers, competitors, approved technological service institutes, consulting organizations, companies from other industries (excluding customers and suppliers), universities, public research institutions, public services, and other public institutions) and by this covers the complete innovation process from invention to commercialization; the

Table 2.1 Distribution of firms on industry

Technology intensity	Classification of manufacturing industry	Number of firms (% of total)	Product innovative firms in 2008 (% within industry)
Low-technology manufacturing industries	Food and beverages, tobacco (15, 16) Textiles, leather, footwear (17–19) Wood, paper, paper products (20, 21) Furniture (22)	136 (27.7)	55 (40.4)
Medium-technology manufacturing industries	Non-metallic mineral products (26) Metal products (27, 28) Rubber and plastic products (25) Machinery and equipment (29)	225 (45.8)	109 (48.4)
High-technology manufacturing industries	Chemical industry (24) Electrical apparatus, computing machines, communication equipment (30–32) Medical, precision and optical instruments (30–32)	130 (26.5)	96 (73.8)

Adapted from OECD (2003)—NACE codes in brackets, innovative firms in Danish manufacturing averages 53.0 % in 2008 and for 2010 the share is 51.3 %

Table 2.2 Distribution of firms on size

Size class	Number of firms (% of total)	Innovative firms (% of total)
Small firms (1–249)	354 (72.1)	153 (43.2)
Medium-sized firms (250–499)	85 (17.3)	56 (65.9)
Large firms (more than 500 employees)	52 (10.6)	51 (98.1)
Total	491	260 (52.9)

respondents were asked to indicate whether they collaborate with the above-listed partners in Denmark, Europe, the USA, China/India and/or other locations (yes/no). The variable *domestic innovation collaboration*

Table 2.3 Utilization of open innovation strategies in 2008 (as % of total number of firms)[a]

	Frequency	% of total
No R&D and no openness	143	29.1
Internal R&D	323	65.8
...Only internal R&D	91	18.5
Domestic external R&D	131	26.7
International external R&D	80	16.3
Domestic innovation collaboration	217	44.2
International innovation collaboration	184	37.5
Total number of firms	491	

[a]The numbers do not add up to 491 firms; this is because the firms may perform several of the strategies in the same year

refers to the number of innovation collaboration partners in Denmark, whereas *international innovation collaboration* stands for the number of innovation collaboration partners abroad. The number of cooperation cases in the USA, China/India, and other locations is very small; therefore, we combine all partnerships into one, indicating that international innovation cooperation counts the number of collaboration partners in Europe and in other countries (the USA, China/India, and others). The variable receives the value 1 if a firm has at least one (but may have more) innovation partner abroad. We ignore the type of innovation collaboration, whether customer, university, or otherwise and only focus on the geographical location. In total, 217 firms have collaborated with a domestic partner (44.2 %) and 184 have collaborated with an international partner (37.5 %). It is therefore a substantial collaborative activity that the firms carry out (Table 2.3).

In parallel, we investigate firms' contract R&D from consultants and the like. In the CIS, the questions are formulated as investments in contracting R&D. These figures are converted into binary variables (for comparative reasons). Hence, if a firm has accessed external R&D from a Danish provider, the variable *domestic external R&D* takes a value of 1 ($n = 131$; 26.7 %), and if a firm accesses external R&D from an international provider, we give the variable *international external R&D* a value of 1 ($n = 80$; 16.3 %) (Table 2.3). On this basis, in a comparative perspective, we observe that firms more frequently collaborate than contract R&D; however, these figures do not provide indications as to whether the collaborative relationships or the contracted R&D are better at facilitating innovation.

We include in our analysis a variable for whether a firm has terminated an innovation project without a result (*abandoned projects*) in 2008. Firms often fail to complete an innovation project due to the gap between their existing resources and those needed to execute the innovation project successfully (Cooper and Kleinschmidt 1990). To cope with this issue, firms collaborate with external actors to acquire the necessary resources and to improve their innovation processes (Keupp and Gassmann 2009). Abandoned innovation projects are measured on whether a given firm started innovation activities in the period 2006–2008 and later abandoned them without result (0 = no/1 = yes). In total numbers, 79 firms abandoned projects in 2008, which corresponds to 16.1 % of all firms.

As to firm performance, we use the introduction of product innovation on the market in the last three years and distinguish them by the degree of novelty. To measure the novelty of new products, the CIS asked the respondents to indicate whether a company introduced a product that was *new to the firm*, but known on a market (1), *new to the firm's own market* (2), or *new to the world* (3). The first question relates to product imitation rather than to product innovation. The second question describes whether firms introduced a product that was new to their own market, but might already have been introduced into other markets in which these firms do not perform. In the final question, firms were asked to indicate whether they had introduced a completely new product to the world. We consider a product that is new to the world to be characterized by a higher degree of novelty than the other two. Thus, we use three measures of product innovation. In total, 168 firms introduced a product that was *new to the firm* in the period 2007–2009, equalling 34.2 %; 126 firms introduced products that were *new to the market*, which is equal to 25.7 %; and finally, the third is products that were *new to the world*. 82 firms introduced radically new products (16.7 %) (Table 2.4).

Table 2.4 The innovativeness of firms in 2010 based on their open innovation strategies in 2008[a]

	Internal R&D	Domestic external R&D	International external R&D	Domestic innovation collaboration	International innovation collaboration	Total
New to the World	76 (23.5)	40 (30.5)	30 (37.5)	57 (26.3)	55 (29.9)	82
New to the Market	107 (33.1)	58 (44.3)	37 (46.3)	77 (35.5)	72 (39.1)	126
New to the Firm	138 (42.7)	70 (53.4)	48 (60.0)	104 (47.9)	95 (51.6)	168
Number of firms	323	131	80	217	184	
Abandoned projects	77 (23.8)	46 (35.1)	29 (36.3)	69 (31.8)	63 (34.2)	

[a]The percentages do not add up to 100 % column-wise because some firms may have no product innovations and other firms several ones that differ in their degree of newness

2.4   Open Innovation Strategies and Innovation Performance: An Explorative Analysis

In the following, we explore how the four different open innovation strategies—introduced above—as well as the internal innovation strategy of Danish firms in 2008 facilitated their different innovation outcomes in 2010. We pursue that via three steps by looking first at the different innovation strategies, by secondly distinguishing between closed and open innovation strategies, and by thirdly focussing on the distinction between domestically and internationally oriented open innovation strategies.

In the first comparison, we directly observe the different strategies and analyse how likely it is that a firm has subsequently introduced a new product, whether new to the firm, new to the market, or new to the world. From Table 2.4, it can be taken that for each of the five innovation strategies, firms are most likely to introduce products that are new to the firm (from 42.7 % with internal R&D to 51.6 % with international innovation collaboration); the more radical in nature innovation becomes—new to the market and new to the world—the lower the likelihood of a product innovation gets. Further, we checked how the open innovation strategies are related to the firms' likelihood of abandoning innovation projects. Here it can be observed that the firms with international external R&D have the highest share of failed projects (36.3 %), closely followed by domestic external R&D (35.1 %), indicating that firms contracting R&D are also more likely to abandon some projects. The lowest share of abandoned projects is found for firms with internal R&D.

Finally, it can be taken from Table 2.4 that looking at the relevance of each of the five innovation strategies in innovations success, internal R&D ranks highest followed by the two innovation collaboration dimensions, and then the external R&D options. For example, firms investing in internal R&D are better in converting the investments into products that are new to the world (76 out of 82 firms); compared to that with respect to international innovation cooperation, 55 out of 82 firms scored in introducing new to the world products, and only 30 out of 82 firms

Table 2.5 The distribution of firms based on their degree of openness in 2008

	Frequency	Percent
No internal or external innovation strategies	143	29.1
Closed innovation: only internal R&D	91	18.5
Open: both internal and external innovation strategies	257	52.3
Total	491	100.0

when it comes to having invested in international external R&D. That kind of ordering holds as well for the other two dimensions of newness of product innovations. Hence, we find a first indication of a differential usefulness of various innovation strategies for product innovation success.

To refine this analysis, in a second step, following the literature on the benefits of open innovation, we commence by investigating openness in general versus a more closed mode of innovation strategy (Table 2.5).

These modes are defined as *closed* following the definition of Chesbrough (2003) if they only pursue own internal R&D, but neither collaborate in innovation nor acquire external R&D. An *open* mode is followed when at least one of the open innovation strategies is pursued. Applying this distinction to our data, firms in the first row of Table 2.5 have no internal R&D and no external R&D irrespective of the form of activity. In total, 234 firms (47.6 %) are not pursuing any external knowledge sourcing, which correspond to the two first strategies (Table 2.5). The second row shows those firms that pursue own internal activities but neither follow domestic nor international *open* innovation strategies; therefore they are closed. 91 firms (18.5 % of the total) are of that type. Finally, the 257 open innovation firms in the third row pursue external innovation strategies either with combined internal innovation strategies or not; they are open.

When we investigate the success of open innovation strategies (Table 2.6), we find the 257 open firms stand for 274 indications of product innovations in the past three years, on the average 1.07, whereas the 91 closed firms indicated in 58 cases product innovations in the past three years, on the average 0.64. Even the 143 firms that do engage neither in internal R&D nor in any open innovation count for 0.31 new products on average (interestingly, a very small share of firms (3.5 % of those with no R&D) is still able to introduce products that are new to the world). This higher innovativeness of open firms applies

Table 2.6 The innovativeness of firms (in 2010) based on their degree of openness[a] in 2008 (as % of total within column[b])

Product innovation	Strategy			
	No R&D	Closed innovation	Open innovation	Total
New to the World	5 (3.5)	13 (14.3)	64 (24.9)	82
New to the Market	15 (10.5)	22 (24.2)	89 (34.6)	126
New to the Firm	24 (16.8)	23 (25.3)	121 (47.1)	168
Total number of firms	143	91	257	
Abandoned projects	0 (0.0)	7 (7.7)	72 (28.0)	

[a]The percentages do not add up to 100 % column-wise because some firms may have no product innovations and others several ones that differ in their degree of newness

[b]All differences between no R&D, closed, and open firms are statistically significant (at 1 % level) when applying *t*-tests

also to each degree of newness of product innovations. We have tested these pairwise differences of the means on the three groups: no R&D, closed innovation, and open innovation. In all cases, the pairwise differences are significant at the 1 % level; this indicates that for open innovation strategies it is more likely that a higher share of firms will pursue products that are new to the firm, new to the market, or new to the world. Hence, there is a significant increase in the share of firms that are innovative, if these firms apply open innovation strategies.

But, as Table 2.6 shows in the bottom row, at the same time, firms with open innovation strategies are also more likely to abandon innovation projects. These results are not necessarily linked, but it can be a sign that firms with more open strategies face higher demands on coordination or that their projects are more risk-oriented and therefore more likely to fail.

In order to disentangle the success of open innovation strategies, in a third step, we seek to understand the importance of domestic versus international relationships (whether contracting or collaborating) for innovation success. For that we identify those firms that have *only* used domestic collaboration partners (and not international ones); they may have used domestic collaboration or external R&D or both of them. In Table 2.7, it is found that this group contains 58 firms, from which 34 showed domestic external R&D and 39 were engaged in domestic cooperation. The comparison group comprises firms that show any of the

Table 2.7 Distribution of firms (in 2008) on domestic and international firms

	Overall category	Divided on activities
Only domestic	58 firms	34 firms domestic external R&D
		39 firms domestic collaboration
Both domestic and international	182 firms	97 firms domestic external R&D
		178 firms domestic collaboration
		70 firms international external R&D
		174 firms international collaboration

two internationally oriented innovation strategies. Again from Table 2.7, this group amounts to 182 firms, which show various combinations of open innovation strategies where domestic and international innovation collaboration are by far most frequent. Firms which where only engaged in internationally oriented open innovation strategies are not considered further (these are 17 firms out of which three firms (17.6 %) were introducing innovations that were new to the world) because we find that the most natural movement is from domestic to international rather than directly international (following Johanson and Vahlne 1977, on internationalization of sales in firms).

In Table 2.8, the innovative performance of these two groups of firms is compared—row "total no. of product innovations" and row "total no. of firms". The 58 firms oriented purely domestically indicated in 44 cases— or 0.76 cases per firm—that they had product innovations in the past three years; compared to that, the 182 internationally oriented firms reported 216 indications of new products in the past three years, which is equivalent to 1.19 cases per firm. Hence, firms that are internationally oriented are more innovative compared to those firms that are only domestically oriented.

This overall result also holds for the three degrees of newness of product innovations separately when one compares the shares in brackets in the a-rows of each newness dimension [e.g., for products new to the world, the 13.8 % under "domestic" and the 29.1 % under "international"; for new to the market, 24.1 % versus 38.5 %; and for new to the firm,

Table 2.8 The innovativeness of firms (in 2010) based on their domestic and international open innovation strategies[b] in 2008 (as % of firms that show the respective degree of product innovation[a])

Product innovation…	Only domestic		International				Total
Strategy	Domestic external R&D	Domestic collaboration	Domestic external R&D	Domestic collaboration	Intern. external R&D	Intern. collaboration	
New to the World[b]							
a	8 (13.8)		53 (29.1)				82
b	5 (14.7)	6 (15.4)	35 (36.1)	51 (28.7)	27 (38.6)	52 (29.9)	
New to the Market[b]							
a	14 (24.1)		70 (38.5)				126
b	11 (32.4)	9 (23.1)	47 (48.5)	68 (38.2)	35 (50.0)	67 (38.5)	
New to the Firm[b]							
a	22 (37.9)		93 (51.1)				168
b	14 (41.2)	14 (35.9)	56 (57.7)	90 (50.6)	45 (64.3)	90 (51.7)	
Total number of product innovations	44		216				
Total number of firms	58		182				
Number of firms in the subcategory	34	39	97	178	70	174	
Abandoned projects	8 (13.8)		64 (35.2)				

[a]The percentages do not add up to 100 % column-wise because some firms may have no product innovations and others several ones that differ in their degree of newness

[b]Percentages in the a-row refer to the total number of firms; percentages in the b-rows refer to the number of firms in the respective subcategory

Note: All differences between domestic and international open innovation strategies are statistically significant (at 1 % level) when applying t-tests

37.9 % versus 51.1 %; all differences are statistically significant (at 1 % level; t-test)].

Moreover, splitting up the broad orientations of "domestic" and "international" into their constituting strategies—as shown in the b-rows to each newness dimension—not only are the results of above confirmed, but also a sort of complementarity effect shows up. For that one compares the shares of innovative firms that also implement domestic external R&D or domestic innovation competition under "international" with their counterparts under "domestic"; quite evidently the former shares are considerably higher than the latter ones (e.g., under "new to the firm" the 57.7 % and 50.6 % under "international" compared to 41.2 % and 35.9 % under "domestic"), all the differences being statistically significant (at 1 % level; t-test). These results suggest that implementing internationally oriented knowledge sourcing strategies on top of domestic sourcing strategies improves the efficiency of the latter. Certainly, this issue deserves further and deeper analysis in the future.

Moreover, internationally oriented firms are also more likely to abandon projects in the same period. This may indicate that pursuing international open innovation is both more rewarding, but also more challenging. Here also, the difference with respect to abandoned projects is statistically significant.

2.5 Conclusion

This chapter has investigated how firms may benefit from not only organizing their open innovation strategies based on the type of strategy, whether internal R&D or full openness, but also that the geographic location of the partnership for openness matters. In general, applying more open and more internationally oriented strategies is better in terms of a firm's ability to introduce new and more radical products to the market, which supports the results of Löof (2009) and Arvanitis and Bolli (2013). These findings may be explained by the possibility to access valuable knowledge from abroad that may even be characterized as superior technological expertise. Most interestingly, this main result holds especially in the case of introducing more radical new products—it sheds some light on the preferable combination of innovation strategies under which innovation leadership positions can be attained. As a second major result, firms with more open innovation strategies and with more internationally oriented strategies also have a higher tendency to abandon innovative projects. This may be explained by previous research on abandoned innovation projects, which showed that R&D intensive firms have a higher likelihood of abandoning innovation projects (Garcia-Vega and Lopez 2010) due to the higher number of innovation projects, and therefore a higher likelihood of abandoning projects. In addition, issues and challenges related to firms finding the right partner for collaboration (Garcia-Vega and Lopez 2010) and problems with management of open innovation relationships (Lhuillery and Pfister 2009) may offer an explanation.

The opportunities to access inter-organizational collaborations and contract with external R&D providers whether domestic or international are all part of a wide array of organizing opportunities for a firm's innovation activities. The complexities of managing open innovation in an international perspective immediately become obvious. In particular, we argue that organizing innovation activities while taking into account both acquisition (external R&D contracting) and collaboration with both domestic and international orientations for innovation revolutionizes the tasks and challenges of innovation managers. When innovation managers face the choice of whether to do it alone by internal R&D or to design a strategy based on open innovation mechanisms that seeks to obtain a good match of acquisition and collaboration, the latter is clearly superior.

With firms opening in innovation, their traditional concern to appropriate the new knowledge generated as best as possible (by IPR, secrecy, etc.) is substituted by an at least as complex task, namely to balance knowledge sourcing strategies in terms of appropriation, external participation, and external sharing. Going external here refers in the first instance to the boundaries of the firm (which in an open innovation context become fuzzy anyway); proximities to the external partners have to be managed, be that mainly cognitive or social ones (Boschma 2005). Furthermore, of interest for future studies will be to investigate—as suggested in the theoretical part–, whether firms relying on external R&D (both/or domestic and international) will exhaust firms' internal innovation potential. Furthermore, when an international orientation is added, compared to staying entirely domestic, institutional proximities in terms of culture and habits gain importance (Boschma 2005), and the geographical or spatial dimension cannot be neglected.

Even though this study rested primarily on a descriptive empirical investigation, the results clearly add to the literature on open innovation and innovation management by investigating the added value of going from domestic towards international sources of knowledge, a perspective yet unexplored in the literature (Arvanitis and Bolli 2013; Beers and Zand 2014). However, further research should be initiated to investigate whether the complementarity effect of domestic and international strategies does in fact exist and what the implications of such complementarities are for innovation management. The opportunities identified in widening the open innovation strategies to benefit from globalization through internationalization strategies apparently also come at a risk in potentially opening and abandoning further innovation projects. This link between internationalization of innovation activities while risking further failures leading to abandoning projects is another topic for further research.

Moreover, the analysis in this study did not go so far as to compare different open innovation strategies. Our data seem to suggest slight advantages of collaboration compared to external R&D and also of going international compared to source at home—and this seems to go hand in hand with studies like Arvanitis and Bolli (2013). Certainly, comparisons like this require further in-depth analysis where also the scope of countries, e.g., the impact of culture, and the type of innovation partners are to be taken into account. The case in this study is Denmark, a relatively small country, for which internationalization is a rather normal issue. But how do these relationships hold in countries considered as large like the USA or Germany?

Furthermore, besides the distinction between domestic vs. international openness, future studies will also benefit from adding, as suggested by Bogers (2011), the influence of the characteristics of the openness/collaboration and the knowledge type on firms' outcomes from innovation projects. Hence, these results open new important research questions for understanding open innovation in an international perspective, as well as for strengthening our implications for handling the emerging revolutionary innovation management tasks.

Last but not least, due the design of the CIS survey and the use of a sample of manufacturing firms across industries, the study is limited from discussing the impact of the environment on innovation performance.

Note

1. The paper acknowledges the access to the Danish CIS data from the Danish Statistical Office.

References

Arvanitis, S., and T. Bolli. 2013. A Comparison of National and International Innovation Cooperation in Five European Countries. *Review of Industrial Organization* 43(3): 163–191.

Barge-Gil, A. 2010. Cooperation-based Innovators and Peripheral Cooperators: An Empirical Analysis of Their Characteristics and Behavior. *Technovation* 30 (3): 195–206.

Becker, W., and J. Dietz. 2004. R&D Cooperation and Innovation Activities of Firms—Evidence for the German Manufacturing Industry. *Research Policy* 33 (2): 209–223.

Belderbos, R., M. Carree, and B. Lokshin. 2004. Cooperative R&D and Firm Performance. *Research Policy* 33(10): 1477–1492.

Berchicci, L. 2013. Towards an Open R&D System: Internal R&D Investment, External Knowledge Acquisition and Innovative Performance. *Research Policy* 42(1): 117–127.

Bertrand, O., and M.J. Mol. 2013. The Antecedents and Innovation Effects of Domestic and Offshore R&D Outsourcing: The Contingent Impact of Cognitive Distance and Absorptive Capacity. *Strategic Management Journal* 34(6): 751–760.

Bettis, R.A., S.P. Bradley, and G. Hamel. 1992. Outsourcing and Industrial Decline. *Academy of Management Executive* 6(1): 7–22.

Boschma, R. 2005. Proximity and Innovation—A Critical Assessment. *Regional Studies* 39(1): 61–74.

Bogers, M. 2011. The Open Innovation Paradox: Knowledge Sharing and Protection in R&D Collaborations. *European Journal of Innovation Management* 14(1): 93–117.

Cassiman, B., and R. Veugelers. 2006. In Search of Complementarity in Innovation Strategy: Internal R&D and External Knowledge Acquisition. *Management Science* 52(1): 68–82.

Chesbrough, H.W. 2003. *Open Innovation—The New Imperative for Creating and Profiting from Technology*. Boston, MA: Harvard Business School Press.

Cooper, R.G., and E.J. Kleinschmidt. 1990. New Product Success Factors: A Comparison of 'Kills' versus Successes and Failures. *R&D Management* 30(1): 47–63.

Deeds, D.L., and C.W.L. Hill. 1996. Strategic Alliances and the Rate of New Product Development: An Empirical Study of Entrepreneurial Biotechnology Firms. *Journal of Business Venturing* 11(1): 41–55.

Enkel, E., O. Gassmann, and H. Chesbrough. 2009. Open R&D and Open Innovation: Exploring the Phenomenon. *R&D Management* 39(4): 311–316.

Fey, C., and J. Birkinshaw. 2005. External Sources of Knowledge, Governance Mode and R&D Performance. *Journal of Management* 31(4): 597–621.

Freeman, C. 1995. The 'National System of Innovation' in Historical Perspective. *Cambridge Journal of Economics* 19(1): 5–24.

Garcia-Vega, M., and A. Lopez. 2010. Determinants of Abandoning Innovative Activities: Evidence from Spanish Firms. *Cuadernos de Economía y Dirección de la Empresa* 13(45): 69–91.

Gassmann, O., E. Enkel, and H. Chesbrough. 2010. The Future of Open Innovation. *R&D Management* 40(3): 213–221.

Gilley, K.M., and A.A. Rasheed. 2000. Making More by Doing Less: An Analysis of Outsourcing and Its Effects on Firm Performance. *Journal of Management* 26(4): 763–790.

Griliches, Z., and J. Mairesse. 1984. Productivity and R&D at the Firm Level. In *R&D, Patents and Productivity*, ed. Z. Griliches, 339–374. Chicago, IL: University of Chicago Press.

Grimpe, C., and U. Kaiser. 2010. Balancing Internal and External Knowledge Acquisition: The Gains and Pains from R&D Outsourcing. *Journal of Management Studies* 47(8): 1483–1509.

Hagedoorn, J. 1993. Understanding the Rationale of Strategic Technology Partnering: Inter Organizational Modes of Cooperation and Sectoral Differences. *Strategic Management Journal* 14(5): 371–385.

Henttonen, K., and P. Ritala. 2013. Searching Far and Deep: Focus of Open Search Strategy as Driver of Firm's Innovation Performance. *International Journal of Innovation Management* 17(3): 1–20.

Henttonen, K., P. Ritala, and T. Jauhiainen. 2011. Exploring Open Search Strategies and Their Perceived Impact on Innovation Performance—Empirical Evidence. *International Journal of Innovation Management* 15(3): 525–541.

Hillebrand, B., and W.G. Biemans. 2004. Links between Internal and External Cooperation in Product Development: An Exploratory Study. *Journal of Product Innovation Management* 21: 110–122.

Holste, J.S., and D. Fields. 2010. Trust and Tacit Knowledge Sharing and Use. *Journal of Knowledge Management* 14(1): 128–140.

Inauen, M., and A. Schenker-Wicki. 2011. The Impact of Outside-In Open Innovation on Innovation Performance. *European Journal of Innovation Management* 14(4): 496–520.

Jaklic, A., J.P. Damijan, and M. Rojec. 2008. Innovation Cooperation and Innovation Activity of Slovenian Enterprises. *LICOS Centre for Institutions and Economic Performance Discussion Paper*, Vol. No. 201.

Johanson, J., and J.-E. Vahlne. 1977. The Internationalization Process of the Firm. *Journal of International Business Studies* 8: 23–32.

Keupp, M.M., and O. Gassmann. 2009. Determinants and Archetype Users of Open Innovation. *R&D Management* 39(4): 331–341.

Knudsen, M.P. 2007. The Relative Importance of Interfirm Relationships and Knowledge Transfer for New Product Development Success. *Journal of Product Innovation Management* 24(2): 117–138.

Knudsen, M.P., and T.B. Mortensen. 2011. Some Immediate—But Negative—Effects of Openness on Product Development Performance. *Technovation* 31 (1): 54–64.

Laursen, K., and A. Salter. 2006. Open for Innovation: The Role of Openness in Explaining Innovation Performance among U.K. Manufacturing Firms. *Strategic Management Journal* 27(2): 131–150.

Lewin, A.Y., S. Massini, and C. Peeters. 2009. Why are Companies Offshoring Innovation? The Emerging Global Race for Talent. *Journal of International Business Studies* 40(6): 901–925.

Lhuillery, S., and E. Pfister. 2009. R&D Cooperation and Failures in Innovation Projects: Empirical Evidence from French CIS Data. *Research Policy* 38(1): 45–57.

Lööf, H. 2009. Multinational Enterprises and Innovation: Firm Level Evidence on Spillover via R&D Collaboration. *Journal of Evolutionary Economics* 19(1): 41.

Miotti, L., and F. Sachwald. 2003. Co-operative R&D: Why and with Whom?: An Integrated Framework of Analysis. *Research Policy* 32(8): 1481–1499.

Mudambi, S.M., and S. Tallman. 2010. Make, Buy or Ally? Theoretical Perspectives on Knowledge Process Outsourcing through Alliances. *Journal of Management Studies* 47(8): 1434–1456.

Nelson, R.R., and S.G. Winter. 1982. *An Evolutionary Theory of Economic Change*. Cambridge, MA: Harvard University Press.

Nieto, M.J., and A. Rodriguez. 2011. Offshoring of R&D: Looking Abroad to Improve Innovation Performance. *Journal of International Business Studies* 42 (3): 345–361.

Nieto, M.J., and L. Santamaria. 2007. The Importance of Diverse Collaborative Networks for the Novelty of Product Innovation. *Technovation* 27(6–7): 367–377.

OECD. 2003. http://www.oecd.org/sti/ind/48350231.pdf

Pakes, A., and Z. Griliches. 1984. Patents and R&D at the Firm Level: A First Look. In *Patents and Productivity*, ed. Z. Griliches, 55–72. Chicago: University of Chicago Press.

Pisano, G.P., and R. Verganti. 2008. Which Kind of Collaboration is Right for You? *Harvard Business Review* 86(12): 78–86.

Powell, W.W. 1990. Neither Market nor Hierarchy: Network Forms of Organization. *Research in Organizational Behavior* 12: 295–336.

Powell, W.W., K.K. Koput, and L. Smith-Doerr. 1996. Inter-organisational Collaboration and the Locus of Innovation: Network Learning in Biotechnology. *Administrative Science Quarterly* 41(1): 116–145.

Quinn, J.B. 1999. Strategic Outsourcing: Leveraging Knowledge Capabilities. *Sloan Management Review* 40(4): 1–9.

———. 2000. Outsourcing Innovation: The New Engine of Growth. *Sloan Management Review* 41(4): 1–13.

Rosenkopf, L., and A. Nerkar. 2001. Beyond Local Search: Boundary-Spanning, Exploration, and Impact in the Optical Disc Industry. *Strategic Management Journal* 22(4): 287–306.

Tranekjer, T.L., and M.P. Knudsen. 2012. The (Unknown) Providers to Other Firms' New Product Development: What's in It for Them? *Journal of Product Innovation Management* 29(6): 986–999.

van Beers, C., and F. Zand. 2014. R&D Cooperation, Partner Diversity, and Innovation Performance: An Empirical Analysis. *Journal of Product Innovation Management* 31(2): 292–312.

Vega-Jurado, J., A. Gutierrez-Gracia, I. Fernández-de-Lucio, and L. Manjarrés-Henríquez. 2008. The Effect of External and Internal Factors on Firms' Product Innovation. *Research Policy* 37(4): 616–632.

Von Zedtwitz, M., and O. Gassmann. 2002. Market versus Technology Drive in R&D Internationalization: Four Different Patterns of Managing Research and Development. *Research Policy* 31(4): 569–588.

Von Zedtwitz, M., O. Gassmann, and R. Boutellier. 2004. Organizing Global R&D: Challenges and Dilemmas. *Journal of International Management* 10(1): 21–49.

Weigelt, C. 2009. The Impact of Outsourcing New Technologies on Integrative Capabilities and Performance. *Strategic Management Journal* 30(6): 595–616.

3

Chaebols' Innovation Management without an Economic Miracle

Ingyu Oh

3.1 Introduction

Economic miracles are few and far between in modern human history, suggesting that world economic affairs have persistently upheld a biased division between a few haves and majority of have-nots. Over the post-war years, the Cold War, an era of freer trade, and US hegemony, only eight countries have successfully ascended to the status of what the IMF calls "developed" (i.e., countries exhibiting full political independence with a highly-developed infrastructure, health care facilities, education, culture, a strong middle class, and affluence as measured by national and per capita GDP). These are Israel in the Middle East; South Korea (hereafter, Korea), Taiwan, Hong Kong, and Singapore in East Asia; and the Czech Republic, Slovakia, and Slovenia in the former Soviet bloc. In this short list of newly developed countries (two of them being city states), only four are non-European, adding further bleakness to the already gloomy picture of north-south inequality.

I. Oh (✉)
Korea University, Seoul, Korea

© The Author(s) 2017
A. Brem, E. Viardot (eds.), *Revolution of Innovation Management*,
DOI 10.1057/978-1-349-95123-9_3

Among the four so-called East Asian tigers, Korea stands out because it is the only non-Chinese country without prolonged interaction with European colonial forces. Hong Kong and Singapore were modernized by the British colonial administration, whereas Taiwan was first exposed to Portuguese and Dutch colonial, or long distance, explorers. Furthermore, while Korea has survived a massive civil war with North Korea, Taiwan, Hong Kong, and Singapore have not fought any major wars since 1949. In addition, Korea is not a territorial part of China, whereas Hong Kong and Taiwan are under the constant threat of being annexed to the socialist regime. In fact, Korea has maintained that it plans to unify the peninsula in tandem with the expected collapse of the North's communist rule. In contrast to Singapore, Korea is a fully democratized country that has faithfully conformed to the Lipsetian rule of democratization through economic affluence, whereby we see a correlation between democratization and economic growth. With regards to economic growth, Korea's GDP per capita was just around twice that of Sub-Saharan Africa in 1960 but almost 24 times as high in 2005 (Pillay 2010). Finally, Korea underwent a long period of military dictatorship between 1961 and 1987 after Japanese colonial rule of a similar length (1910–1945). This pattern cannot be found in Hong Kong, Singapore, or Taiwan, where civilian dictatorship or UK-style colonial administration had been the norm (Table 3.1).

Qualifying the Korean economic miracle is therefore a complicated task, given its unique presence in East Asia on the one hand and its superficial resemblance to Japan, Taiwan, Hong Kong, and Singapore on the other. Koreans share similar physical features with the Chinese populace, elements of Chinese and Confucian culture, and use many Chinese expressions and terminologies in their language. On the surface, the Korean economic miracle seems to be Chinese in origin, as was much propagated by scholars who touted a Confucian work ethic and Confucian capitalism (Rozman 1990; Lew et al. 2011; Bae and Form 1986). To others, however, Korea also resembles Japan. Koreans also share similarities with the Japanese and hold on to the Japanese cultural concept of *senpai* (senior) and *kōhai* (junior) in hierarchical human relations. Like the Japanese, Koreans have respected and followed the pre-war system of selecting public officials or *kōmuin* through national exams. Indeed,

Table 3.1 Korean GDP growth, 1960–2013

Year	GDP ($)	Year	GDP ($)	Year	GDP ($)
1960	156	1980	1778	2000	11,948
1961	91	1981	1969	2001	11,256
1962	104	1982	2076	2002	12,789
1963	142	1983	2268	2003	14,219
1964	120	1984	2474	2004	15,922
1965	105	1985	2542	2005	18,657
1966	129	1986	2906	2006	20,917
1967	156	1987	3628	2007	23,101
1968	193	1988	4813	2008	20,475
1969	237	1989	5860	2009	18,339
1970	292	1990	6642	2010	22,151
1971	317	1991	7676	2011	24,156
1972	339	1992	8140	2012	24,454
1973	426	1993	8869	2013	25,977
1974	589	1994	10,275		
1975	646	1995	12,404		
1976	875	1996	13,255		
1977	1106	1997	12,197		
1978	1468	1998	8134		
1979	1858	1999	10,432		

Source: World Bank Group, World Development Indicators
Accessed October 24, 2014. http://data.worldbank.org/country/korea-republic

many precedent studies of the Korean and Japanese economic miracles have highlighted bureaucratic efficiency in a developmental state as a key factor for success (Johnson 1982; Hattori 1987; Lie 2000).

Despite these cultural proximities between greater China and Korea as well as between Korea and Japan, the lynchpin of the Korean economic miracle was an idiosyncratic institutional and cultural framework that cannot be found in its neighboring nations. For one thing, neither greater Chinese (Hong Kong, Taiwan, Singapore) nor Japanese economic development necessitated the development of the *chaebol*, or family-owned and -controlled inter-market conglomerates that competed over a small domestic market during the heyday of post-war capitalism. The key aspect of the *chaebols'* birth, development, and maturity involves monopolistic competition under the behest of military dictatorship (see *inter alia* Lie 2000; EM Kim 1997; Oh 1999; Cumings 1984). In East Asia and elsewhere, family conglomerates, which dominate global export and foreign direct investment (FDI) markets in addition to the domestic market, are rarely sustainable under military dictatorships, unless they have blood ties with the military itself (Khanna and Yafeh 2007; Hattori 1997; Mo and Weingast 2013). For another, these *chaebols* have maintained their strong market position through both radical (i.e., either profit growth of more than 30 percent in one fiscal year or cost reduction by the same scale due to the introduction of new technology) and incremental innovation. While innovation occurs in all advanced and globally competitive firms in export markets, the kind of innovations that have occurred and are still occurring in the *chaebol* are considerably different from those found in the Japanese *keiretsu* (interlocked business groups) or in the *guanxi* firms based on personalized social networks in greater China. Briefly, Japanese innovations are process-based with institutional complementarity that emphasizes a combination of malleable skills between management and shop floor teams (Aoki 1990). In greater China, firms manage to innovate through collaboration between *guanxi* groups in the motherland and in North America through inter-faction competition (Saxenian 1999; Hsu and Saxenian 2000; Oh 1999; Wong 2005). But in the *chaebol*, innovation is more radical and patent-oriented than in Japan, while few *chaebol* groups maintain *guanxi* networks with Korean Americans for technological innovations (L. Kim 1997; Oh et al. 2005; Ghoshal 1988; Chang 2011). Innovative *chaebols* are therefore the fundamental institutional rubric of the Korean miracle (Table 3.2).

Furthermore, no East or Southeast Asian country that underwent an economic miracle featured Korean-style macroeconomic policies of rapid industrial restructuring, which required forcible closure of old industrial sectors to bet on new, untested alternatives in the global export market (Song 2003; World Bank 1993; Pirie 2008; Eichengreen et al. 2012). This means that large-scale population displacement, massive unemployment between stages of restructuring, and geographical transfiguration involving landscape destruction and environmental pollution were far more rampant and disparaging in Korea than in Japan, Taiwan, Hong Kong, or Singapore. While predominantly agrarian in the 1950s and the 1960s, the political economy of Korea (or its peculiar state-business relations) managed a rapid, abrupt, and far-reaching movement of young people from the rural to urban areas to create the urban proletariat

Table 3.2 Top five Korean *chaebols*, 2003 vs. 2013

2003			2013		
Company	Assets (KRW trillion)	Employees	Company	Assets (KRW trillion)	Employees
Samsung	83.5	130,750	Samsung	306.1	257,091
LG	58.6	92,283	Hyundai Motor	166.7	147,714
SK	47.5	29,127	SK	140.6	78,593
Hyundai Motor	44.1	98,706	LG	102.4	141,722
KT	30.8	48,344	Lotte	87.5	85,010

Source: South Korea Fair Trade Commission
Accessed October 24, 2014. http://www.businessweek.com/articles/2013-09-26/for-south-koreas-top-students-chaebol-are-the-place-to-be

class in the 1970s (Koo 2001; Lie 2000). Farmlands were converted into factory complexes in a matter of years, if not months, for light industries (e.g., textiles, wigs, toothpaste, soap), which were then bulldozed and replaced with new factories for heavy and chemical industries (e.g., oil refinery, automobiles, shipbuilding, electronics). In the 1980s and 1990s, employees of heavy and chemical industries were laid off in large numbers due to factory automation and robotics, while tertiary sector jobs (or what we call "McJobs") were created in vast numbers to jumpstart a new era of the service sector economy. As a consequence, geographical and environmental metamorphoses were most dramatic in Korea, while labor union movements were and still are the most militant among East Asian miracle economies (Lie 2000; Hart-Landsberg 1993; Cumings 1984; Pirie 2008).

The net result of the innovation management within the *chaebol* during the Korean economic miracle was radical (i.e., both in terms of rapid catching up and taking-over global industrial leaders by either reducing costs by more than 20 percent or salvaging profits by the same rate). The Korean innovation management during that period was marked by the semi–world-class process and technological innovation. However, as the miracle has stopped by 2015 with an annual GDP growth rate of less than three percent (compared to 8–12 percent during the miracle years), *chaebols* are now faced with a new mandate of continuing radical innovation with a different innovation management strategy that has to go beyond the level of catching up and taking over. *Chaebols* are asked to introduce genuine technological and/or process innovations that are radically new and fresh to the industry they are leading. In this chapter, I will first explain *chaebols'* innovation management during the miracle years, followed by their new innovation strategy in recent years with a suggestion on what they should emphasize during the post-miracle years.

3.2   Innovation Management During Miracle Years (with a Case Study)

The most peculiar institutional arrangement of the Korean economic miracle was based on the lack of credible commitment among economic actors and organizations to deliver a guaranteed quantity of goods and services at agreed-upon prices. Amid the absence of the most fundamental element of the Anglo-American concept of the free market and its mechanism of credible commitment (see Williamson 1983; North 1993), Korean economic actors and organizations had to rely on the credible threat, which appears in the context of conflict and rivalry. In Korea, credible threats were realized only through the mafia/predatory state, which was willing to exercise either legitimate or illegitimate power to enforce agreements (for credible threats, see Konrad and Skaperdas 1997; Gambetta 2000; for Korean credible threats, see Oh 1999; Oh and Varcin 2002).

The mafia state can take many forms, although the most distinctive property is its peculiar way of collecting revenue. While extortion is a typical mafia means of collecting revenue from street merchants in exchange for property protection, extortion by the mafia state can be institutionalized on an ongoing basis through either rent-seeking or rent-sharing. Unlike rent-seeking, where interest groups and individuals seek bigger rent in exchange for co-opting state actors (Buchanan et al. 1980; Krueger 1974), rent-sharing requires an opposite arrangement of state actors seeking a larger share of the rent than the one garnered by interest groups and individuals (Oh and Varcin 2010). In fact, throughout the miracle years, Korean state actors tried hard to raise the portion of rent they shared with the business sector. For example, in one year, total rent of 100 may be divided between the state and firms at a ratio of 20 and 80, respectively. If the state demands a greater portion of rent that exceeds rent generated for firms, firms would have to increase total output dramatically to meet the state demands, while maintaining an adequate share of the rent for themselves. As such, total rent may increase to 200 in the next period, with the state receiving 80 and firms receiving 120.

What did the mafia state do to maximize its (legitimate or illegitimate) share of rent? First and foremost, dictators of the first military regime (1961–1979) pursued macroeconomic policies to boost economic growth rates via higher real interest rates. Savings ratios were high (i.e., the K effect) throughout the regime's lifecycle, but the state quickly moved into the banking sector to own and control most Korean financial institutions. Savings went into state-controlled banks that lent money out to select clients, such as *chaebol* families. Unlike in Japan, where savings rates were also high, the Korean mafia state maintained high interest rates to induce savings from the working class. Although savings ratios were high, the absolute need for capital far exceeded what state banks could provide to *chaebol* groups. As such, the state had to underwrite most of the foreign loans and aid money to fund *chaebol* projects, which in turn promised paybacks to the state. Simultaneously, the state suppressed wages while improving labor productivity (i.e., the L effect). Firms subsidized night schools for workers while jailing thousands of union leaders and their supporters, and wholesale relocation of rural youth to urban factories progressed quickly thanks to government and factory buses and recruiters. Finally, the state actively subsidized firms that licensed foreign technologies, especially from Japan (i.e., the T effect). With the K, L, and T effects combined, the Korean mafia state boasted GDP growth rates between eight and ten percent during the 1960s and the 1970s (Eichengreen et al. 2012).

On the other side of macroeconomic policies was the *chaebol* that contributed extorted money to the predatory mafia state. *Chaebol* literally means "families with enormous wealth." How the families accrued and expanded their wealth may remain a family secret, although all top ten *chaebol* families were connected to each other and to key politicians through marriage (Hattori 1987; Chang 2003). The *chaebol* differs significantly from other East Asian conglomerates on several accounts. First, *chaebol* groups have a dual ownership structure. On paper, owning families do not possess more than two to six percent of total shares, but in reality, they own more than sixty percent of total equity through a pseudo holding company system (Chang 2003; Campbell and Keys 2002; Kim et al. 2004; Trautvetter 2010). It is a pseudo holding company system because *chaebol* holding companies indirectly own shares of *chaebol* member firms without publicly listing the holding company itself. The reason behind a dual ownership structure is the thorny issue of succession. Succession from the *chaebol* founder to his son was not seriously challenged during the military regime under the mafia-clientele arrangement. But since rapid democratization since 1987, the civilian government began heavily taxing *chaebol* inheritances (e.g., shares) while concomitantly demanding ownership diffusion according to Anglo-American standards of corporate governance, particularly after the 1997 Asian financial crisis. In order to safeguard succession without paying massive taxes, *chaebols* have experimented with different varieties of dual ownership structures (Chang 2003).

Second, ownership and control are fused instead of separated, unlike in many *guanxi* corporations in greater China and Japanese *keiretsu* groups. Although managerial professionalization has progressed rapidly in Korea, *chaebol* families have actively educated male heirs in preparation to succeed their fathers as CEOs and/or chairmen and neutralize external criticism of nepotism, such as Samsung's heir-apparent Lee Jaeyong's education at Harvard University. Unlike in North American or European family businesses, it is not uncommon to see many *chaebol* heirs attending or having graduated from Ivy League schools in the United States, not to mention prestigious Korean and Japanese undergraduate programs.

Third, *chaebols* have increased the market value of their companies through massive diversification and tunneling. Diversification was a bulwark or insurance against state hostility to *chaebols* in the form of destruction or confiscation (i.e., no property right protection). In fact, *chaebols* such as Yulsan, Kukje, and Daewoo disappeared during the first and second military regimes and even under the civilian government, in addition to seven *chaebols* that were closed down after the inauguration of the first military regime. The *chaebol* logic was that the government would not confiscate their property if they were big in size and highly-diversified into industries such as automobiles, textiles, and even military (EM Kim 1997). Tunneling is an illegal means of manipulating the price of *chaebol* holding company stocks by actively buying out unrelated firms through mergers and acquisitions (M&As). If unrelated firms are bought out, the *chaebol*'s stock prices go up artificially with market rumors about potential revenue growth through new acquisitions (Baek et al. 2006). These practices are either illegal or uncommon in other East Asian countries.

Fourth, unlike other conglomerate groups in neighboring countries, *chaebol* groups relied heavily on labor exploitation for profit, using both workplace patriarchy and police crackdowns on militant labor unrest. Labor unrest was an anticipated response to harsh working conditions. Often, these organizations functioned as sweatshops or prison labor camps, where workers from the countryside worked in often unhealthy and poorly ventilated workspaces, eating and sleeping on the same premises. Wages were 20 to 40 cents an hour, far below recommended rates for factory workers in export processing zones of many developing countries (Hart-Landsberg 1993; Lie 2000; Pirie 2008). Workers in Korean *chaebols* were denied union rights, minimum wage laws, or lifetime employment during the military regime, while labor union movements instigated by the self-cremation of Jeon Taeil in 1970 were quashed by brute police force. What distinguished the *chaebol* from other family businesses in East Asia was the suppression of one of the world's most militant labor movements, either unionized or unorganized, arguably resembling a massacre of one social class by another. To this point, labor strikes reached a record high of more than 3600 incidents in 1987 (EM Kim 1997).

Finally, the *chaebol* has maintained a huge network of interlocking ownership (not director interlocking), where the financial firm in the secondary finance market (e.g., insurance, stock brokerage, leasing, credit cards) and former holding companies (i.e., holding companies before the 1961 military coup) in general trading, construction, and electronics (e.g., Samsung Mulsan, Hyundai Construction, Samsung Electronics) own one another's stock to protect ownership of the *chaebol* group by one family. This system of mutual stock ownership is different from that of the *keiretsu* in Japan or *guanxi* firms in greater China; the use of financial and former holding firms within the *chaebol* is to protect the *chaebol* family, in contrast with the ban on owning *keiretsu*-style main banks or *guanxi*-style holding companies (Chang 2003; Oh and Park 2001).

The birth of the mafia state and the *chaebol* after the 1961 military coup created a new business culture of what we call "credible threats," contrasting with the Anglo-American or Japanese culture of credible commitment (see Williamson 1983; North 1993). The culture of credible threats is the third element of the Korean post-war economic miracle. Credible commitment works in two ways. First, in the Anglo-American tradition, formal contractual relations in the market and between firms reduce room for opportunism. But given that contractual relations in the UK and the USA cannot be institutionalized without administrative fiat or organizational (or sometimes legal) safeguarding, actual inclination to opportunism looms large. To offset opportunism rampant in the market, Anglo-American firms use institutions of administrative fiat to induce credible commitment between contractual parties. Second, in the Japanese tradition, room for opportunism is always very high given the relative absence of formal contractual relations in business practice. But given that Japanese business networks are based on long-term trust rather than short-term contracts, actual inclination to opportunism is surprisingly rare between business partners and firms, thus leading to credible commitment between liable business parties. Either system of inducing credible commitment, whether based on institutional complementarity of functional specificities (e.g., functional specialization) or structural stochasticity (e.g., shop floor communication between blue and white collar workers or between mother firms and supplier firms), would be an acceptable institutional solution to the problem of transaction costs (Aoki 1994; Nooteboom 2001).

However, in post-coup Korea, neither system of prompting credible commitment worked. For one thing, Korean business and economic actors did not possess functional specificities to lead to high levels of organizational (both technological and procedural) standardization. They also failed to build a business network that was based on a long-term trust. Structural stochasticity, or effective management–labor/buyer–supplier communication, did not exist within such networks because the actors lacked a sufficient level of tacit knowledge to run organizations constrained by qualitative, if not functional, standardization. In a nutshell, Korean business firms were organized and run under the principle of informal solidarity and group norms, although they tried to quickly learn and apply American-style technological know-how and work procedures (see Oh and Varcin 2010). Amid the welter, both military rulers and *chaebol* owners agreed upon a new rule of using credible threats in the form of brute force to realize organizational goals. Between the state and the *chaebol*, credible threats worked to induce the *chaebol*'s commitment to economic growth and payments (both legal and illegal) to the state, and the punishment if either failed was to close down the *chaebol* (i.e., withdrawal of state protection of *chaebol*'s property rights). Between labor suppliers and the *chaebol*, credible threats worked in a fashion to induce labor/supplier commitment to economic growth and sacrifice (e.g., supplier bribery to the *chaebol*, low salaries for workers) for the *chaebol*, and punishment in the case of failure, such as destroying the supplier firm or laying off workers in large numbers (Oh 1999). In order to institutionalize credible threats, both the state and the *chaebol* routinely punished inexorable partners. For example, 1653 mergers and acquisitions (M&As) of small firms by the *chaebol* groups were reported throughout the 1980s. Although all these M&As were illegitimate under the M&A law, only one case was ruled illegal by the court (Chung and Yang 1992).

The final element of the Korean economic miracle was technological and organizational innovation, a key feature of the economic success throughout the miracle period. In order for real GDP to grow quickly, developing states need to secure either momentous labor productivity or technological innovation, whether radical or incremental (see Tsuru 1996; Eichengreen et al. 2012). For Korea, labor productivity was not always something that the government could quickly increase due to various structural difficulties and constraints. Fundamentally, the state faced low levels of skill attainment among young rural boys and girls who were almost forcibly shifted from rice paddies to urban factories. Educating the new urban proletariat class required substantial investment in education and long-term training programs, and the military state had no intention of doing either. Instead, the state and the *chaebol* spent enormous effort on technological and organizational innovation (or the T factor of GDP growth). To many Anglo-American economists and innovation scholars, this option would have been more difficult for Korea than that of increasing labor productivity (the L factor of GDP growth). However, Korean firms had the option of copying to improve their T factor quickly. Copying and piracy had occurred widely from the 1960s to the 1990s before Korea joined the WTO (World Trade Organization). Korea was fortunate due to its close proximity to Japan, where highly sophisticated technologies ranging from textiles and construction to shipbuilding, electronics, and automobiles, were available for either licensing or outright copying (L Kim 1997).

Cases Study: Samsung Electronics

An anecdote regarding the effect of the T factor on Korean GDP growth includes that of Samsung Electronics during the 1970s. In the early days of electronics development at Samsung, the *chaebol* successfully garnered a loan from the Long Term Credit Bank of Japan. With the borrowed money, the firm rented a two-story house in the Tokyo neighborhood of Akihabara, a well-known shopping district for the most advanced Japanese electronic goods. In the house, Samsung technicians bought and disassembled Japanese electronic goods (mostly household appliances such as refrigerators, washing machines, range ovens, and TVs) to uncover secrets behind Japanese electronic technology (i.e., reverse engineering). Although they were patented in Japan and elsewhere, patents proved to be ineffective in Korea.

In addition to outright piracy, the Korean *chaebol* also actively sought licensing opportunities with Japanese and American companies, such as Sony, Panasonic, and Corning, with the hopes of learning both standardized and tacit knowledge from advanced firms. Licensing is a fast way of learning advanced technologies in a legitimate way, although it is vulnerable to knowledge theft by licensees (Davis 2008). In return for Samsung's active T-factor improvements, the state provided R&D subsidies in tandem with a silent negligence over patent infringement. In less than four decades since the 1960s, Korean *chaebol* firms defeated Japanese competitors in steel (POSCO became the fifth biggest global steel company by the 1980s), shipbuilding (Korean shipbuilders are the second largest shipbuilding country in the world), household appliances, electronic hardware and semiconductors (among the top ten global semiconductor suppliers, two are Korean—Samsung Electronics and SK Hynix—while just one is Japanese), and mobile phone markets. Electronics constitutes one of the most fascinating success cases of the *chaebol*, in that Samsung and LG Electronics alone make more annual revenue and profit than what all Japanese electronics firms generate combined (Chang 2011). The T-factor growth story is a secret formula for an export-led development strategy and cannot be easily emulated by other developing nations that do not have neighboring countries with advanced technologies for patent pirates. To this extent, China is a case in point. With Korea, Taiwan, and Japan right next to the mainland proper, it could easily emulate Korea's development through its own version of export-led development schemes. This is also why countries like the Philippines could not develop as quickly as China or Korea, despite the fact that the island nation was under the US Cold War protection program: it simply did not have any neighbor that was technologically advanced.

Be that as it may, Samsung now holds the second largest number of patents in the USA, only second to IBM (U.S. Patent and Trademark Office 2014). Despite its phenomenal track record of R&D and patenting, various rivals in the market, including Apple and Microsoft, have sued Samsung for patent infringement. While this indirectly illustrates how the *chaebol* is least innovative with its own Korean version of ingenuity, it remains an organizational structure that is extremely efficient in learning others' technologies in a short period of time. In this sense, the *chaebol* is probably the most efficient learning organization in the world.

3.3   Innovation Management After the Miracle (with a Case Study)

Having explained in detail *chaebols'* innovation management during the miracle years, I now present their comprehensive transformation they introduced in the 2010s in order to continue radical innovations for the post-miracle years. I also add my own suggestions dovetailed here for their future success.

Continuous economic development during the second military regime (1979–1987) mobilized the masses more than ever toward nationwide democratization movements, which included intellectuals, university students, outlawed labor union organizers, and even white-collar workers at *chaebol* firms. Democratization in 1987 and the subsequent election of the first civilian president in 1992 signified the victory of the capitalist market economy and its juggernaut, the *chaebol*, in Korea's history of modernization and economic development. The *chaebol*'s strategy of "too big to fail" proved to outwit the brute force of the mafia state. Coase's theorem gives us some clues to understand this seemingly ironic outcome. If there is a dog in the flat next door that barks early in the morning and wakes up all the residents on the same floor, complaints from building tenants would not stop the dog owner from disowning him as no law has yet been institutionalized to penalize causing public nuisance (or perhaps the dog owner is a beloved daughter of a neighborhood mafia boss who would send horse heads to those threatening to report his daughter to the police). Coase suggested that money would resolve this issue: a rich building tenant can offer a price for the dog that she cannot refuse. The rich neighbor can then safely put the dog away after buying it from the owner (Coase 1937; for the dog anecdote, see Mankiw 2014: 210).

In a similar vein, the *chaebol* has technically put the menacing mafia state in Korea to death. The monopoly of violence by the capitalist democratic state is not complete unless its capitalist class buys out competing groups of violence (e.g., the military, the mafia, the police, bandits, rebels, terrorist groups) from state apparatuses (Mo and Weingast 2013). The *chaebol* has not only grown too big to fail, but they can now financially co-opt and manipulate holders of violence and power for their own benefit as well. It is not a shocking revelation in Korea that Samsung and other leading *chaebol* groups continuously hire ex-judges and state attorneys to protect the *chaebol* family from state indictments for any wrongdoing (Yonhap 2012). The end of the developmental state in Korea effectively opened up a new era of the instrumental state, whose biggest beneficiary is the *chaebol*.

The *chaebol* garnered its legitimacy from the mafia state itself, which later became a key source of illegitimacy to the Korean people (e.g., workers, consumers, conscientious elements, intellectuals) after democratization. Although it was the *chaebol* that defeated the mafia state in the fight over the control of the property protection market, its lack of legitimacy within the new Korean democratic state has forced the *chaebol* to actively buy institutional raison d'être from civilian bureaucrats, their bosses, elected politicians, and even intellectuals. Simultaneously, the *chaebol* colluded with the state to bust labor unions through violent means. Today, a new form of state-business complicity under the democratic government is not over the issue of property protection; it is over the question of the *chaebol*'s institutional legitimacy. Globalization, the 1997 financial crisis, widening class polarization, and increasing economic concentration by the few *chaebol* groups have combined to threaten *chaebol* legitimacy in Korea, especially from the perspective of disgruntled Korean voters over illegal ownership succession plots by *chaebols* to turn over property to biological heirs (Ilyo Weekly 2014). The neoliberal policies forced upon the Korean government after the 1997 crisis also worked against the *chaebol*, the latter of which promotes concentration and monopoly more than free market competition, accounting transparency, and managerial professionalism (Kang 2002; Siegel 2007).

Consequently, the Korean political economy still suffers from a lack of trust among business actors (buyers vs. suppliers; owners vs. managers; employers vs. employees; consumers vs. marketers; the state vs. business) in the market. Rent-sharing is now replaced by rent-seeking as the annual GDP growth rate during the post-miracle years has remained less than six percent since 2003, and has fallen below the three percent level in recent years. Rent-seeking is a means of prolonging *chaebol* corporate governance (i.e., family control) despite the democratic institution of guaranteed private property protection. Corrupt politicians, state bureaucrats, and *chaebol* owners have worked closely for this purpose. As such, we can argue that rent-seeking has been responsible for the lackluster performance of Korean innovation (both technological and institutional) in the 2010s. It is not surprising that during the 2010s Samsung Electronics had one of the most difficult times in the global market over the issue of patent infringements. Despite their splendid and sustained track records of radical innovation in the 1970s and 1980s, Korean *chaebol* groups do not own any world-class technology, although Samsung owns US patents that are only second to IBM in quantity (Hankyung 2013). Therefore, quantities do not matter as much as the quality of the patents. Although Korean scientists publish lots of research results and are ranked number six in the world in terms of citations, no Korean university is ranked in the top thirty in the world in terms of scientific reputation. Consequently, *chaebol* groups have been buying research results from North American, European, and Japanese scientists, while Korean scientists are rapidly forming a fourth group of rent-seekers who embezzle government research funding for their own personal use (Oh 2013).

The only possibility of raising GDP through rent-seeking is both increasing labor productivity and introducing rapid technological innovation, while also pursuing monopolies by lobbying the state. In other words, monopolies like *chaebols* had to create national wealth through both L and T factors and pay off exponentially growing amounts of both legal and illegal rents to the state. As explained above, increasing the L factor takes a long time and requires radical education reforms. Therefore, the *chaebol* chose to exploit the labor force instead of nurturing them through increasing hours of leisure and retraining. However, we have also seen that the *chaebol* could easily ensure a T factor growth through Japan and the USA, either under licensing agreements or piracy. As licensing and piracy no longer generate sufficient rents for the *chaebol*, they now have to augment the T factor through radical innovation as an industry leader, not as a catch-up follower and late developer.

Case Study: Post-miracle Radical Innovation by Samsung

The benefit of the rent-seeking system where the *chaebol* is in the driver's seat is its ability to separate the political side of business from the all-out innovative efforts within the firm. During the miracle economy, such separation was impossible, as the state controlled innovation as a political agenda with centralized R&D resources of funds and talents. Innovation as a non-political agenda of the firm, independent from state interventions and controls, means that *chaebols* can utilize both domestic and foreign sources of innovation resources. It is therefore not surprising to see the upsurge of foreign investments and foreign R&D employees within Samsung in the post-miracle years. While the state has emphasized concentrated efforts in promoting and developing university-led R&D efforts, Samsung has continuously sought after international sources of innovation, particularly from the EU, Japan, and the USA (Oh 2013). The globalization of R&D efforts is not motivated by the top-down pressure from the Korean government that has lost most of its dynamic fervor as a mafia state. Rather, it is motivated by Samsung's own needs to survive in the global monopolistic market, where the *chaebol* has continuously faced harsh competition from global leaders that no longer treat the former as an infant original equipment manufacturer (OEM) or original design manufacturer (ODM) partner in the global division of labor. Samsung is now an equal competitor with global leaders in each industry, where technological superiority through monopolistic R&D capacities would secure its market leadership and competitiveness.

Samsung's solution to the problem of maintaining its competitiveness in the global market is its revolutionary transnational strategy, by which the *chaebol* can hold on to its winning edge through the competitive prices obtained by the economies of scale and the superior quality secured by the economies of scope. Again, this strategy was executed with relative success due to the opening of Samsung's innovation system to global R&D resources that enabled scale economies in countries like BRICS and Southeast Asia on the one hand and scope economies in countries like the USA (e.g., Silicon Valley), Japan, and the EU on the other. The gargantuan financial resources that required product globalization (i.e., scale economies) and quality localization (i.e., scope economies) were funneled into Samsung from both local and global bases. For example, it is not surprising to find that 52.33 percent of Samsung Electronics is owned by foreign investors (Yonhap 2014).

The downside of Samsung's transnational strategy with transnational innovation (i.e., innovative cooperation between home country firms with multinational corporation (MNC) subsidiaries in host, supplier, customer, and competitor country firms), however, is manifested when the capacities of explorative research at the home country firm is significantly diminished due to MNC subsidiaries' salient contribution to radical innovation (in terms of novel combinations). Learning capabilities at Samsung were probably one of the best among all types of conglomerates in the world during the catch-up phase (i.e., learning by technology transfers). However, the reason why Samsung's home country firms find it difficult to learn from MNC subsidiaries that generate exploratory research is mostly due to the cultural discordances between the firms in Korea and their subsidiaries in the USA, the EU, and Japan. The same pattern is also observed among Japanese MNCs that eschew the EU and North America for their transnational innovation research partially because of such cultural and/or learning deficiencies (Gerybadze and Reger 1999).

The transition from exploitation as a main strategy for innovation during the miracle years to exploration for radical innovation for the post-miracle years was fraught with difficulties within Samsung. First, leadership succession within the *chaebol* created unnecessarily strenuous pressures on the entire business group that had to concentrate its efforts on diverting the national-level legal attention from Samsung's legal problems. Lots of Samsung resources were spent in the co-optation of the legal and political regulators and overseers who would otherwise have applied severe legal sanctions to Samsung's illegitimate leadership successions. The organizational resource management for legal and political co-optation therefore created a sudden need of lessening transnational R&D management for the entire *chaebol* group creating financial imbalance between political/legal management and R&D investments.

Second, although catch-up was possible through quick learning capabilities within the *chaebol* during the miracle years, tacit or explorative knowledge requires much longer time in learning and digesting unstandardized information. While Samsung was excellent in absorbing global standards and creating standardized products, it was inefficient in introducing explorative knowledge learning. To ameliorate this problem, Samsung decided to rely on transnational R&D, especially utilizing Korean-American scientists and project managers in the USA. Although this new strategy can bring in new talents for the *chaebol* innovation with emphases on "exploration" rather than "exploitation," the cultural discordance between Korean-American (or other foreign) R&D researchers and *chaebol* managers is too huge to forge an ongoing productive relationship. Samsung's future innovation success therefore hinges on multicultural management, which appears to be a difficult task to many inside the *chaebol*.

Third, without any institutional framework based on functional specificities or structural stochasticity, Samsung has to find yet another institutional formula for its future innovative projects. Although the transnational strategy was emulated by learning new global market drives from leading competitors in the world, the *chaebol* is still stuck in the process of family succession issues, while its shop floor remains inefficient and unproductive due to new labor conflicts between temporary and permanent workers. The temporary worker system that was introduced to the *chaebol* during the 1997 financial crisis reduced labor costs without increasing productivity. Job insecurities after the first two years of fixed term awarded to the temporary workers, who are not allowed to join labor unions, exacerbated the shop floor communication situation that has already been hampered by the lack of either functional specialization or structural stochasticity.

At the moment, Korean *chaebols* have no solution to these problems, although they keep spending 2.8 percent of GDP annually in R&D, which is the second largest in the world next to Israel (3.51 percent in 2010). This figure is disappointing rather than promising, because Korean *chaebols* are ranked only 15 in the world in terms of their own-funded R&D investments. Furthermore, although Korean *chaebols* rank world's number six in terms of patent applications, their actual trademark applications are ranked 22nd, indicating low track records of successful commercialization. In the following section, I provide some suggestions for future innovation in *chaebol* firms (OECD 2012).

3.4   Future of the Miracle: Suggestions

The issue of *chaebol* reform will continue to fetter the development of Korea's political economy beyond the economic miracle. The *chaebols* no longer seem to generate national economic wealth through the T factor, while Korean labor productivity is not increasing as fast as it needs to. Korean corporate workers work the second-longest number of hours, whereas their income is the lowest among all OECD countries (OECD

2012). Creativity remains a central question to the future viability of the Korean economy. With current *chaebol* organizations, creativity remains sparse, although it was the most efficient form of learning and catch-up of all industrial organizations during the miracle years. This suggests that corporate Korea should experiment with varieties of organizational forms that allow for diversity, multiculturalism, and organizational freedom (i.e., freedom to pursue individual goals within organizations). As such, *chaebol* reform must include not only corporate governance reform, but organizational transformation as well. In order to achieve these new sets of goals, I suggest the following reforms that need to be taken thoroughly within the *chaebol* in next decade or two in order for them to remain as viable as they are now.

First, *chaebol* organizations must be reformed to accommodate creative talents into their rigid and highly competitive intra- and inter-organizational politics. Most *chaebol* firms are highly diversified into several unrelated markets creating a dense web of both horizontal and vertical networks of subsidiaries and their main firms. Inter-organizational politics is usually played out to expand their organizational clout over other networked subsidiaries in areas of securing project financing, human resource management, and the overall control of the domestic and overseas markets. In their efforts to protect their own turf, new creative talents from unknown backgrounds are often considered organizational threats more than future assets. It is not overstating to emphasize the fact that creative talents are usually misunderstood as destructive talents by many clique leaders within each *chaebol* firm. Therefore, what is urgently needed to reform this catch-up style turf protectionism is to destroy such power cliques on the one hand and to open up the organization to outside talents. This task is revolutionary from the *chaebol* owners' point of view, the very people who need these cliques to protect their illegitimate succession projects for their sons. Therefore, creativity requires the separation of ownership from control of the *chaebol* to begin with allowing external managers to carry out genuine reforms much akin to the Japanese post-war reforms under the American occupying forces.

Creativity for the *chaebol* in the 2010s and beyond certainly requires explorative postures in their R&D decisions; however, exploration should be directed toward a new combination of knowledge based on the new global division of labor. Unlike in the previous periods, the *chaebol* is now facing competition from both BRICS (Brazil, Russia, India, and China) countries that are rapidly catching up with South Korea and from G7 (the UK, the USA, Germany, Japan, France, Canada, and Italy) countries that are trying to enlarge the innovative gap with South Korea. As a semi-peripheral economy with high R&D capabilities comparable to those of Israel, the *chaebol* firms must cultivate importing creativity from G7 countries and Israel into their world class production system that is more efficient and productive than BRICS nations. To do this, *chaebol* firms first have to open up their firms to G7 creative talents even relocating their R&D centers to G7 countries. Instead of reverse engineering during the catch-up periods, these G7-based R&D centers must focus on explorative research, not on copying the advanced technologies.

Second, for a new global division of labor to occur in *chaebols'* favor, where it is stipulated that G7 talents should genuinely lend their creative talents to *chaebol* firms, it is mandatory to introduce multicultural management to *chaebol* management teams. According to the government statistics, although 12,689 foreign researchers and professionals were working in Korea in 2014, most of them were mainly Japanese (4777), Indians (1744), Americans (1037), Chinese (1201), and Russians (326). Among the Americans, a large number of them were no doubt Korean Americans. Japan and the USA being the only two G7 countries that send researchers and professionals to Korea (two nationalities comprising close to 50 percent of the total), Korean multiculturalism in *chaebol* for creativity is far and few between. What *chaebol* firms need to do is to open up their R&D facilities to G7 researchers and professionals, even if that requires relocating R&D centers to G7 nations. Simultaneously, *chaebol* firms should shy away from hiring Korean American and Japanese researchers only and instead diversify their talent pools from all of the OECD countries for globalization purposes.

Given that *chaebol* firms have a very strong corporate culture of Korean-style Confucianism that emphasizes hierarchy according to organizational power (both formal and informal), seniority based on organizational power, and the collective suppression of powerless individual talents, it is almost impossible to convert the *chaebol* into a multicultural organization that promotes individual creativity. Furthermore, *chaebols* have culturally different norms of performance evaluations from those of the G7 countries. Instead of valuing innovativeness through breakthroughs that would lead to relatively long periods of profitability, *chaebols* cherish short-term profitability without having to be radically innovative. Therefore, they do not know how to perceive long-term profitability in the commercialization of their R&D results. This also means that they lack the capability of finding and nurturing creative talents for their R&D projects. For these problems, the first thing *chaebols* have to do is to open up their R&D facilities to G7 talents with new guidelines of cultural management that is acceptable to these new talents.

Third, the product commercialization of their explorative research must be managed by G7 talents, as Korean *chaebol* firms have never introduced radically new products in the global market. The four leading Korean industrial exports in 2015 were semiconductors, cars, ships, and chemical products, none of which were radically commercialized. This means that Korean corporations are good at leading existing industries (especially, semiconductors and ships), whereas they are incapable of introducing new ones. To commercialize radically new products based on explorative research, *chaebol* firms must rely on G7 talents who have long experience of developing new industries (e.g., radios, TVs, cars, bullet trains, spaceships, smart phones, etc.).

Explorative R&D and commercialization being in the hands of G7 talents, *chaebol* firms can concentrate on manufacturing new products on a global scale and scope, simultaneously learning explorative R&D and commercialization skills. Whether this new process will make *chaebols* shy away from their rent-seeking behaviors with the Korean state remains a separate issue. However, their behavior with the state will no longer be "rent-seeking" as the GDP will grow rapidly once again, auguring a new form of state-business relations under the radical innovation scheme.

3.5   Conclusion

In this chapter, I identified four important elements of the Korean economic miracle that surfaced between 1965 and 1987. During this period, the Korean economy recorded annual GDP growth rates in excess of eight percent. But unlike neoclassical explanations, we argued that the Korean miracle was marked by: (1) a mafia/predatory state that espoused GDP growth with escalating class polarization; (2) *chaebol* groups that could not survive without political protection extended to them by the mafia/predatory state; (3) a social and institutional culture that could not maintain or organize human business and social relations without resorting to credible threats amid rampant distrust among organizational members; and (4) semi–world-class process (institutional) and technological innovations through parodying. I also argued that the theoretical principle of the country's economic growth was rent-sharing, an institutional process of engendering phenomenal growth based on state-business collusion and credible threats. In so doing, I explained that rent-sharing was fundamentally different from rent-seeking due to actual economic growth through corruption.

However, this chapter also noticed that credible threats had discouraged creativity and innovation in the Korean economy despite political democratization and economic development, presenting a bleak picture for the future of Korea's economic miracle. Consequently, the Korean economy is suffering from outright rent-seeking behavior by economic and political actors under the new democratic state that is dominated by corrupt politicians and bureaucrats. When the economy is in the hand of the *chaebols*, which remain too big to fail, economic development is hampered because credible threats are not replaced with creditable commitment. We need to explore when and why credible commitments are made possible.

The lesson of the Korean economic miracle is twofold: the global capitalist regime that started in the 1500s was critical in shaping the exogenous basis of industrial transformation, although the endogenous basis of an economic system that was founded on the principle of the credible threat was equally pivotal in bringing about the miracle. At the same time, globalization in the same world system has substantially delimited the creative potential of the Korean miracle in much the same way it has curtailed Japan's efforts to hammer out creative solutions to its prolonged recession, following a period of high-powered growth and mass consumption. Thus, going forward, there will be great academic and practical interest in how to improve the relationship between credible threats and commitments via theory-building and empirical testing.

The lack of radical innovation in Japan and Korea therefore originates from their culture. For Korea they have to refurbish cultural management in order to tap into a new global division of labor that necessitates a new influx of G7 talents for explorative research and radical commercialization of new products.

References

Aoki, Masahiko. 1990. Toward an Economic Model of the Japanese Firm. *Journal of Economic Literature* 28: 1–27.

———. 1994. The Contingent Governance of Teams: Analysis of Institutional Complementarity. *International Economic Review* 35: 657–676.

Bae, Kyu Han, and William Form. 1986. Payment Strategy in South Korea's Advanced Economic Sector. *American Sociological Review* 51: 120–131.

Baek, Jae-Seung, Joon-Koo Kang, and Inmoo Lee. 2006. Business Groups and Tunneling: Evidence from Private Securities Offerings by Korean Chaebols. *The Journal of Finance* 61: 2415–2449.

Buchanan, James M., Robert D. Tollison, and Gordon Tullock. 1980. *Toward a Theory of the Rent-Seeking Society.* College Station, TX: Texas A&M University Press.

Campbell, Terry L., and Phyllis Y. Keys. 2002. Corporate Governance in South Korea: The Chaebol Experience. *Journal of Corporate Finance* 8: 373–391.

Chang, Sea Jin. 2003. Ownership Structure, Expropriation, and Performance of Group-Affiliated Companies in Korea. *The Academy of Management Journal* 46: 238–253.

———. 2011. *Sony vs. Samsung: The Inside Story of the Electronics Giants' Battle for Global Supremacy.* Singapore: John Wiley & Sons.

Chung, Byung Hyu, and Yung-sik Yang. 1992. *Hankuk Chaebol Bumun ui Gyungje Bunseok* [An Economic Analysis of Korean Chaebols]. Seoul: KDI.

Coase, Ronald H. 1937. The Nature of the Firm. *economica* 4: 386–405.

Cumings, Bruce. 1984. The Origins and Development of the Northeast Asian Political Economy: Industrial Sectors, Product Cycles, and Political Consequences. *International Organization* 38: 1–40.

Davis, Lee. 2008. Licensing Strategies of the New 'Intellectual Property Vendors'. *California Review Management* 50: 6–30.

Eichengreen, Barry, Dwight H. Perkins, and Kwan-ho Sin. 2012. *From Miracle to Maturity: The Growth of the Korean Economy*. Cambridge: Harvard University Asia Center.

Gambetta, Diego. 2000. Mafia: The Price of Distrust. In *Trust: Making and Breaking Cooperative Relations*, ed. Diego Gambetta, 158–175. Oxford: Basil Blackwell.

Gerybadze, Alexander, and Guido Reger. 1999. Globalization of R&D: Recent Changes in the Management of Innovation in Transnational Corporations. *Research Policy* 28: 251–274.

Ghoshal, Sumantra. 1988. Environmental Scanning in Korean Firms: Organizational Isomorphism in Action. *Journal of International Business Studies* 19: 69–86.

Hankyung. 2013. Korea Falls from Number Two to Eleven in Technology Competitiveness: Best in R&D Success Rates but Last in Commercialization. *Hankyung News*, June 6. Accessed September 14, 2014. http://www.hankyung.com/news/app/newsview.php?aid=2013060621851

Hart-Landsberg, Martin. 1993. *The Rush to Development: Economic Change and Political Struggle in South Korea*. New York, NY: Monthly Review Press.

Hattori, Tamio. 1987. Formation of the Korean Business Elite during the era of Rapid Economic Growth. *The Developing Economies* 25: 346–362.

———. 1997. Chaebol-style Enterprise Development in Korea. *The Developing Economics* 35: 458–477.

Hsu, Jinn-Yuh, and AnnaLee Saxenian. 2000. The Limits of Guanxi Capitalism: Transnational Collaboration between Taiwan and the USA. *Environment and Planning A* 32: 1991–2006.

Ilyo Weekly. 2014. Chaebol Management Succession: Wealth Succession without Social Approval, a League of Their Own. *Ilyo Weekly*, May 27. Accessed September 14, 2014. http://www.ilyoweekly.co.kr/news/articleView.html?idxno=9796

Johnson, C. 1982. *MITI and the Japanese Miracle: The Growth of Industrial Policy: 1925–1975*. Stanford, CA: Stanford University Press.

Kang, David C. 2002. Bad Loans to Good Friends: Money Politics and the Developmental State in South Korea. *International Organization* 56: 177–207.

Khanna, Tarun, and Yishay Yafeh. 2007. Business Groups in Emerging Markets: Paragons or Parasites? *Journal of Economic Literature* 45: 331–372.

Kim, Eun Mee. 1997. *Big Business, Strong State: Collusion and Conflict in South Korean Development, 1960–1990*. Albany, NY: State University of New York Press.

Kim, Hicheon, Robert E. Hoskisson, and Jaebum Hong. 2004. The Evolution and Restructuring of Diversified Business Groups in Emerging Markets: The Lessons from Chaebols in Korea. *Asia Pacific Journal of Management* 21: 25–48.

Kim, Linsu. 1997. *Imitation to Innovation: The Dynamics of Korea's Technological Learning*. Cambridge: Harvard Business Review Press.

Konrad, Kai A., and Stergios Skaperdas. 1997. Credible Threats in Extortion. *Journal of Economic Behavior and Organization* 33: 23–39.

Koo, Hagen. 2001. *Korean Workers: The Culture and Politics of Class Formation*. Ithaca, NY: Cornell University Press.

Krueger, Ann O. 1974. The Political Economy of the Rent-Seeking Society. *The American Economic Review* 64: 291–303.

Lew, Seok-Choon, Woo-Young Choi, and Hye Suk Wang. 2011. Confucian Ethics and the Spirit of Capitalism in Korea: The Significance of Filial Piety. *Journal of East Asian Studies* 11: 171–196.

Lie, John. 2000. *Han Unbound: The Political Economy of South Korea*. Stanford, CA: Stanford University Press.

Mankiw, Greg, N. 2014. *Principles of Economics*. Stamford, CT: Cengage Learning.

Mo, Jongryn, and Barry R. Weingast. 2013. *Korean Political and Economic Development: Crisis, Security, and Institutional Rebalancing*. Cambridge: Harvard University Asia Centre.

North, Douglas C. 1993. Institutions and Credible Commitment. *Journal of Institutional and Theoretical Economics* 149: 11–23.

Nooteboom, Bart. 2001. *Learning and Innovation in Organizations and Economies*. Oxford: Oxford University Press.

OECD. 2012. *STI Country Profiles*. OECD. Accessed November 23, 2015. http://www.oecd.org/sti/outlook/e-outlook/sticountryprofiles/korea.htm

Oh, Ingyu. 1999. *Mafioso, Big Business, and the Financial Crisis: The State-Business Relations in South Korea and Japan*. Surrey: Ashgate Publishing.

———. 2013. Joining Innovation Efforts Using Both Feed-Forward and Feed-back Learning: The Case of Japanese and Korean Universities. In *Evolution of Innovation Management: Trends in an International Context*, ed. Alex Brem and Eric Viardot, 208–235. New York, NY: Palgrave Macmillan.

Oh, Ingyu, and Hun-Joon Park. 2001. Shooting at a Moving Target: Four Theoretical Problems in Explaining the Dynamics of the Chaebol. *Asia Pacific Business Review* 7: 44–69.

Oh, Ingyu, Hun-Joon Park, Shigemi Yoneyama, and Hyuk-Rae Kim. 2005. *Mad Technology: How East Asian Companies are Defending their Technological Advantages*. New York, NY: Palgrave Macmillan.

Oh, Ingyu, and Recep Varcin. 2002. The Mafioso State: State-Led Market Bypassing in South Korea and Turkey. *Third World Quarterly* 23: 711–723.

———. 2010. Rent-Sharing: Organizational and Technological Innovations under Military Regimes in South Korea and Turkey. *International Journal of Technology Management and Sustainable Development* 9: 77–94.

Pillay, P.N. 2010. *Linking Higher Education and Economic Development: Implications for Africa from Three Successful Systems*. New Cape: Centre for Higher Education Transformation.

Pirie, Iain. 2008. *The Korean Developmental State: From Dirigisme to Neo-liberalism*. New York, NY: Routledge.

Rozman, Gilbert. 1990. *The East Asian Region: Confucian Heritage and Its Modern Adaptation*. Princeton, NJ: Princeton University Press.

Saxenian, AnnaLee. 1999. *Silicon Valley's New Immigrant Entrepreneurs*. San Francisco, CA: Public Policy Institute of California.

Siegel, Joel. 2007. Contingent Political Capital and International Alliances: Evidence from South Korea. *Administrative Science Quarterly* 52: 621–666.

Song, Byung-Nak. 2003. *The Rise of the Korean Economy*. Oxford: Oxford University Press.

Trautvetter, Christoph. 2010. Transitions to Good Governance: A Case Study of South Korea. *Hertie School of Governance Working Paper* No. 18.

Tsuru, Shigeto. 1996. *Japan's Capitalism: Creative Defeat and Beyond*. Cambridge: Cambridge University Press.

U.S. Patent and Trademark Office. 2014. *All Technologies Report: January 1, 1989–December 31, 2013*. U.S. Patent and Trademark Office. Accessed September 14, 2014. http://www.uspto.gov/web/offices/ac/ido/oeip/taf/all_tech.pdf

Williamson, Oliver E. 1983. Credible Commitments: Using Hostages to Support Exchange. *The American Economic Review* 73: 519–540.

Wong, Bernard P. 2005. *The Chinese in Silicon Valley: Globalization, Social Networks, and Ethnic Identity*. Washington, DC: Rowman & Littlefield Publishers.

World Bank. 1993. *The East Asian Miracle: Economic Growth and Public Policy.* Washington, DC: World Bank.

Yonhap News. 2012. From Chief Prosecutor to High Court President: Ex-Senior Judicial Officers Overflow in Chaebol Ranks. *Yonhap News*, January 30. Accessed September 14, 2014. http://www.yonhapnews.co.kr/bulletin/2012/01/27/0200000000AKR20120127210800008.HTML

———. 2014. Foreign Ownership of Samsung Electronics Now 52.33 Percent: A Historical High in Eight Years. *Yonhap News*, November 2. Accessed November 11, 2015. http://www.yonhapnews.co.kr/economy/2014/11/01/0301000000AKR20141101037700008.HTML

4

Innovation in China: The State of Art and Future Perspectives

Jin Chen and Rebecca Wenjing Lyu

4.1 Introduction

Over the past decades, China has performed well in innovation. For now, the Chinese government has made innovation-driven development its national strategy in its Thirteenth Five Year Plan. Chairman Jinping Xi especially emphasizes the essential position of technological innovation and proposes the "three-step" goal for developing science and technology in China: the first step is to become an innovative nation in 2020; the second step is to become a major leading innovative nation in 2030; while the third step is to guarantee China becoming the world's leading power in science and technology by the 100th anniversary of the founding of the new China (Xi 2016). Such an innovation-driven developmental

We thank Yanyan Wang, Linbo Sun, Ximing Yin, and Yongqian Duan for their help of collecting cases and insightful comments.

J. Chen (✉) • R.W. Lyu
School of Economics and Management, Tsinghua University, Beijing, China

Research Center for Technological Innovation, Tsinghua University, Beijing, China

© The Author(s) 2017
A. Brem, E. Viardot (eds.), *Revolution of Innovation Management*,
DOI 10.1057/978-1-349-95123-9_4

strategy, according to Xi, is the inevitable choice to maintain sustained and healthy economic development in China.

In fact, despite its irreplaceable and essential role in economy, innovation also enjoys an important position in theoretical research in China. Based on unique innovation management practices in Chinese enterprises, Chinese scholars have proposed several unique innovation theories, such as "3-I pattern" (imitation, improvement, and innovation, see also from Xu et al. 1998), indigenous innovation (Chen 1994), Total Innovation Management (Xu et al. 2007), etc. As during the transition from major innovative nation to super innovative nation, China is now facing the challenge of how to stimulate more major innovation patterns which would "change the world" in the era of the knowledge economy; thus, it is in need of going through the whole innovation journey in China and proposing future perspectives for a Chinese innovation paradigm.

In this chapter, we establish an innovation timeline in view of a summary of innovation patterns across different periods; generalize the internal connection among these innovation practices through representative case studies; and propose a new innovation paradigm based on Chinese "Yin Yang" culture and its practices in enterprises. Our study proceeds in three parts: first, we describe the basic view of innovation in China. Next, after a panoramic description of the innovation journey in China, and a brief discussion of Chinese innovation policies, we review related innovation theories proposed by Chinese scholars. We conclude this part by noting the promising and exciting innovation practices happening in Chinese enterprises through representative case studies, and pointing out the gap between innovation literature and practice. In the third part, we turn to a new innovation paradigm which represents "the best practice" for enterprises in the new era, and perform concluding remarks and propose future perspectives for innovation in China.

4.2   The Whole Picture of Innovation in China

Since the 1990s, China has been the world's fastest growing economy, enjoying an about 10% GDP growth rate during many years, which contributed to the so-called "Chinese economic miracle". During the same period, technological innovation has received more and more attention in China. Annual R&D expenditure keeps steady growth, without being affected by fluctuations in the economy. In 2015, R&D expenditure is more than 1400 billion RMB, which makes China the world's second largest country in R&D expenditure, just below the USA (China National Bureau of Statistics, see Fig. 4.1). Meanwhile, in 2015, expenses on basic research were 67.06 billion RMB, which shows an annual growth of 10.4%, and the proportion of basic research made up 4.7% of total R&D expenditure. Moreover, Chinese basic research witnessed tremendous achievements, such as major breakthroughs in the field of quantum anomalous Hall effect, iron-based HTS, dark matter particle detection satellites, heat shock protein 90α, chemically induced pluripotent stem cells (CiPSCs), Weylfermions, etc., not to mention Ms. Tu Youyou as the first Nobel Laureate in Physiology or Medicine due to her contribution of finding artemisinin to effectively reduce malaria mortality, which finally fills China's gap in Nobel Prizes on hard science.

Meanwhile, sustained steadily increasing R&D investment has indeed had its effect on innovation. Seen from patents application, which could be regarded as a proxy of a nation's innovative power, domestic patents application numbers keep growing dramatically, especially for invention patents in recent years. However, China is still far from a "super

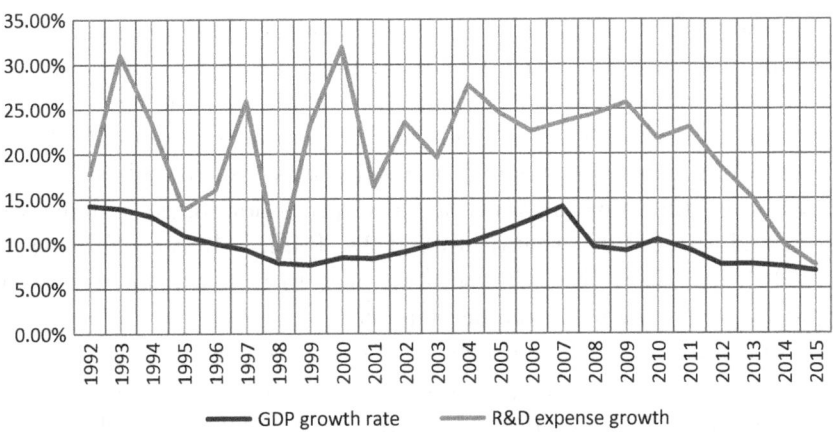

Fig. 4.1 GDP growth rate and R&D expense growth during 1992–2015 in China. Source: Sorted from China National Bureau of Statistics

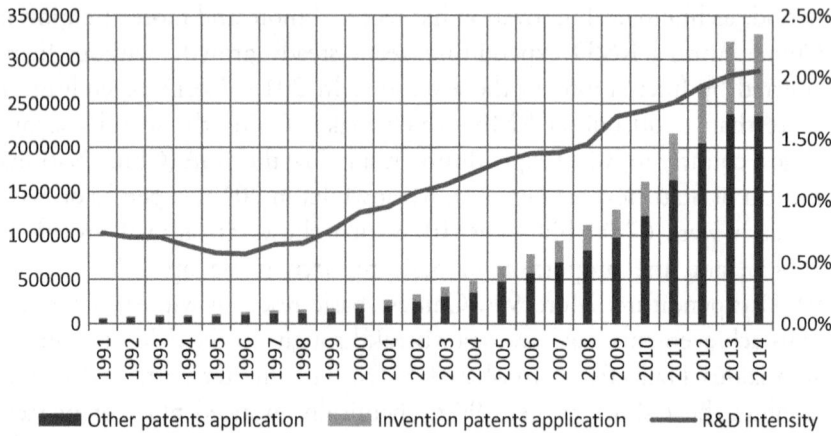

Fig. 4.2 Patents application and R&D intensity during 1991–2004 in China. Source: China National Bureau of Statistics

innovative nation", especially in innovation quality. R&D intensity (measured by the R&D expenditure as a percentage of GDP) is still relatively low in China, especially compared to developed countries (Fig. 4.2). In 2014, R&D intensity in China was only 2.046%, still lagging behind Korea (4.292%), Israel (4.109%), Japan (3.583%), and other major innovative countries, and even lower than the average indicator (2.371%) for total OECD countries (OECD 2016).

However, as the Chinese government has made a goal to increase R&D intensity to 2.5% in 2020, Chairman Jingping Xi also points out the important position of technological innovation, and the clear demand to build the world's super technological innovative nation (Xi 2016). Meanwhile enhancing original innovative capacity through a national high-level innovative platform and enterprises-dominated and market-oriented innovation is also stressed by Prime Minister Keqiang Li (2016), it is likely that Chinese firms need to play a major role in the process of innovation-driven development.

Still, as for now, Chinese firms need to compete in an environment of radical technological change and sophisticated customer needs (Xu et al. 2007); thus it is important to develop their own innovative capabilities. As China has an unique cultural and social environment, innovation in

Chinese domestic enterprises cannot be wholly described, explained, or forecasted by Western innovation theories, such as disruptive innovation (Christensen 1997), user innovation (von Hippel 1998), open innovation (Chesbrough 2006), architectural innovation (Henderson and Clark 1990), radical/incremental innovation (Abernathy and Utterback 1978), etc. Innovation theories developed by Chinese scholars might be more appropriate to examine and study Chinese innovation practices, due to the fact that they are deeply rooted in Chinese culture and context.

Thus, this chapter summarizes and evaluates the innovation journey in China, not only through assessing innovation theory development, but also through reviewing innovation practices in Chinese enterprises.

4.3   Innovation Journey in China

The "3-I Pattern" (Imitation-Improvement-Innovation)

The "3-I pattern"—an acronym for imitation, improvement, and innovation—once was recognized as a suitable innovation pattern for developing countries in the Asia-Pacific Rim like China (Kim 1997; Xu et al. 1998). This pattern is also described as "Introduction, Digestion, Absorption and Innovation" (Wang and Lu 2013) or "secondary innovation" (Wu 1997; Wu and Ni 2001). The first emphasized step of this pattern, imitation, is realized through the acquisition and introduction of higher level technology from developed countries (Levitt 1966). Due to a lack of technological capabilities, imitation was the most suitable way for Chinese enterprises, and thus was encouraged from the 1980s. This path is realized mainly through tremendous investment in technology importation, and multidimensional technology acquisition with the strategic purpose of import substitution and export promotion.

The second step of the "3-I pattern" is technology improvement through digestion and absorption. During this step, the emphasized point is to analyze and obtain the introduced foreign technology and knowledge, in order to understand and master the operation of the technology, and then develop improved and localized technology, which could fit the domestic context and market well.

The third step of the "3-I pattern" is innovation based on previous technology adoption and improvement, and fostering high-level technological capability on its own to develop leading products.

The "3-I pattern" was developed under a special context: during its popular period, China lacked original innovation and core technology, making the role of imported technology and knowledge seem essential to economic development. During that period, in order to realize "latter comer advantage" (Lin 2003), it was reasonable to learn from introduced advanced technology, as Chinese low-level self-design and development was less competitive and lacked efficiency compared to imitation from high-level imported technology.

The "3-I" pattern is truly suitable for enterprises which lacks core technology or resources to build their own competitiveness (Yip and McKern 2016). Based on these enterprises' comparative advantage, the "3-I" pattern from imitation to innovation is their optimal choice to maximize resource endowments (Lin 2003). However, the "3-I pattern" is not an ideal innovation pattern for a country in the long run. It is important to develop one's own core technology and competitiveness, especially to a major economy like China. Thus, with the development of both technology and economy in China, the "3-I pattern" seems out-of-date for ambitious Chinese enterprises, and might not be suitable for enterprises want to compete in the new era.

Indigenous Innovation

To improve the shortcomings of the "3-I pattern", Chen (1994) firstly proposed the theory of "indigenous innovation", which was then recognized as a national strategy in China's Eleventh Five Year Plan. At that time, indigenous innovation was thought to be the key to transfer from the developmental mode of completely relying on natural resources and imitation of foreign technology and knowledge, to innovation-driven development. The key factor emphasized in indigenous innovation is to realize technological breakthroughs relied on independent research and development efforts, and thus to achieve original scientific and technological achievements (Chen 2005; Chen et al. 2010). After that, the concept of "indigenous innovation" was developed into a full system covering "secondary innovation, integrated innovation, and original innovation" (Wu et al. 2009).

Integrated Innovation

However, indigenous innovation remains a "black box" to enterprises, without clear sources of innovative capability (Xu et al. 2003). Thus, in order to resolve specific operational issues of indigenous innovation, especially in enterprises, integrated innovation was developed and became an interconnected part of indigenous innovation (Jiang and Chen 2000). The basic argument of integrated innovation is rooted in Iansiti's concept of technology integration (Iansiti 1998), which proposes that in order to improve R&D efficiency and effectiveness, enterprises need to integrate resources, instruments, and solutions through organization to realize technological applications. Based on this construct, Jiang and Chen (2000) firstly introduced three constituent features of enterprises in integrated innovation: technology integration, knowledge integration, and organization integration. Besides Iansiti's technology integration, integrated innovation also emphasizes the importance of enterprises' own knowledge base through systematically integrated knowledge sources and activities, alongside the importance of using integrated organization to realize "effective communication" between different departments inside enterprise (Chen 2002).

Total Innovation Management (TIM)

However, in integrated innovation, the influence of the environment is not considered, which makes it seems not appropriate to some industries, especially when stepping into the twenty-first century, some scholars realized the importance of outsourcing knowledge and cooperation to enterprises' innovation. Thus, "total innovation management" (TIM) was developed to describe the new trend in enterprises' innovation management (Xu et al. 2003).

Unlike previous innovation theories, TIM stressed every factor in innovation patterns, including technology, market, organization, management, culture, institution, etc. The five dimensions emphasized in TIM are to realize innovation (1) in the whole time; (2) during the whole process; (3) dependent on total members; (4) through the total value chain; and (5) from globalization. Thus, in TIM, everyone could act as an innovation engine on everything in everywhere at any time (Xu et al. 2014).

However, it is hard to measure and truly realize TIM, especially for small and medium enterprises (SME), as there are too many dimensions to notice at the same time. Meanwhile, as in the new era of knowledge economy and sharing economy, motivating innovation power not only from inside enterprises, but also from outsourcing stakeholders to realize interdependent and interconnected innovation system, is the new trend. Thus, this research proposes a new innovation paradigm of "dual source innovation", which is deeply rooted in Chinese Yin Yang culture.

Dual-Source Innovation Based on Chinese Yin Yang Culture

In Chinese Yin Yang culture, the most essential factor is to keep balance between two types of force, which is recognized as the codependency between Yin and Yang, that is:

> Yin and Yang not only coexist in everything, but also could give rise to, complement and reinforce each other; meanwhile, everything embraces Yin and Yang, and Yin and Yang exist within each other and interplay with each other to form a dynamic and paradoxical unity. (Fang 2012)

Recommended by several Chinese scholars, Yin Yang could be used to understand the dynamics of culture context in management (Fang 2010; Faure and Fang 2008). As management practices, especially in a dynamic management context, are deeply dependent on the cultural context, it is necessary to study Chinese culture from a Yin Yang perspective in order to better grasp dynamic management practices (Hong et al. 2000).

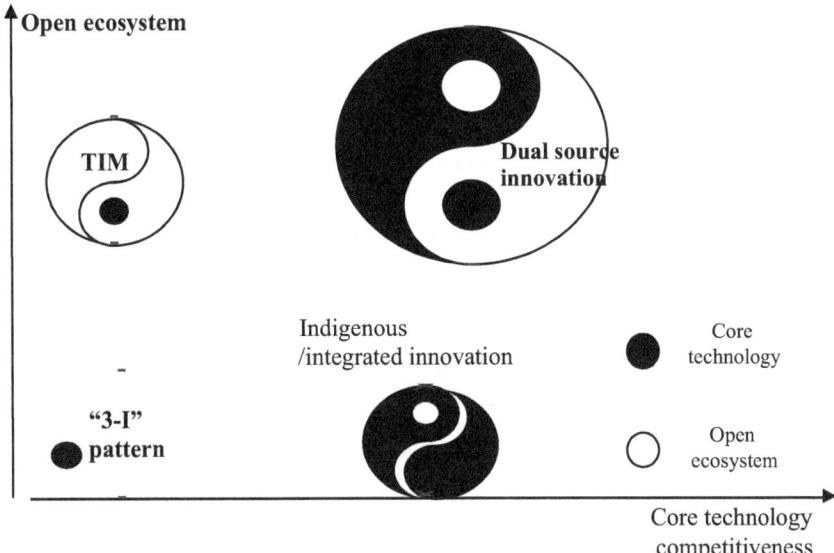

Fig. 4.3 Comparison of four innovation patterns from a Yin Yang perspective. Source: authors' own

Meanwhile, as the innovation process is regarded as a "dynamic, nonlinear, and systematic process" (Dosi 1982), thus it is appropriate to use a Yin Yang perspective to analyze the innovation process.

From a Yin Yang point of view, the most important thing is to keep balance between Yin and Yang, which are two essential forces. Thus, for firms deeply rooted in Yin Yang culture, it is necessary to realize the importance of keeping balance between two essential innovative sources. For Chinese enterprises, based on previous analysis, these two essential forces are core technology competitiveness, and open ecosystems (Fig. 4.3).

As shown in Figure, the black part in the Yin Yang circle stands for a firm's core technological competitiveness, whereas the white part in the Yin Yang circle stands for a firm's open ecosystem. Evaluated from a Yin Yang perspective, the three previous innovation patterns respectively have their own shortcomings. As for the "3-I" pattern, technology is overemphasized, without even considering open ecosystems, thus there is only one little black circle that stands for the "3-I" pattern, which indicates its lack of open ecosystems, and low technology competitiveness. Meanwhile, as for indigenous innovation, core technology competiveness is also overemphasized, although an open ecosystem is slightly mentioned in indigenous innovation, especially in integrated indigenous innovation. Thus, based on a Yin Yang perspective, an unbalanced circle which lacks of enough white part stands for indigenous innovation, which indicates its lack of open ecosystem, whereas core technology competitiveness is overemphasized. However, for total innovation management, an open ecosystem is overemphasized, without enough consideration of core technology competitiveness: thus, based on a Yin Yang perspective, there is an unbalanced circle which lacks of the black part that stands for TIM, indicating its lack of core technology competitiveness and overemphasized open ecosystem. Thus, from a Yin Yang perspective, only dual source innovation could simultaneously guarantee core technology competitiveness and open ecosystems, and keep balance between these two major innovative sources.

4.4   Methods

Research Design and Settings

In this chapter, we used an inductive, multi-case studies design (Eisenhardt 1989). This kind of research design could generate more robust and generalizable results and conclusions than single cases (Eisenhardt and Graebner 2007), by using multiple cases to permit a replication logic by trading cases as experiments in order to testify inferences (Yin 2013). The research setting is representative of innovative Chinese enterprises which could best reflect the above innovation theories. This setting was attractive and reasonable because each enterprise stands for the "best practice" in innovation management.

To guarantee the generalizability of our research, we selected both State Owned Enterprises (SOEs), Collective Owned Enterprises (COE) and Private Owned Enterprises (POEs). We also selected firms addressing five distinct markets: display monitor, railways, information

Table 4.1 Description of sample firms and case data

Characteristic	BOE	CRRC Zhuzhou Institute	Huawei	Haier	Letv	Midea
Domain	Display monitor	Railways	ICT	Household appliances	On-line video	Household appliances
Ownership type	SOE-POE	SOE	POE	COE	POE	COE-POE
Archival data						
Number of audio/video	1	2	3	3	2	3
Internal sources	100 pages	200 pages	300 pages	300 pages	200 pages	300 pages
External sources	150 pages	100 pages	500 pages	700 pages	300 pages	400 pages
Number of interviews	1	2	2	2	2	2
Internal informants	Chairman	Technology department minister	CEO CMO	CEO VP	Strategic VP	ClnO of research institute VP
External informants	Industry expert Academic researcher	Industry expert Academic researcher	Industry expert Academic researcher	Industry expert Academic researcher	Industry expert Academic researcher	Industry expert Academic researcher

and communication technology, online video, and household appliances. Table 4.1 summarizes the diverse characteristics of the sampled firms. Such a diverse set of sample firms enabled our grounded theory to be more robust than developing from a homogenous sample set (Harris and Sutton 1986).

Given our aim of understanding the innovation pattern change among these enterprises, our design comprehensively tracks the development periods of all the sampled firms, which required rich, archival, historical data and first-hand interviews.

Data Collection

To triangulate our data source, we collected data relied on two sources: second-hand archives including enterprises' annual reports, external analysis reports by consulting companies, and video and audio archives of presentations made by enterprise representative or executives on media; and first-hand interviews with internal informants and external informants. Our secondary sources are based on official data released by respective enterprises, complete with firms' annual reports, analyst reports, and media articles.

We got our in-depth, semi-structured interviews with internal informants in a technology innovation meeting. Each interview lasted about 30 minutes. We chose external informants from academic researchers and industry experts. This use of multiple informants enabled our investigation to be richer and more trustworthy through complementary views from different resources (Dougherty 1990).

Analysis

We began our analysis of each case through previously summarized major innovation types, to see which type of innovation could best describe and forecast innovation patterns in each firm. We then used the most suitable innovation theory to figure out major characteristics and make comparisons between each firm. To facilitate our analyses, we used tables and graphs (Miles and Huberman 1994). We then turned to cross-case analysis, and developed a new innovation paradigm to better predict innovation practices in the new era.

4.5　Innovation Pattern Comparison and Future Perspective

The "3-I Pattern" (Imitation-Improvement-Innovation) in BOE

BOE (Beijing Oriental Electronics) is a representative enterprise which successfully realized innovation through the "3-I pattern". Founded in April 1993, BOE is the successor of Beijing Electronic Tube Factory, which holds five main business units: display system business; energy and environmental business; electronic materials business; monitor tube business; and technology park business. Due to its closed relationship with local government, BOE gained a large amount of subsidies to support its daily business and technology introduction through overseas M&A.

In 2002, when it recognized huge business potential in the field of TFT-LCD (Thin Film Transistor-Liquid Crystal Display), which is the core tube of display monitors, BOE made a decision to quickly acquire high-level technologies and occupy the domestic market in TFT-LCD through acquiring the Korean company HYDIS, at the price of $380 million. This technology-driven acquisition made BOE the only one domestic enterprise which held TFT-LCD technology, and at the same time benefited from tacit assets such as 450 patents, large amounts of R&D talents, and marketing distribution of HYDIS.

Stage of Imitation

In order to realize innovation through imitation (Levitt 1966; Kim 1997), BOE first built a display technological park in Beijing, and utilized technology imitated from HYDIS. At first, to quickly learn from HYDIS, BOE invited a Korean technology expert to be COO, and imitated from learning.

Stage of Improvement

The TFT-LCD production line of BOE was put into use in 2005, quickly after acquisition of HYDIS. This pattern enabled BOE to realize a leapfrog development in technology in a very short time. Based on HYDIS's acquired leading technology, BOE made several technological improvements to adapt to the domestic market better. In October 2003, BOE developed AFFS technology, which could be used in tablets, and had several functional improvements compared to previous technologies.

Stage of Innovation

After the technology improvement stage, BOE began to develop technology through cooperative innovation with competitors, as well as with customers and research institutes. In order to develop independent innovation based on absorptive technologies, BOE built a technology alliance with IBM, and set up 5 overseas R&D centers to realize cooperative innovation. Meanwhile, BOE had set up a talent training program with Tsinghua University, to integrate technology resources among research institutes. Through connection both with suppliers and customers, BOE not only integrated a distribution network inherited from HYDIS, but also steadied its advantageous position in the whole value chain of TFT-LCD, and finally realized an industry upgrading through the "3-I" pattern (Fig. 4.4).

Seen from above case of BOE, the "3-I" pattern is truly suitable for enterprises which lack core technology or resources to build their own competitiveness. Based on these enterprises' comparative advantage, the "3-I" pattern from imitation to innovation is their optimal choice to maximize resource endowments (Lin 2003). However, the "3-I pattern" is not an ideal innovation pattern for a country in the long run. It is important to develop its own core technology and competitiveness, especially for a major economy like China. Thus, with the development of both of technology and the economy in China, the "3-I pattern" seems out-of-date to ambitious Chinese enterprises, and might not suitable for enterprises want to compete in the new era.

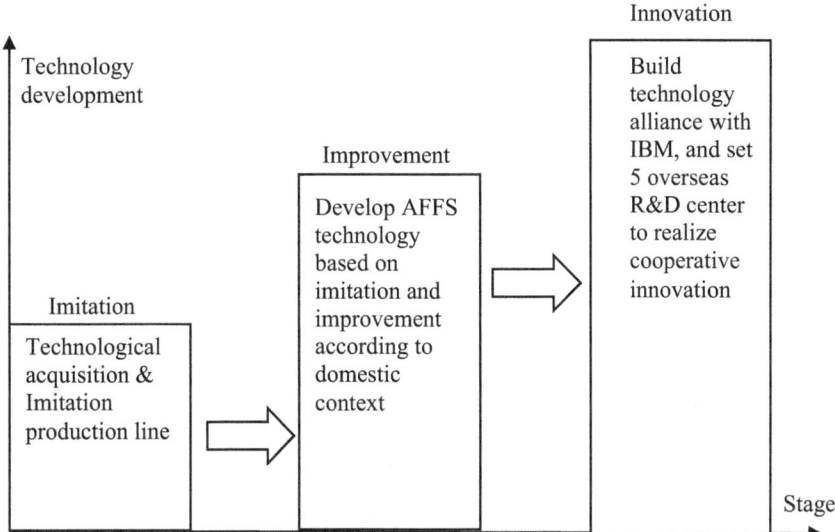

Fig. 4.4 BOE's "3-I pattern" of innovation. Source: adapted from Xu et al. (1998) and Liu and Jian (2007)

Indigenous Innovation in Huawei

Huawei Technologies Co., Ltd. is a leading global information and communications technology (ICT) solutions provider. Huawei has established a competitive ICT portfolio of end-to-end solutions in telecom and enterprise networks, devices, and cloud computing. The solutions, products, and services of Huawei are used in more than 170 countries and regions, serving over one-third of the world's population.

As such a successful and huge technological company, Huawei is an outstanding representative Chinese company, which successfully realized "technology catch-up" innovation. Since it was founded in 1988, Huawei has been making constant, high-efficiency R&D investment, and has not only achieved a global leading position for patent quantity and market share in the field of core technology, but has also achieved a continuously high investment–output efficiency while maintaining its constant and large amount of R&D in investment. For now, its output elasticity of

R&D investment is 0.85, which is much higher than that of Ericsson (−1.0), which was the benchmark company Huawei pursued for a long time (Liu 2010). Recently, Huawei proposed a vision of "integrating global resources and building a wholly connected new world", and formulated the innovation strategy of "utilizing wisdom of the world to serve for Huawei".

Independent Innovation Capability

To realize catch-up and leapfrogging faced with competition with multinational giant enterprises, it is important for Chinese indigenous companies to develop an independent innovation capability and self-developed technologies (Fan 2006). Huawei has been focused on developing its own technologies from the very beginning, and benefited from its wise prioritized innovation strategy.

In order to build an independent innovation capability, Huawei started with continued, intense, in-house R&D development. Taking the "pressure" principle, Huawei has always poured enormous investment and effort into technical fields it wants to enter, without considering the cost. According to related reports, Huawei has kept R&D expense as high as 10% of annual sales continuously for several years. In 2013, Huawei's R&D expenses were 30,672 million RMB, accounts for 12.8% of its revenue. The accumulated R&D expenses in the last decade are more than 151,000 million RMB. Besides its steady high R&D expenditure, Huawei attracts and brings up a large amount of highly-skilled technology personnel (more than 70,000, taking up 45% of the total employees), with relatively low cost. As proposed in "Huawei Basic Law", the basic spirit of Huawei's technology innovation is to adhere to the "pressure" principle, by focusing on key factors and selected strategic growth points, and allocating more resources than its main competitors. Thus, Huawei can realize its aim "to be the best or not to be", that is, once determined to develop and enter into specific market, Huawei will assemble exclusive manpower, financial resources, and other necessary resources to achieve major breakthroughs.

Besides its "pressure" principle to develop an independent innovation capability, and combined with its operation strategy and advanced technology management, Huawei focuses on low-cost differentiation strategies in order to adapt to environmental change, and aims to become the industry leader through incremental innovation rather than radical change.

Meanwhile, Huawei realized the importance of intellectual property (IP) a long time ago. As early as 1995, Huawei established the department of intellectual property, and built an IP group that consists of more than 100 specialized, IP-related researchers and lawyers and is responsible for all of the company's IP strategy decisions, including patents applications, maintenance and analysis, trademarks management, R&D contract review, and negotiations and litigations involving IP. Specifically, through patent strategy and trade secret protection strategy, Huawei has clarified the value of IP, and maintained sustainable competitive advantage through the maintenance and promotion of IP, avoiding the loss of intangible assets.

Through paying attention to IP and intense R&D investment, Huawei has harvested a huge patents pool. As of December 31, 2013, Huawei has cumulatively applied for 44,168 Chinese patents, and 18,791 foreign patents, and has 36,511 licensed patents for all, which makes it number one in patents application across the world (World Intellectual Property Organization).

Internationalized R&D Cooperation

Since 2002, Huawei began transferring its closed innovation strategies to R&D internationalization. At the beginning, SHAI (the share for a given country of patents with a foreign inventor and a domestic applicant in the country's total domestic applications, Guellec and de la Potterie 2001) dominated Huawei's international R&D activities, whereas the proportion of SHII (the share for a given country of patents with a foreign resident as co-inventor in the population of patents with a domestic inventor) has increased as time goes by, which indicates that Huawei now realizes R&D internationalization mainly through cross-border cooperation between R&D organizations, and aims to enhance its technical capabilities through participation in international R&D activities.

Huawei's R&D internationalization process reflects the common internationalization strategy of Chinese enterprises; that is, entering into global markets by using foreign innovation resources at first, and then building its own brand image to acquire long-term competitiveness. Due to historical reasons, Chinese enterprises always have a long way to go, since they began with a huge technological gap from global counterparts. Huawei's experience shows that obtaining access to global markets through patents purchase is the first step for Chinese technological enterprise. By altering and reforming purchased foreign patents and technologies, Huawei could develop its own original core patents, begin R&D internationalization cooperation to improve local R&D employees' innovation capabilities, and then realize mutual learning through international cooperation.

Customer-oriented Innovation Strategy

To Huawei, R&D is divided into four categories: product development, product preparatory research, technology development, and technology preparatory research. To develop customer-centered products, Huawei pours its major resources and manpower into development, meanwhile utilizing product and technology preparatory research to get customer insights (Table 4.2).

To sum up, based on its independent innovation capability, R&D internationalization cooperation, and customer-centered innovation strategy, Huawei develops world-leading products, realizes key technological innovation, and guarantees its rapid growth.

Integrated Innovation in CRRC Zhuzhou Institute

Developed from the research institution on electric locomotives of the Railways Ministry founded in 1959, CRRC Zhuzhou Institute always devotes itself to the development of railway electrification in China. It owns eight key national-level engineering laboratories and a world-class

Table 4.2 Huawei's customer-centered R&D typology (Source: authors' own)

	Product development	Product preparatory research	Technology development	Technology preparatory research
Purpose	To guarantee product success in finance and market, according to demands of project	To test or guide customer's potential needs and seize the right market direction	To develop public technology and platform to satisfy user's needs	To verify technology scheme and make technology reserve
Market	Aims at recent target market with clear market needs	Aims at future development and market, with unclear market prospect	Aims to satisfy technology needs of current products	Aims at future development, without clear customer needs
Risk and technical difficulties	Relatively low	High	Relatively low	Relatively high

R&D team with 6000 talented and experienced experts, including several Chinese Academy of Engineering members, 100 senior engineers at professor grade, and 151 doctors. It has also attained over 4500 patents and won the State Preeminent Science and Technology Award of China three times in the past three years.

Integrated Technology Development Through Cooperation

Based on the industry-university–research cooperation, Zhuzhou Institute insists on exploiting advanced technology, building core competence and establishing international influence in the field of rail transportation. From learning and repetition to controlling independent mature technologies, Zhuzhou Institute now is dominant in the development of 128 international or national standards related to the core technologies in high-speed railway manufacturing. The success of Zhuzhou Institute can also be regarded as a milestone, where high-speed technology and core equipment technology in China has exceeded the international advanced level.

Integrated Development Through MOTIF Innovation System

Though the industry-university–research and traditional R&D models, Zhuzhou Institute has benefited in its development in recent years. In order to better fit market needs and absorb external advanced knowledge, Zhuzhou Institute founded the MOTIF technological innovation system, coordinating different industrial processes and reshaping internal orientations and structures. Combined with the previous industry-university–research system, MOTIF further strengthened the adaptive and independent innovative competences of Zhuzhou Institute. According to the requirements of industrial development, the MOTIF system contains three technological platforms: a manufacturing platform, product technology development, and a designing technology platform. The management in these platforms follows three principals: market-oriented, customer-centered, and open innovation.

The first principal, market-oriented, enhances the understanding toward the market of Zhuzhou Institute, improves the flexibility of product development and manufacturing processes, and also increases its profitability and market share. The customer-centered principal changes the previous expert-centered model so that the designs are more connected to needs in reality rather than the imagination of researchers. What is most important is that Zhuzhou Institute dares to open its closed system to absorb much more external knowledge and technology. By learning from the product development system in IBM, Zhuzhou Institute has formed a more practical R&D procedure, from the laboratory to the market (Fig. 4.5).

Seen from the above two cases, both indigenous and integrated innovation are most suitable for enterprises which already possess technology competitiveness and have the urge to compete in technological innovation. Meanwhile, core technology competitiveness is overemphasized in both indigenous and integrated innovation, without considering outsourcing innovation from stakeholders. Thus, as China is entering into a cooperative era, it is likely that total innovation management through focusing on every aspect of innovation is suitable for some enterprises.

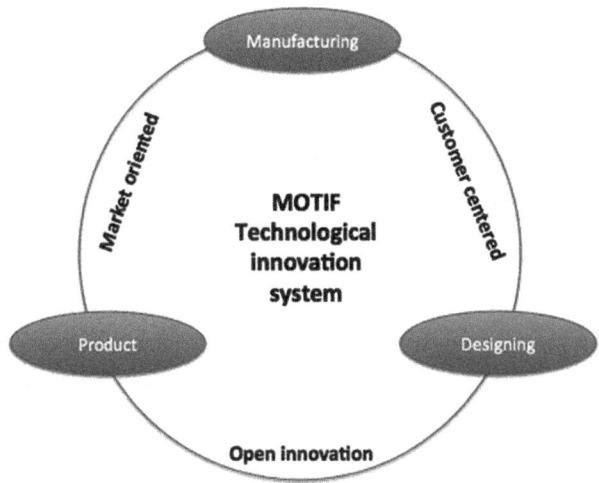

Fig. 4.5 CRRC Zhuzhou Institute's MOTIF technological innovation system

TIM in Haier

Haier Group was founded in 1984, and started its business in fridge manufacture. As for now, Haier focuses on providing the whole package of life service solutions. In 2014, Haier reached a global revenue of 200.7 billion yuan, with profit as high as 15 billion, which makes Haier Group continue to be the No.1 among global large household appliances enterprises for the 6th year.

In 2009, Haier founded its mass innovation platform called "Haier Open Partnership Ecosystem (HOPE)" to integrate global R&D resources, and provide resource support for Haier Group through open innovation, thus enhancing Haier's brand image and global reputation. HOPE is an online platform, which aims for technology exchange and innovation. This online community is an active hub of innovation where companies, start-ups, inventors, academia, and anyone interested in technology interact to solve technology challenges. In HOPE, companies looking for technologies and users offering technologies can post their needs and capabilities by its accurate matching system. Besides, its offline professional innovation team ensures all processes of collaboration (Jiang et al. 2016).

Open Platform in Innovation During the Whole Process and in the Whole Value Chain

Based on HOPE, Haier encourages open innovation by building an interdependent network connecting idea providers, inventors, and support staff for technology transfer, with end users. This open platform encourages multi-level and cross-level collaborations based on different technologies, and integrates social resources and conduct, thus accelerating both knowledge inflows and outflows and expanding the markets for external exploitative innovation (Chesbrough 2006).

Massive Innovation Through Total Members in the Whole Time

HOPE holds two sections for now: one is the NEEDS section, which is the place where not only HAIER, but also any interested companies, can post their technology requirements; the other is the TECHNOLOGIES section, which is the place where technology providers, which can be large companies, start-ups, SMEs, R&D centers, inventors, etc., show what they can do, maybe with an innovative product or service. Besides these two sections, HOPE still has a group of more than 30 engineers with an average of ten years of work experience providing supporting services, such as technical consulting, commercial planning, and a full range of services of technology transferring.

Massive innovation is a new innovation type in the new era in the Chinese context. Thanks to positively taking part in the Internet economy, China has made enormous progress in terms of knowledge diffusion and sharing. Massive innovation is rooted in user innovation (von Hippel 2005, 2007), and inherits the characteristics of user innovation, which is user-centered, and adapting to a knowledge society (Xu et al. 2013). Like user innovation, permitting the masses, especially grassroots or even

Bottom of Pyramid (BoP) groups, to join in the innovation process is the key factor to improving innovation efficiency for enterprises passing the mass innovation paradigm.

Globalization Through HOPE

Haier insisted its vision was to regard "the world as Haier's R&D center". Based on that belief, Haier initiated users and resources across the world to take part in the R&D process of products through HOPE (Fig. 4.6). HOPE is a real global platform, attracting top universities, research institutes, Fortune 500 companies, and other innovative business units from all over the world. For now, global technological resources on HOPE beyond more than 130,000 (Crainer 2015).

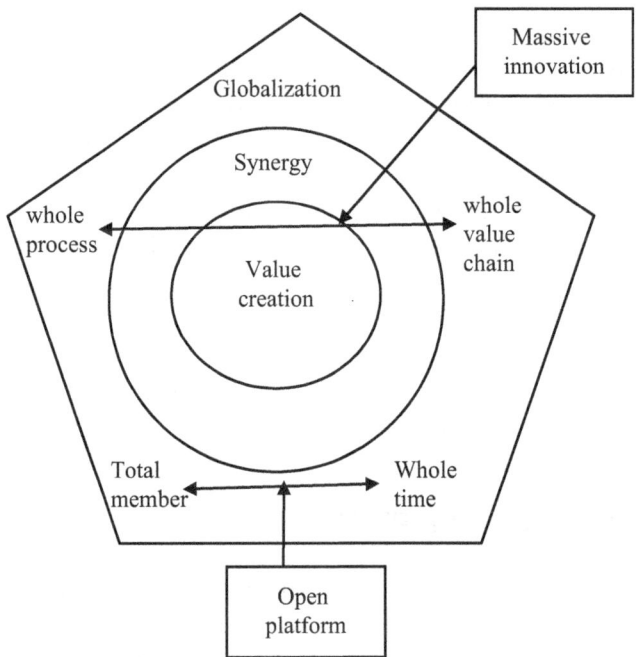

Fig. 4.6 Simplified Haier's TIM framework. Source: Adopted from Xu et al. (2007)

To conclude, Haier has gained lots of benefits through TIM in its HOPE platform. However, in TIM framework, an open ecosystem is overemphasized, without considering the important role of a firm's own technology competitiveness. Thus, it is likely that dual source innovation, which underlines open ecosystem and core technology competitiveness at the same time, is more suitable for enterprises competing in technology-intense industries.

Dual Source Innovation in Letv

Founded in 2004, Letv has become a major player in the online video/TV industry in China. Besides its core business, Letv is now building a user-centered innovation ecosystem which covers four core sub-ecosystems and is striving to become the industry leader through its open innovation ecosystem.

Based on its core ecosystem (i.e., online video, content related services) and hardware terminals, Letv is now pushing forward in seven major ecosystems based on Internet technology, which are: technology, content, big screen TV, smartphones, sport media, smart cars, and internet financial system. It seems that Letv is in strategic confusion at first glance; however, Letv has its own reasonable logic in designing these seven ecosystems, and aims to realize coordinated development through such an innovation ecosystem. The vertically integrated closed-loop ecosystems of Letv have made it the No.1 enterprise holding the highest market value in today's Chinese internet/TV industry. The key drivers of Letv's success are its clear strategy to occupy the submarket quickly at the cost of short-term profits, and its innovation ecosystem.

Core Technology Competitiveness

Letv has three aspects to its core technology competitiveness: its unique contents as well as copyright dataset; its technology development capability; and its licenses through good government relations.

Letv's content ecosystem has two main modules: one is content operation, which includes an accumulated massive video copyrights base built from the beginning, and television program channels and theaters; the other is content production, which consists of Letv Picture, Flower Picture, and other television production subsidiaries.

Based on its content ecosystem, Letv successfully attracts users and keeps user stickiness as its core resources. In the online video industry, Letv is now ranked No. 1 in terms of daily unique visitors, total amount of video playing, and total video playing time. The largest video copyright base it holds has become the major profit resource for Letv.

In recent years, the market size of smart hardware terminals such as smartphones and smart TVs has been expanding rapidly, and has now become the important user entrance to internet video. Thus, this business unit is essential for Letv to attract users from the beginning. Letv has also recognized this problem, and is pouring lots of effort into build ecosystems for smart hardware terminals. According to its 2015 annual report, this business has contributed as much as 46.78% to total profits, making it the largest business unit of Letv. Meanwhile, more than 4.5 million smart TVs, and more than 3 million smartphones were sold cumulatively. The numerous users through these hardware terminals will definitely contribute a sizeable cash flow to Letv.

In Letv's business ecosystem empire, platform ecosystems should not be neglected. Sports media acts as an advertising platform, whereas Letv has also built the open platform of cloud computing, a user operation platform, the online business platform, and the platform of big data. Among them, Letv's cloud computing platform is an independent subsidiary providing video cloud computing services, including the whole package "video hosting" business for partners, such as helping video uploads, video publishing, marketing, and other services based on cloud computing, which aims to become a new public infrastructure service platform. Meanwhile, the cloud computing platform of Letv attracts content providers through its value-added services so as to increase the competitive advantage of Letv's business ecosystem. In addition to that, Letv has now holds four online business platforms, and sells Letv's smartphones, smart TVs, accessories, and other hardware terminals of Letv through these online business platforms, which not only contributes to its hardware terminals ecosystem by advertising and accelerating sales, but also builds strong connections between platform ecosystems and hardware terminals ecosystems.

Open Ecosystem

Learning from Apple, Letv tries to create a profitable combination between hardware and software. For now, the app ecosystem of Letv, i.e., Letv store, is an open application platform based on Android system, providing services for smart TVs, ifacetv explorer, and leso the searching engine. Taking leso the searching engine as an example, this app is focused on video searches through smartphones, and tries to build the largest and most comprehensive genuine video search platform. This app, without doubt, is quite fit for Letv's smartphones, and has helped popularize Letv's genuine video and other video-related contents, meanwhile the search results are based on Letv's platform of big data, which would also offer precise matching of contents to users.

To conclude, the four major sub-ecosystems of Letv are interconnected and interdependent (Fig. 4.7). The content ecosystem, as the core business

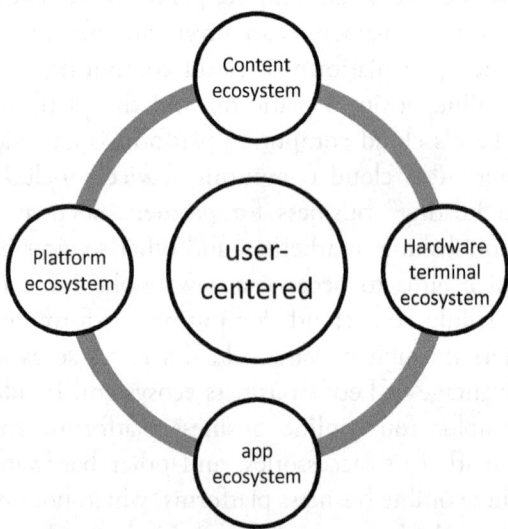

Fig. 4.7 Letv's innovation ecosystem

of Letv, offers genuine video and is in charge of the operation of video broadcasting across all platforms. The platform ecosystem, besides helping advertise Letv's videos, offers unique customer insight through big data analysis and cloud computing. Meanwhile, the smart hardware terminal ecosystem and the app ecosystem together attract end users and guarantee user-stickiness and loyalty through controlling the entrance to the internet.

Based on its complete innovation ecosystem, Letv is developing rapidly and healthily as an internet ecosystem company, with its outstanding performance both in capital markets and commercial markets, and has the potential to be the next generation of Internet unicorn companies, after Baidu, Alibaba, and Tencent (BAT).

In Letv's business model, the completeness of its ecosystem is better than Apple, and other companies which succeed based on perfect ecosystem design and operation. Apple has its own interconnected hardware and software ecosystem, and has for a long time been seen as the outstanding representative of using a closed-loop business ecosystem to realize enormous profits. However, compared with Letv, Apple lacks its own content or platform ecosystem to help attract end users and analyze them. Starting as a content-generation provider, Letv has approached it in an unique way to disruptively change the traditional television industry through a combination of internet and video. The interconnected innovation ecosystem in contents, platforms, smart hardware terminals, and software helps Letv influence more and more end users' consuming habits, thus successfully dominating the mainstream market.

Dual Source Innovation in Midea

While open innovation helps companies to build an ecosystem so that companies like Haier and P&G can use more external resources for R&D and innovation, there are two kinds of potential risks for the company that applies open innovation. The first one is when the degree of openness is too high, then the managerial cost of the open innovation would be much higher and thus might decrease the efficiency of making use of external innovation resources. The second one would be that if the company pays much attention to building and maintaining the open innovation ecosystem instead of building its core capability, then it must risk losing its competitive advantage compared to its rivals and even its core members in the same ecosystem. As a result, the company with an open innovation strategy but without core capability might lose its position of control and give the power to later movers.

Midea is a traditional air-conditioning manufacture company that made a huge success during its translation of business strategy through core-capability–based open innovation. Since being established in 1968, Midea has grown from what was once a local workshop into a leading consumer appliances and heating, ventilation, and air-conditioning (HVAC) systems manufacturer, with operations around the world. After 40 years of persistent growth, its global turnover was over US$22 billion in 2015. Consequently, Midea has about 100,000 employees in China and throughout the world.

Core Technology Competitiveness

Midea continues to invest in R&D for its products technology and seeks to catch next generation trends. Also, it achieves market advantage through a customer-oriented, fast-responding strategy. Midea believes in creating value through responding rapidly to market demands, cost-efficient operations, and consumer satisfaction. As a result, Midea wields a comprehensive product portfolio and a vast production capacity to meet these demands. Midea's integrated research and manufacturing process helps to enrich lifestyles worldwide through a distinct range of innovative, yet affordable products.

Midea continues to globalize its operations with production bases in Vietnam, Belarus, Egypt, Brazil, Argentina, and India, to be followed by additional plants in some other countries. Midea is also expanding its distribution network in several countries to offer better services to local consumers in those locations. Through globalizing its operations and collaboration around the world, Midea builds an open innovation ecosystem to strengthen its ability for market information, R&D profitability, and future development.

Open Ecosystem

On one hand, Midea tries to make the best of an open innovation strategy. On the other, Midea continues to address core technology development and strengthens its innovation system. Midea puts R&D as the company's first-order aim and then reorganized its organization structure to fit the needs of innovation. At the same time, Midea continues to introduce elite members from the outside environment—including cooperating with universities, R&D centers, and international associations—to its innovation system so that it can maintain a consistent innovative ability.

By combining open ecosystem and core technology competitiveness, Midea benefits both from external innovation resources and its own capability. Today, Midea is a leading brand in China and a rising giant around the world. Since Midea's public listing in 1993, the company has maintained a record of uninterrupted profitable operation and dividends payments every year. The accumulated dividend payment from 2013 to 2015 amounts to RMB 12.7 billion. The dividend payout was RMB1.2/share in 2015.

Based on previous analysis, in order to win in the new era, enterprises need to cultivate two major resources/capabilities: one is core technology competitiveness; the other is open ecosystems. Such a dual source innovation paradigm has witnessed its success in "best innovation practice" in Letv and Midea. Seen from Fig. 4.7, our six representative enterprises possess different positions in the dual source of core technology competitiveness–open ecosystem innovation prospect, thus enjoying different performances, as shown in Fig. 4.8 and Table 4.3.

As shown in Table 4.3, among our six representative enterprises, only Letv and Midea adopt the dual source innovation paradigm, which emphasizes open ecosystems as well as core technology competitiveness at the same time, thus enjoying the best innovative performance. Midea ranked No. 1 in the top ten innovative household appliances companies in the world; the patents application number for Midea in 2015 was 5427, much higher than that of Haier (Thomson Reuters Derwent World Patents Index 2015). However, as TIM was adopted by Haier, core

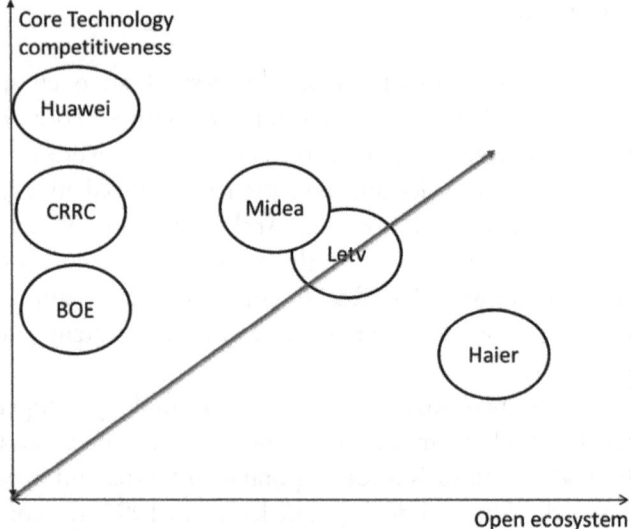

Fig. 4.8 Dual source innovation picture and case enterprise's position

Table 4.3 Analysis of representative cases

	Open ecosystem	Core technology competitiveness	Innovative performance
BOE	−	+	Fine
CRRC Zhuzhou	−	++	Good
Huawei	−	++	Good
Haier	++	+	Good
Letv	++	++	Best
Midea	++	++	Best

technology competitiveness in Haier does not receive the attention deserved, thus Haier could only enjoy good innovative performance. Meanwhile, as Huawei mainly adopts an indigenous innovation paradigm, an open ecosystem, to some extent, is neglected. Thus, like Haier, Huawei could enjoy good innovative performance. Despite its large amounts of R&D expense and its huge number of R&D talents, Huawei does not enter into basic research for now, and inevitably become confused in the face of the challenge of the artificial society (Ren 2016). The case of CRRC Zhuzhou research institute is just like Huawei. At last, for BOE, the "3-I pattern" of innovation it adopts just focuses on technology, without even considering open ecosystems, which ensures BOE could only enjoy a not too bad innovation performance.

4.6   Concluding Remarks and Future Perspective

Conclusion and Contribution

As innovation itself is a dynamic, nonlinear, and systematic process (Dosi 1982), innovation theories also need to be dynamic through nonlinear development to reflect and to predict innovation practices in enterprises. In this chapter, we reviewed the innovation journey in China through examining four representative innovation theories developed by Chinese scholars and analyzing their use in enterprises. We considered that these innovation theories cannot suit enterprises which need to compete in intense technology industries in a knowledge economy, thus, based on Chinese Yin Yang culture, we proposed a new innovation paradigm possessing two key innovative sources: open ecosystems and core technology competitiveness, and named the paradigm dual source innovation. We analyzed the use of dual source innovation in two representative enterprises in China, and compared them with other enterprises undertaking different innovation patterns. Our theoretical framework based on case studies could offer beneficial references to study Chinese enterprises' innovation.

Limitation and Future Perspective

The dual source innovation paradigm proposed in this chapter, although it covers the two major innovation sources in enterprises, still lacks elaboration and generalization. Enterprises need to balance between open ecosystems and core technology competitiveness, but how to acquire these two key factors at first is not discussed in this chapter. Meanwhile, our framework still needs to adjust to specific industries and enterprises. For example, in several industries such as mining or service industries, core technology competitiveness seems not as important as open ecosystems. We will further modify and complete the dual source innovation paradigm in our future works.

References

Abernathy, W.J., and J.M. Utterback. 1978. Patterns of Industrial Innovation. *Technology Review* 64: 254–228.

Chen, J. 1994. The Learning Pattern from Technology Introduction to Indigenous Innovation. *Science Research Management* 15(2): 32–34.

———. 2002. The Theoretic Mode of Integrative Innovation. *China Soft Science* 12: 23–29.

———. 2005. Towards Indigenous Innovation: Pathways for Chinese Firms. In *Workshop of Technology Innovation and Economic Development*.

Chen, J., X.Z. Yu, and S. Wang. 2010. The Pathway and Policy of Chinese Indigenous Innovation. *Journal of Industrial Engineering and Engineering Management* 15: 12–22.

Chesbrough, H.W. 2006. *Open Innovation: The New Imperative for Creating and Profiting from Technology*. Boston, MA: Harvard Business Press.

Christensen, C.M. 1997. *The Innovator's\Dilemma: The Revolutionary Book that Will Change the Way You Do Business*. New York, NY: Collins Business Essentials.

Crainer, S. 2015. Haier Calling. *London Business School Review* 26(1): 24–30.

Dosi, G. 1982. Technological Paradigms and Technological Trajectories: A Suggested Interpretation of the Determinants and Directions of Technical Change. *Research Policy* 11(3): 147–162.

Dougherty, D. 1990. Understanding New Markets for New Products. *Strategic Management Journal* 11(1): 59–78.

Eisenhardt, K.M. 1989. Building Theories from Case Study Research. *Academy of Management Review* 14(4): 532–550.

Eisenhardt, K.M., and M.E. Graebner. 2007. Theory Building from Cases: Opportunities and Challenges. *Academy of Management Journal* 50(1): 25.

Fan, P. 2006. Catching Up Through Developing Innovation Capability: Evidence from China's Telecom-Equipment Industry. *Technovation* 26(3): 359–368.

Fang, T. 2010. Asian Management Research Needs More Self-Confidence: Reflection on Hofstede (2007) and Beyond. *Asia Pacific Journal of Management* 27(1): 155–170.

———. 2012. Yin Yang: A New Perspective on Culture. *Management and Organization Review* 8(1): 25–50.

Faure, G.O., and T. Fang. 2008. Changing Chinese Values: Keeping Up with Paradoxes. *International Business Review* 17(2): 194–207.

Guellec, D., and B.V.P. de la Potterie. 2001. The Internationalisation of Technology Analysed with Patent Data. *Research Policy* 30(8): 1253–1266.

Harris, S.G., and R.I. Sutton. 1986. Functions of Parting Ceremonies in Dying Organizations. *Academy of Management Journal* 29(1): 5–30.

Henderson, R.M., and K.B. Clark. 1990. Architectural Innovation: The Reconfiguration of Existing Product Technologies and the Failure of Established Firms. *Administrative Science Quarterly* 35(1): 9–30.

Hong, Y.Y., M.W. Morris, C.Y. Chiu, and V. Benet-Martinez. 2000. Multicultural Minds: A Dynamic Constructivist Approach to Culture and Cognition. *American Psychologist* 55(7): 709.

Iansiti, M. 1998. *Technology Integration: Making Critical Choices in a Dynamic World.* Boston, MA: Harvard Business Press.

Jiang, H., and J. Chen. 2000. Integrated Innovation Patterns. *Science Research Management* 21(5): 31–39.

Jiang, S., Z. Wang, and Y. Hu. 2016. Core-firm Based View on the Mechanism of Constructing a Corporate Innovation Ecosystem: A Case Study of Haier Group. *Technological Forecasting and Social Change.*

Justin, Y.L.P.Z. 2005. The Advantage of Latter Comers, Technology Imports, and Economic Growth of Developing Countries. *China Economic Quarterly* 4.

Kim, L. 1997. *Imitation to Innovation: The Dynamics of Korea's Technological Learning.* Boston, MA: Harvard Business Press.

Levitt, T. 1966. Innovative Imitation. *Harvard Business Review* 44(5): 63–70.

Li, K. Q. 2016. Speech at the National Science and Technology Innovation Conference.

Lin, J.Y. 2003. Development Strategy, Viability, and Economic Convergence*. *Economic Development and Cultural Change* 51(2): 277–308.

Liu, X. 2010. China's Catch-Up and Innovation Model in IT Industry. *International Journal of Technology Management* 51(2–4): 194–216.

Miles, M.B., and A.M. Huberman. 1994. *Qualitative Data Analysis: An Expanded Sourcebook.* Thousand Oaks, CA: Sage.

Ming-jue, L.X.L.J. 2007. How to Upgrade Technological Capability through International Acquisition: The Case of BOE. *China Soft Science* 12: 10.

OECD. 2016. Gross Domestic Spending on R&D (Indicator). Accessed June 5, 2016. doi: 10.1787/d8b068b4-en.

Ren, Z. F. 2016. Speech at the National Science and Technology Innovation Conference.

Thomson Reuters Derwent World Patents Index. 2015.

von Hippel, E. 1988. *The Sources of Innovation.* New York, NY: Oxford University Press.

von Hippel, E. 2005. Democratizing Innovation: The Evolving Phenomenon of User Innovation. *Journal für Betriebswirtschaft* 55(1): 63–78.

———. 2007. *The Sources of Innovation,* 111–120, Gabler.

Wang, Y., and L. Lu. 2013. Export-oriented Economy as Moderator of the Relationship between Technology Acquisition Model and Independent Innovation. In *2013 6th International Conference on Information Management, Innovation Management and Industrial Engineering (ICIII),* vol. 3, 34–37. IEEE, November.

Wu, X., R. Ma, and G. Xu. 2009. Accelerating Secondary Innovation through Organizational Learning: A Case Study and Theoretical Analysis. *Industry and Innovation* 16(4–5): 389–409.

Xi, J. P. 2016. Speech at the National Science and Technology Innovation Conference.

Xiaobo, W. 1997. The Evolutionary Process of Secondary Innovation. In *Innovation in Technology Management-The Key to Global Leadership. PICMET'97: Portland International Conference on Management and Technology,* 183. IEEE, July.

Xiaobo, W., and N. Yifang. 2001. Secondary Innovation and Strategies for China's Manufacturing Industry in the Global Competition. *Science Research Management* 3: 006.

Xu, Q.R., J. Chen, and B. Guo. 1998. Perspective of Technological Innovation and Technology Management in China. *IEEE Transactions on Engineering Management* 45(4): 381–387.

Xu, Q.R., J. Chen, Z. Xie, J. Liu, G. Zheng, and Y. Wang. 2007. Total Innovation Management: A Novel Paradigm of Innovation Management in the 21st Century. *The Journal of Technology Transfer* 32(1–2): 9–25.

Xu, Q.R., Z.P. Wang, and L.T. Chen. 2013. An Analysis of the Evolution Path to and the Driving Factors of, the Independent Innovation of Enterprises in the Transitional Economy: A Longitudinal Case Study on Haier Group from 1984 to 2013. *Management World* 4: 014.

Xu, Q. R., Z. Y. Wu, S. P. Zhang, and S. Y. Liu. 2014. Total Innovation Management Paradigm for Firm Innovation System. In *2014 I.E. International Conference on Management of Innovation and Technology (ICMIT)*, 359–364. IEEE, September.

Xu, Q.R., G. Zheng, Z.D. Yu, and W. Shen. 2003. Towards Total Innovation Management (TIM): The Emerging New Trend of Innovation Management—A Case Study of Haier Group. *Science Research Management* 24(5): 1–7.

Yin, R.K. 2013. *Case Study Research: Design and Methods*. Thousand Oaks, CA: Sage Publications.

Yip, G.S., and B. McKern. 2016. *China's Next Strategic Advantage: From Imitation to Innovation*. Cambridge, MA: MIT Press.

5

Looking at Business Model Innovation and Innovation Ecosystems and How They Are Evolving

Arvind Sahay and Arunaditya Sahay

This chapter deals with business model innovation (BMI) and innovation ecosystems. Across all countries and industries in the EU, approximately 1 out of 20 SMEs was classified as a business model innovator with CIS data (EC Research 2014). And BMI leads to higher profitability and growth. A 2006 study by IBM on Global Chief Executive Officer (CEO) suggests that that BMI had a higher correlation with operating margin growth than any other type of innovation. Evidence from the USA suggests that 40 % of the 27 companies founded in the 25 years to 2008 that grew their way into the Fortune 500 in the 10 years to 2008 did so through business model innovation (Johnson et al. 2008). Relatedly, an IBM Global Services Study suggests that business model innovators enjoy an operating margin increase that is 5 % more than that of competitors

The inputs of Eric Viardot, EADA, and Sunil Sharma, IIM, Ahmedabad, are gratefully acknowledged.

A. Sahay (✉)
Indian Institute of Management Ahmedabad, Vastrapur, India

A. Sahay
Birla Institute of Management Technology, Greater Noida, India

© The Author(s) 2017
A. Brem, E. Viardot (eds.), *Revolution of Innovation Management*,
DOI 10.1057/978-1-349-95123-9_5

compared with a differential of only 1 % for product innovators (Gleed 2009). Moreover, the success of product innovations, process innovations, and other forms of innovations is also dependent on whether these innovations are consistent with the dominant business model of the firm that has created the product or process innovation. Hence, business models and innovations in business models provide a superstructure for the success or failure of other innovations. In addition, research findings also suggest that business model changes are one of the most sustainable forms of innovation (Sosna et al. 2010).

The ideas presented in this chapter are meant for the managers of a focal firm that is interested in designing new business models with a view to improving its competitive position. The chapter is organized as follows. First, we briefly describe business models: what is a working description of a business model and what are the different kinds of business models? Why is clear thinking, design, execution, and suitable change of business models so critical for firms today?

Second, we look at the main drivers of change and innovation in business models. Among other things, changes in customer behavior and technological change, both of which are interrelated, are driving BMI.

Third, we develop a framework that connects the types of business models to drivers of change in business models and to different innovations in business models that have worked successfully. We provide examples of different starting points of business models and the finish points within a framework. Finally, we extend innovation in business model to innovation ecosystems—or the context in which BMI takes place and its impact on business model innovation. Indeed, how can one leverage and use the innovation ecosystem to maximize the effectiveness of the BMI?

5.1   Business Models and Business Model Innovation

While there are many definitions of business models, we take an amalgam of definitions. We define a business model as a configuration (activity systems) of what the business does (activities) and what it invests in (resources). The logic is that BMI drives the profits for a business by creating and capturing value (Chatterjee 2013). It is the way in which a firm gets its revenues and defines value for different stakeholders. It is the content, structure, and governance of transactions that are designed to create and capture value through interactions with collaborators, partners, and customers. A successful business model is one that fulfills a compelling customer need.

BMI, therefore, refers to the search for new logics and new activity systems of the firm. BMI is about the decisions that enable new ways to create and capture value for its stakeholders through new resource allocation; it focuses primarily on finding new ways to generate revenues and define value propositions for customers, suppliers, and partners (Zott and Amit 2008, 2010). In other words, since a business model is essentially a set of key decisions that collectively determine how a business earns its revenue, incurs its costs, and manages its risks, BMIs are changes to those decisions. What will your offerings be, when are decisions made, who makes them, and why. A BMI would, therefore, do one or more of the following: change the way a firm earns its revenues; change the value chain configuration; change the cost structure of the firm; or change the configuration of activities within and/or across the firm or its set of customers. BMI, therefore, can be characterized by one or more of the following: (a) a fundamental change in the customer value proposition; (b) a fundamental change in the operating model of the firm; or (c) a fundamental change in the business architecture of the firm.

Thus, South West Airlines in the USA has deployed a unique business model that changed the operating model for an airline firm and its business architecture. South West uses one make of plane, secondary airports, point to point flights, no interlining of baggage, no meals, and long term flexible union contracts to develop the lowest cost structure in terms of cost per seat mile that cannot be equaled by other airline firms unless they replicate all elements of the model—an extremely difficult task. Ryanair earns a good share of its revenues not from ticket prices but from such ancillary sources as subsidies from secondary airports or payments from bus companies taking passengers from those airports to city centers. Both these firms changed the configuration of activities within the firm, the value chain configuration, and the cost structure of the firm and catered to a different set of customers.

Somewhat differently, in the same industry, Indigo Airlines in India has employed an asset-light balance sheet–based business model where it keeps giving new orders for planes that, once bought, are quickly sold and leased back. A constantly large order pipeline (its roster of planes as at September 2015 was 97 and it had pending firm orders for 300 more with Airbus) allows it to induct new planes to keep its fleet young (the average age is 4 years) and fuel costs low; a laser focus on standardization of operational process and the use of front and rear doors for entering and exiting passengers keep turnaround times for planes at 30 minutes and operating costs low due to low maintenance costs and highly fuel-efficient planes, an innovation in the business model based on a different operating model and a different business architecture for airlines in India that no other airline has been able to match.

In addition to commercial organizations, business models also apply to non-commercial organizations as well. Nonprofits, government agencies, social enterprises, schools, and nongovernmental organizations (NGOs) also use different ways to create, deliver, and capture value, and, therefore, have a business model. It does not matter whether an organization is in the public or private sector. It does not matter if it is a nonprofit or a for-profit enterprise. All organizations have a business model. Nonprofit corporations may not be providing a financial return to investors or owners, but they still capture value to finance activities with contributions, grants, and service revenue. Social enterprises may be mission-driven, focused on delivering social impact versus a financial return on investment, but they still need a sustainable model to scale. Government agencies are financed by taxes, fees, and service revenue, but are still accountable for delivering value to citizens on a large scale.

BMI, therefore, not only is applicable to different kinds of enterprises but also affects all types of enterprises. Without thinking and execution on business models, an organization will likely lose its way, as customers, technologies, regulations, and enabling infrastructures change over time. Very successful BMI can redefine the rules of the game in the market. Successful BMI leads to successes like Dell in the late twentieth century with its build-to-order business model (against the existing build-to-stock and sell-through-retail store). Successful BMI is an Apple in the early twenty-first century with its foray into mobile phones with a new value chain configuration of service providers and an ecosystem, and IBM in the mid-twentieth century with its large enterprise class computers. A lack of BMI at an appropriate time, however, can lead to the near death of a firm like IBM in the early 1990s. Changes in customer eating habits under way in many markets mean that restaurants like McDonalds need to change their back-end kitchens. These kitchens look like a mini-factory for serving mass-produced frozen patties and French fries and need to change to a kitchen that serves freshly prepared meals with locally sourced vegetables and grains; and the changed kitchen should still provide tasty and affordable meals. Such change will require a change in the business model of these fast-food outlets.

What makes BMI powerful? Competitors can more easily copy a product or a process innovation; but they find it a lot harder to copy a BMI that incorporates many different activities, target customers, revenue flows, value chain configuration, and levels of information concentration. The sheer scale of the effort (including organizational change and change management) required to replicate and improve on a BMI will frequently preclude imitation in any meaningful way.

5.2 Types of Business Models

Classifying business models (BMs) is important to any discussion on BMs to enable a better understanding (Lambert 2015). We describe business models on three dimensions.

The first dimension is premised on strategic logic. Strategic logic has two components—the competitive basis (or basis of customer value) and the value chain configuration.

Is the value generation for customers and value capture from customers and the profit logic primarily on the basis of efficiency or on the basis of "value?" The Indigo business model is predicated on efficiency—efficient use of planes, of manpower, of resources; its success depends critically on reduction of costs that provides value to customers. When a firm like SouthWest Airlines is able to ferry its customers at a cost of 8 cents a seat mile[1] as a consequence of a business model that is based on efficiency and low costs, then competitors find it difficult to catch up with a business model when the alternate business model cost per seat mile is more than 12 cents a seat mile.

On the other hand, the business model of British Airways and Unilever depends on perceived value and value network for the customer; customers need to like Surf detergent; customers need to like the experience of flying on British Airways above and beyond the functional benefit of flying from point A to B. The output is a "want" item and commands a price premium. The value drivers behind the "want" can be objective (such as drug or medical devices) or subjective/perceived (such as movies, music, video games, cosmetics, and fresh/organic food). This component in a sense defines the nature of the customer value proposition in the business model.

The second component of strategic logic that defines a business model is the value chain configuration that deals with the nature of players and the nature of links between them. A typical automobile manufacturer has a vertical value chain with components coming in from the supply chain, which gets assembled in the factory, from where the product goes to the distribution system and then the customers. In the online retail space, however, we now also have a horizontal component in the value chain, where the telecom operator has become an important player in the value chain configuration through the provision of data services through mobile apps to the customer and the retailer that enables individual customers to shop directly at the e-retailer bypassing the public internet. A mobile app provider like Affle is also an additional horizontal entity in the value chain configuration. The value chain configuration of Apple includes vertical providers like Foxcom, horizontal providers of content like music, games, and information providers, horizontal enablers like mobile app providers, and a network of vertical dealers. This component brings together the activities that the firm does and the linkages between the activities and includes the governance structure of the business model.

The second dimension of a business model is whether the markets and customers that are served are one-sided or two-sided (or indeed multiple-sided) and where the revenues come from. Hindustan Unilever and GE serve a set of customers that belong to "one set." GE Health Care, for example, will sell medical facilities with equipment and services of different kinds and the revenue is from the sale of this equipment and the associated services to customers that are some sort of health-care–providing facility. There is no other set of "customers."

In contrast, a television broadcaster like Astro Malaysia, a job recruitment portal like naukri.com, or firms like Uber, Ola, or Google have business models with two-sided markets. Astro has television viewers as one set of customers and advertisers as another set. And the value of the product that it sells to advertisers (airtime) depends on the number of customers in the other set that view programs, very unlike a GE or a Hindustan Unilever. Similarly, naukri.com has two sets of customers— recruiters and job seekers. And the value that a customer in one set gets is a function of the number of customers in the other set. The greater the number of job seekers that upload their resumes on naukri, the more recruiters flock to naukri; similarly, the more recruiters that come to naukri, the greater the number of job seekers that come to naukri. Uber serves drivers and passengers—both are customers and they influence one another. These are two-sided markets with two distinct sets of customers. Newspapers also have a two-sided business model, as do Google and Yahoo. This dimension of the business model defines the value architecture and links the value chain configuration to the customer value proposition.

The third dimension of business model comes from the firm's level of control and/or access to and use of information related to the customer usage of product, the customer experience, the flow of goods or services in the value chain, etc.—in short, any information that is useful and usable in providing the desired service to the customer.

Information can relate to supply chain, customer purchase and customer experience information, to pricing practices in the channel, to the physical location of inventory in the channel, etc. Access to and appropriate use of such business information is essential to keep the business running smoothly. Is this information diffused among different players? Or is it concentrated in one or a few players? A leading information technology company is attempting to put together an Internet Of Things (IOT)-enabled model that concentrates health-care data in the hands of one provider in the ecosystem that provides health care. This provider, therefore, would be able to, if successful, tap into a greater proportion of the revenues associated with the health-care service. This dimension of a business model describes the information context in which the value architecture connects the value chain to the customer value proposition. Taxi hire apps like TaxiForSure and Uber's business model are constructed around capturing information about the location of drivers and the requirements of transportation for a set of customers at any given point in time, and matching the information to create transactions that

	Dimension of Business Model		Direction of Change in Business Model	
1.	Strategic Logic	Customer Value is "Efficiency" Based	⬛➡ ⬅⬛	Customer Value is "Value" Based
		Value Chain Configuration is Primarily Vertical	⬛➡ ⬅⬛	Value Chain Configuration is Both Vertical and Horizontal
2.	Market Structure of Customer set	One Sided Market	⬛➡	Two Sided Markets
3.	Information Concentration	Information about the entire value creation process is diffuse and not available or leverageable by provider or customer	⬛➡ ⬅⬛	Information about the entire value creation process is concentrated / concentrateable, available and leverageable

Fig. 5.1 Business model typology and business model innovation and drivers

create value for drivers, customers and for Uber. L'Oréal's use of an iPad app to capture customers' facial features (a critical piece of information that lay elsewhere with others) and help her customize a makeup solution herself has enabled L'Oréal to come up with a business model that enables a higher value capture.

Figure 5.1 summarizes a typology of business models. Recall that the chapter is about innovation in business models. Just as product innovation can have drivers like technological change and customer trends, BMI also has its drivers. Our next section deals with the drivers of BMI.

5.3 Drivers of Change in Business Models

When Indigo launched its airline in India in 2006 (as of 2015 it had a 37 % passenger share in the Indian market), it chose to order 100 planes (firm orders not options) from Airbus, the largest single order by an airline start-up—something that it managed to do because one of its founders is Rakesh Gangwal, the ex-CEO of US Airlines with a large reputation in aviation circles. Indigo anticipated that to run a low-cost airline in India, the only certain way to decrease costs was to rely on continuously improving technology that would cut fuel costs for new planes and keeping the fleet young would reduce maintenance costs; it anticipated that it could not depend on low landing charges or low fuel prices. A constantly large order pipeline (currently at 300) allows it to induct new planes to keep its fleet young—the average age of its fleet is 4 years; a laser focus on standardization of operational processes keeps turnaround time for planes at 30 minutes and operating costs low due to low maintenance costs and highly fuel efficient planes.

Over the 10 years to 2015, Indigos's A-320s (the only model that it has) have increased their fuel efficiency cumulatively by more than 12 %, leading to large savings on fuel costs that can be as much as 50 % of total costs in India for an airline. So a younger fleet enjoys a disproportionate cost advantage over an older one. Selling and leasing back planes leads to an asset-light business model. A key driver leading Indigo to choose and design its business model was, therefore, technological change in engines and planes. Indigo chose a plain vanilla, straight, efficiency-based model that is driven by riding the technological change of the increasing fuel efficiency of engines.

We categorize drivers of change in business models under the following heads.

a. Changes in Customer Behavior and Demographics (e.g., more women working—ready to eat food; requirement of organic food)
b. Infrastructure Deficiency Filling Models: lack of facilities such as banking, internet access, reliable transport facilities, low affordability offer the scope of new business models (examples are Godrej Chotukool; M-PESA; Airtel)
c. Technological Change–Led Business Model Innovation:

    i. Value Chain Reconfiguration due to Technological Change (Netflix)
    ii. New Players in Value Chain Due to Technological Change (Apple iPod)
    iii. Information Concentration–led Change in Business Model (L'Oréal; iPod)

d. Strategy Driven Innovation in Business Models (GE; Airtel)

1. We shall look at two kinds of changes in customer behavior. The first is demographic change. The second is attitudinal change driven by familiarity with categories.

    a. As more women enter the workforce in India, processing of produce and cooking at home is decreasing. Earlier, customers would buy wheat, get it ground into flour at a flour mill, knead the flour into dough and make the chapatti (Indian bread) at home and then consume the food at home. Each element of this purchase and consumption chain is shifting outside home slowly and surely. More and more consumers are now buying branded flour, ready-made chapattis, and ready-made food that includes chapatti, and they are eating out. This is leading to products like Ashirvaad branded flour and Visakha ready-to-eat meals, products that require new manufacturing and supply chain lines and an increasing number of restaurants. Importantly, the information required by customers to source and manage their eating is getting concentrated in firms like Zomato that are becoming one stop shops for food related information beginning with restaurants. Changing customer behavior is creating the space for new business models that did not exist before. Interestingly, in developed and developing markets, as customers move to more organic, fresh, and natural foods that are sourced locally, there is an increasingly fundamental shift that will be required in the business models of established chains like McDonalds, KFC, and others that have thrived on factory-processed and frozen food sourced from distant places. Statistics like a drop in consumption of orange juice by 45 % (now seen as free sugar without the fiber), and a 25 % drop in the sale of packaged cereal are all pointers to customer movement in the direction of natural and fresh food.

b. Increasingly, what customers want from products is not necessarily ownership, but rather the function that the product provides or the service that it delivers. The underlying assumption is that the value of the product in many cases lies in its utilization and its functional benefits to the customer. In this case, the very notion of economic value is changing from exchange value to utilization value. This new approach is part of the larger move to the provision of services, which, evidence has shown, is linked to higher and more stable profits. Servicizing, then, could be considered as an operation which satisfies customers' needs by selling the usability, functionality, "non-tangible" side of the product rather than the artifact itself (Stahel 1994). More and more, customers are looking for intangibles as an integral part of the value offering from the provider. The Makeup Genius mobile app available from L'Oréal is used on tablets; the mobile app turns a tablet into a mirror and camera and helps young women through the makeup experience. Since its launch in 2014, it has been downloaded more than 14 million times and has driven more than 250 million product trials (Edelman and Singer 2015). The experience of choosing and applying the makeup as a part of the purchase process has been transferred and there is now utilization value in the exchange transaction.

2. The second major driver of BMI tends to emanate from "friction" in the market, or, what can be called as "infrastructural" deficiencies that tend to be common in developing countries. Infrastructure alludes to access to or deficiencies in areas such as transport bottlenecks, electricity supply, regulatory hurdles, etc. that increase the cost of doing business: 4 hours of electricity supply a day requires a different business model to supply refrigeration needs in emerging markets. A weak road and common market network that increases costs of transportation and inventory carrying cost leads to a business model that requires distributed manufacturing to decrease transportation costs. Indian trucks' speed is on average 35 km/h while it is 75 km/h in Europe (AT Kearney 2014). Over the last 60 years, the railway network has grown by 23 % in India while both freight and passenger traffic has increased by more than 1300 %. This has resulted in large congestion and lower train average speed and ultimately to the transport bottlenecks (Indian Railways 2015). Enforcement of contracts can differ widely across countries. It takes on average 1420 days to enforce a contract in India, compared to 395 days in France, 437 in the UK, 394 days in Germany and 510 days in Spain. So firms operating in countries like India need to build in slow contract enforcement into their business models.

   a. Countries like India and Kenya tend to have many infrastructural deficiencies that may not be present in developed markets. For example, a lack of regular supply of electricity and low affordability makes refrigerators present in only 20 % of households in India. Customers still want refrigeration but cannot afford the usual product manifestation that provides the refrigeration benefit because it is too costly, not portable, and over engineered for their purpose.

   b. In Kenya, a small number of bank branches makes it difficult for people to transfer money from one place to another at a low cost. Godrej in India and Vodafone in Kenya have designed new business models and products to deliver new products and services to customers that leverage these infrastructural deficiencies.

3. Frequent use of a new technology allows a firm to reconfigure the value chain and develop a new business model. Netflix, in the USA, was able

to first use a lower technology (DVD Rentals that were delivered to the home through the US Post Office) and then streaming technology to upend Blockbuster that depended on a physical retail chain, rental of physical objects (DVDs and videos) and a limited selection of highly desired movies.

a. From the beginning, Netflix owned its library of movie DVDs that it could legally rent out as many times as it pleased. The core objective of Netflix was to maximize the percentage of its DVD library that was rented out, leading to high asset utilization. Netflix brought a new player—the offbeat movie production house—into the value chain. A secondary core objective was to circulate the movies quickly—quick turnaround measured by one-day delivery—that was a key desired outcome for movie renters; this is typical of the efficiency-based model. Netflix catered to movie aficionados and built up a loyal following. Movie aficionados watch many more movies than the general public and it was critical to keep them happy by delivering the movies quickly. While this implied expenses in building a superb distribution system, this investment was very visible to the subscriber and was instrumental in developing the loyalty. However, movie aficionados also watched more offbeat movies and Netflix endeared itself to this group by being an easy source to find these movies. This was another core objective for Netflix. Why? Offbeat movies could be acquired inexpensively sometimes for only 50 cents.

b. Finally, Netflix started a movie queue on its website where the subscribers would list the movies they wanted to watch. This practically eliminated the risks of acquiring movies that would not be rented out. The customer was co-opted in the value chain and his inputs were used in sourcing of content. In the early stages, Netflix also built an activity system that co-opted other stakeholders such as Indie studios and a small base of engaged movie aficionados. By targeting a niche segment that it became intimately familiar with, Netflix managed to slowly perfect the logistical challenges, its predictive model for movie acquisitions and then over a period of time was also able to source content from the "mainstream studios" and finally graduated to producing its own content.

c. Netflix also used the public internet to start streaming its movies over a period of time and saved on distribution costs for itself, while customers saved on the costs of finding and purchasing the movie. From sourcing movies and programs, Netflix has now become a producer of content and has started dis-intermediating producers, thus changing the nature of the value chain configuration—influenced by the use of new technology that became available in the ecosystem.

4. Sometimes, changes in business models are driven by explicit changes in the strategy of a company. The long time conglomerate GE has over the decade to 2015 changed its business model by following a strategy of divesting all its financial subsidiaries. This has changed the business model because earlier sales used to be financed by the GE subsidiary; now the financial arm of GE is an independent company that will deal at arm's length with the sales of GE's industrial equipment. The business model has changed in terms of the value chain configuration from a straight, value-add model to a straight, efficiency-based model as a deliberate strategy by CEO Inmelt to decrease the volatility of revenues and profits that are inherent in a leveraged financial services business. Another change in the business model for GE flows from its R&D based in emerging markets that is producing products and services that are 40 % to 60 % cheaper to own and operate and that utilizes a different value chain configuration.

To recapitulate, drivers of business model innovation can be summarized as:

a. Changes in Customer Behavior and Demographics (e.g., more women working—ready to eat food; requirement of organic food)
b. Infrastructure Deficiency Filling Models: lack of facilities such as banking, internet access, reliable transport facilities, low affordability offer the scope of new business models
c. Technological Change–Led Business Model Innovation:

   i. Value Chain Reconfiguration due to Technological Change
   ii. New Players in Value Chain Due to Technological Change

iii. Information Concentration–led Change in Business Model

d. Strategy Driven Innovation in Business Models

5.4   Business Model Innovations

An innovation in a business model, therefore, is a change in an element of the business model configuration that hopefully leads to a better competitive position and is motivated by one or more of the factors given in the previous section. Santos et al. define BMI as a reconfiguration of activities in the existing business model of a firm that is new to the product/service market in which the firm competes (Santos 2009). BMI, therefore, can be characterized by one or more of the following: (a) a fundamental change in the customer value proposition and the value chain configuration; (b) a fundamental change in the operating model of the firm—in the value architecture and value capture that links the value chain configuration to the customer value proposition; (c) a fundamental change in the business architecture that the firm operates in—the information concentration and flow and the links to the innovation ecosystem.

BMI, at its heart, is about capturing and providing a larger (than before) share of the value created for customers or about being able to aggregate the value in one or a few providers from a situation where there are millions of providers (individuals). A strong business model will help a firm to capture a significant portion of value that is created in a context and do so in a way that is difficult for other firms to replicate. Although there may be a best business model, depending on the nature of the innovation and the assets of the corporation, there is rarely a single good business model. BMI, therefore, refers to the search for new logics and new activity systems of the firm, and the decisions that enable new ways to create and capture value for its stakeholders through new resource allocation, and focuses primarily on finding new ways to generate revenues and define value propositions for customers, suppliers, and partners (Teece 2010).

Why is BMI becoming increasingly important? Because of the realization that the success of all other types of innovation is dependent on consistency with the business model of the organization. Because BMI leads to new sources of revenues, new activity systems for the firm, new customer groups for the firm, changes in the value chain configuration that the firm operates in, and new types of strategies and customer value propositions that can fundamentally alter the competitive position of the firm. Because changes in technology, various kinds of infrastructural deficiencies in physical transport and information flow and changes in the customer behavior are leading to new possibilities of changes in the business model that a firm can leverage to its advantage. BMI is more difficult to imitate by the competition; certainly, BMI is more difficult to implement, but also more difficult to imitate. Therefore, BMI is more sustainable as compared to other forms of innovation and is, therefore, more likely to lead to a competitive advantage over a longer period of time. In India, naukri.com is now the clear leader in the online recruitment market with a 70 % traffic share and does not have any real competitor to date with its ticking-like-clockwork business model that has proved insurmountable for all competitors like timesjobs.com, shine. com, monsterindia.com, jobstreet.com, and others. Even monster.com, the global leader in online recruitment, is a distant second to naukri.com in India.

Thus, managers need first to understand the kind of business models that they are using and then think about the possible changes that will help to improve the firm's competitive position, and the implications that such changes in the business model would have for product, process, and other innovation forms in the firm.

Below, we explore changes from one form of business model to another as a form of BMI. Recall that the dimensions on which business models are able to change are (see Fig. 5.1):

- "efficiency-based vs. value-based along with changes in value chain configuration,"
- straight one-sided vs. two-sided or multiple-sided markets, and
- diffuse information-based vs. concentrated information-based models.

Recall also that innovations in business models are driven by customer behavior changes, infrastructural deficiencies in the relevant markets, technological change, and the focal firm's strategy change.

From Straight Efficiency-Based to Straight Value-Based Business Model and the Other Way

Swiss farmers were struggling with the cost of producing cheese that was valued mainly on the basis of how efficiently it was produced—a straight efficiency-based business model, which was not being able to produce the product at a cost where it could compete with industrially produced cheese. One Swiss farmer called Paul Wylie decided to take stock of all his assets and not just his productive assets— the cows. The model that came out of this has come to be known as "rent a cow" (www.swissinfo. ch/eng). Wylie decided to put his cows up for lease to be rented by Swiss city folk for 380 SFr/summer in return for: commitment to buy cheese for 16 SFr/kg (min. 30 kg) and 4 hours of work at the alpine farm (20 SFr/kg in case of not working). The lessee got the following: the right to buy the entire cheese production of the rented cow (50–120 kg); a framed certificate of the cow; the right to watch all daily work processes (milking, making cheese); the companionship of the Alpine farmer during first visit; and some catering (coffee, milk, cheese, and bread).

The business model innovation rested on the realization that cross-elasticity of demand for cheese was much lower when it was offered not as a single product but as the opportunity to become part of the Alpine ecosystem. The model proved to be a tremendous success and had spillover effects on the local tourism industry. The model shifted the demand in time and place as well as value. A straight efficiency-based business was converted into a straight value-based business model by adding other "value components" to the original product and getting the customer to think differently about the product. The receptivity of the customer due to his changing profile and requirements enabled the shift to and success of the new business model. In this case, the Swiss farmer created change: (a) in the customer value proposition from the same value chain configuration; and (b) in the value capture mode because now customers were paying for other dimensions of value that they were not paying for earlier.

Zara, the fashion retailer, based out of Spain, did exactly the reverse. A part of the fashion retailer, Inditex, Zara has made many choices that are different from its peers and appears inefficient on most metrics (it is the most efficient on one key metric). In the fashion industry, a key variable that determines if a firm has an edge in the market is the time to market. While almost all competitors have outsourced many of their activities such as dyeing, cutting the fabric, washing, ironing, and ticketing the finished garment, Zara keeps all of these in-house or very close to itself physically (like sewing, which is done in small production facilities very close to Zara). When viewed in isolation, these appear inefficient. However, the totality of all these activities done together enables Zara to bring new fashionable apparel lines from the design stage to the market in a much shorter time than the competition. So, ironically, Zara has moved from a straight value-based model to one that is more efficient in reducing the numbers on a key efficiency metric that matters to Zara, which is time to market in the fashionable apparel industry. Customer behavior is again the driver of this BMI.

Infrastructural deficiency (high transport costs and time) have led Hindustan Unilever (HUL) also to use a BMI in a straight value-based model to an efficiency-based process with a change in the value chain configuration. Because transport costs in India can be substantial and take away narrow margins that are available in categories like a mass market soap and detergent, HUL has chosen to disperse its manufacturing facilities across 230 different locations, of which 150 are franchised (business.mapsofindia.com). The product does not have to travel far to reach the end of the distribution chain, reducing the transportation costs in terms of time and carrying inventory, and saving on margins. This model is difficult to replicate by most other firms because they do not have the scale or the management wherewithal to manage franchisees, nor do they have the organizational expertise or the access to the local multilevel distribution chain that such a dispersed manufacturing set-up depends on. Infrastructural deficiency is the driver of this BMI.

From Straight Efficiency-Based to a Two-Sided, Value-Based Model

NTT DoCoMo launched i-mode in Japan in February 1999—a mobile internet service in a country that had low fixed-line penetration. NTT had been a very traditional telecom service provider providing basic telecom services in a straight efficiency-based model. When it launched i-mode, it moved from serving one set of customers to serving two sets of interrelated customers: the first set of customers were content providers who generated content like ringtones, transaction services for financial products, astrological predictions, etc. for NTT DoCoMo's other customers—individuals. NTT DoCoMo provided content providers a billing service and access to a much larger set of customers through a market platform that they would not otherwise have had access to; content providers were paid a proportion of the revenues that came from the second set of customers. The second set of customers were individuals who bought a phone that was customized by NTT DoCoMo for i-mode services and who bought the services—almost all of which came from the content providers that i-mode aggregated on the DoCoMo platform.

I-mode went from nothing to 30 million subscribers in Japan in less than three years of launch on the back of this new value-based, two-sided business model with a new value chain configuration. Very interestingly, this business model did not use the latest technology at the time (WAP) but a slightly earlier technology (cHTML) in order to make sure that all the different players on the business model (the content providers, the handset makers, and the customers) were aligned. DoCoMo i-mode created a change in the customer value proposition and the value chain configuration; it created a change in the value architecture and value capture that links the value chain configuration to the customer value proposition; it also created a fundamental change in the business architecture that the firm operates in—the information concentration and the links to the innovation ecosystem.

Google and Facebook also created new two-sided market business models. In Google's case, the firm provides information as a service to one of customers—individuals—and it provides eyeballs to the other set—firms that advertise or market to individuals. One could think of Google as the Uber of broadcast media. It has a value-based, two-sided business model where none existed before. Facebook also has two sets of customers—individuals and advertisers—and uses a different play on information as a service—that of providing a platform for human interactions in the digital space—again creating a business model where none existed before (the information exchange in the human interactions that Facebook has captured were earlier done between individuals and at physically co-located aggregations of people).

It will be interesting to watch how the value creation wars between Google and Facebook play out, to see the extent to which Google's value engine advantage offsets Facebook's ability to add new dimensions of customer value. Google's advantages include its ownership and leverage of fiber optics capacity, bought at dot-com fire-sale prices, plus its data center scale, productivity, and energy efficiency, and its software/hardware capabilities to manage more data than any other organization on earth. Google's estimated costs are one third that of its main competitors. It is hard to see how the global telecommunications establishment can escape the margin erosion of price wars, data plan hyper-competition, and dependence on fixed assets.

Naukri.com in India is an online recruitment portal; it upended the traditional recruitment model in India by inventing the two-sided business model based on its platform and set up the virtuous circle where the more resumes that come to it, the more recruiters advertise on its site, and also the more recruiters that come to its site and use its resumes, the more job seekers that come to its web site. Naukri started in 1997 in a bootstrap mode, with no corporate customers, by taking magazine job advertisements and putting them on its web site and a few job seekers coming to its site, at a time when there were only 14,000 web sites in India; by 2015, naukri has grown to having more than 15 million resumes on its servers and more than 1500 corporate clients with a daily traffic of more than 5 million to its web site. Interestingly, naukri employs an offline salesforce[2] to sell its recruitment solutions to companies, unlike Monster that has employed teleselling and came up a distant second. Companies provide 95 % of the revenues and job seekers provide 5 % only; yet both are integral to the business model of naukri. As of early 2016, naukri was the gorilla in the Indian market with a 70 % traffic and revenue share in the online recruitment market in India.

From Straight Value-Based Business Model to a Two-Sided, Value-Based Model

Tesco started out as a straight discount retail business and is now labeled as Walmart's worst nightmare, one of the three largest global retailers, a leading financial services company, one of the most successful mobile phone firms, and by far the most profitable player in online grocery sales. It went from a straight, efficiency-based model to a two-sided, value-based and information concentrated model.

Tesco is now the largest seller of "branded" gas to car drivers and the national price-leader. Its loyalty card is the second currency of the entire UK economy. Tesco's value architecture was designed with the aim of earning the customer's lifetime loyalty, not just selling groceries, at which it is superb. In many ways, Tesco is an opportunity platform readied for the next expansion and looking for the one after that. It is notable that its platform, built for growth, has become key in recovering from the erosion of its basic business as the UK economy grows at a rather tepid rate. Its "dark stores" are a new digital hub for online groceries and it is on track to reach a 50 % market share in the UK online business (Keen and Williams 2013).

From Straight Value-Based With No Information Business Model to a Straight Value-Based, Concentrated Information Business Model

Consider the provision of health-care information in the case of chronic diseases. For a diabetic patient, for example, therapeutic care requires that information about symptomatic parameters, such as blood sugar (fasting and postprandial), HbA1C, lipid profile, insulin, glucagen, ghrelin, Vitamin B12, Potassium, etc., be made available on requirement to the doctor. The more regular and real time the information, the better the quality of care possible to the patient. Currently, the information tends to be fragmented (some in the hands of the patient, some with the family doctor, some with the hospital that the patient may have used, and some with the pathology labs where diagnostic tests have occurred for the patient). "Customer value" in the market happens when the information is aggregated and made available in the right quantity and format to provide the correct course of treatment to the patient.

A new business model that is being sought to be put together will have sensors in a patient's body that track these parameters on a prescribed periodic basis and transmits that data to a designated provider (who owns the sensors and has arrangements with or owns the network that transmits the data). The data remains private to the patient but is made available to the doctor or hospital by arrangement with the patient. The insurance provider's list of health-care providers includes this designated provider for information. The patient's payments are either directly to the doctor or hospital or through the insurer. The hospital/doctor and insurer pay a fee to the designated provider for the information and for the use of the infrastructure. Revenues will therefore come from possibly three sets of customers: hospitals, patients, and telecom operators. It is a two- or three-sided business model, with each set of customers being influenced by the other in terms of their signing on to the platform and with the relevant information getting concentrated in the hands of one player in the value chain.[3]

The final business model in this case should be able to:

a. Monetize effectively the partnerships of various players in the ecosystem;
b. Suggest a primary partner for joint go-to-market for a specific solution or business vertical—should it be a telecom operator, M2M platform provider, device manufacturer, or any other player in the ecosystem?
c. Suggest specific metrics to evaluate & monitor financial profitability of projects;
d. Outline options of revenue sharing model, required for each partner in order to maximize the value delivered to the end customer at the end of the chain and ensure stable returns to a service provider like the ICT firm.

There are several stakeholders in the health-care vertical who are potential customers for this new business model–based solution such as:

a. Hospital management
b. Doctors
c. Patients
d. Health insurance providers
e. Medical equipment manufacturers
f. Health-care regulators/government agencies
g. Elderly care homes/hospices
h. Pharmaceutical companies (digital health care).

Clearly, the putting together of a new business model is a non-trivial task. Clearly, also, the firm that puts together the first working business model in the sector will have innovated a new business model in that space.

Consider another example. Ford Motors has recently set up a lab at Palo Alto in Silicon Valley. The lab is working on ways to better integrate phones and other personal communication devices into cars alongside upgrading safety systems in the car with a view to providing a larger range of information-enabled services to the customer. A part of the remit of the facility in Palo Alto is to look at the car in a similar way as the i-Pad and i-Phone ecosystem. Examples of additional features added to a car that would fulfill consumer needs are:

- Identify deals at nearby restaurants and retailers based on driver's preferences;
- Enable voice commands while using GPS maps, audio books, or other similar applications;
- Alert drivers if it senses a lane change without a signal and nudge the car back into the lane if necessary;
- Find an open parking space using a mobile application and reserve it for the driver;
- Improve weather with a mobile application by transmitting signals when a car's rain-sensing wipers are triggered.

The lab will also study larger issues, including population growth in developing countries like China and India, and how best to handle traffic in those countries. In a straight value-based business model in no information content, Ford is actively trying to build information-based value into the car as a greater proportion of customer "wants" related to a car, at least in a developed economy as a large segment of the population moves from the transportation service that the car provides to other aspects such as comfort and information-based "value add services." So, this change in the business model, which is still in the making, is at least partly driven by the changing requirements of the customer.

From Straight Value-Based with Diffused Information Business Model to a Two-Sided, Value-Based Concentrated Information Business Model

Zomato was started in India on the customer insight that as people move to large towns from their home towns, they need information on places to eat, and restaurants would like to be able to reach such customers. Taking advantage of the customer trend of eating out, Zomato had built a two-sided business model that concentrates information within it as the principal value add for one set of customers (individuals wanting options to eat well). Its second set of customers are restaurants who are looking for patrons and want to make themselves known to the target set of customers on a platform where they are already aggregating.

Zomato revenue is primarily from advertising—by leasing out space on its web/mobile interface to restaurants that place banner ads. It does not do preferential search—except in the category search where the top three results could be paid (featured ads) and these ads would be clearly marked as such. Zomato charges one set of its clients (restaurants) an upfront subscription fee on a quarterly basis. Price revisions happen periodically. Rates vary from Rs. 2000 (US$30) to Rs. 100,000 (US$1500) a month.

Zomato offers no commitment to the restaurants in terms of clicks or leads. In India, around 10 % of the listed restaurant base is monetized. Within India, Zomato is monetizing only seven to eight of the largest cities. Zomato's clients are largely owners of one to ten local restaurants.

Its clientele churn rate is very low and largely attributable to restaurants going out of business and not because clients do not find Zomato value adding.

The vision is to own the communication channel between consumers and restaurants. Zomato (with Urbanspoon) attracts more than 80 million visits per month and has upwards of 48 million user ratings. In all, 45 % of the traffic is from the mobile app while the rest is from desktop and mobile web. Mobile web and app constitutes 70 % of the traffic. This figure was close to 50 % in 2014. Nearly 30 % of traffic into Zomato is from Google, while the rest is organic. Mobile traffic is nearly 70 % and close to 45 % of overall traffic comes from mobile apps.

Restaurants are provided with a dashboard which provides details on page views, calls, map views, menu views, and the number of searches. The key metric that restaurants track is the number of calls through Zomato.

Zomato created a new business model in a market which had a straight value-based business model with diffuse information with many different entities. There was no one party that could provide the information about eating-out places in an easy-to-access manner. Zomato created a concentrated information, two-sided, value-based model for its customers. By doing so, Zomato aggregated the value creation for both sets of its customers through channelized information flow and captured a larger share of the value in the pie than was the case before. Zomato created a new market through its BMI.

From Straight Value-Based with Simple Value Chain Configuration Business Model to a Straight, Efficiency-Based, Changed Value Chain Configuration

Godrej Boyce in India is a manufacturer of refrigerators. It is the number four player in an annual market of 3 million units where the leaders are Korean firms LG and Samsung. The largest selling models until recently in India were the 160–170 liter refrigerator models that retailed for Rs. 6500 to Rs. 8000; however, only one in five households has a refrigerator. Affordability is an issue for the other 190 million households.

Lack of regular electricity and a relative frequent shift of homes is also an issue. Most these households are 4–5 member households in rural or semi-urban areas with one-room tenements where the people shift frequently and earn between Rs. 7000 and Rs. 10,000 per month ($110–150 per month). The need was not to preserve food for a week but to preserve the remains of a meal until the next meal; the need was not to freeze water but to make it cooler than room temperature; the need was to have a refrigerator that was portable and affordable where the person would not have to spend a month's income on a refrigerator. And these requirements could not be satisfied by the stripped down version of current designs.

Godrej has launched a Rs. 3250, 43-liter, 7.8-kilo refrigerator called Chotukool with higher insulation capacity that consumes half the electricity and can maintain a temperature of 4 degrees with no electricity for a few hours. It has no compressor and uses a cooling chip and fan similar to that used in computers and also runs on a battery. The number of parts in Chotukool has been reduced to 20 from 200 in a regular refrigerator. The product innovation also runs hand in hand with a BMI. Godrej had created new ecosystem of suppliers for these parts. These suppliers are completely different from the existing suppliers, changing one part of the value chain configuration.

An integral part of any business model is the channels a company is employing. Most of the performed functions are: (a) the creation of awareness in regards to services or products; (b) helping potential customers evaluate products or services; (c) enabling customers to purchase; (d) delivering the product and/or service physically and the value to customers; and (e) ensuring post-purchase satisfaction through customer support. The channel is also a medium to communicate information to the customer.

For Chotukool, the Godrej group does not use the traditional model of a proprietary channel with a sales force and a distributor–dealer chain and has joined hands with micro-finance institutions and villagers, creating a new distribution ecosystem. The product just does not work with the existing channels and hence the change in the value chain configuration. Village girls are also involved in selling the products at a commission of

Rs. 150 per product sold (something that the company claims will reduce the distribution and marketing costs by 40 %).

The last element of the change in the business model comes from the set of customers addressed. While the business model changes from conventional straight value-based to straight efficiency-based with a different value chain configuration, the customers addressed are also different—more toward the bottom of the pyramid customers per the classification of management thinker, C.K. Prahalad.

From Straight Value-Based with Simple Value Chain Configuration Business Model to a Straight Value-Based, Changed-Value Chain Configuration and Concentrated Information

In Kenya, the number of bank branches was and still is limited. Money transfer as an activity depended on either a costly transfer through a bank branch—time to travel to a branch, make a commission payment that was quite exorbitant, especially for small transfers and then wait for a couple of days for the transfer to happen—or it was a time consuming and risky affair where people physically transported the money. Both these were straight value-based with a simple value chain configuration business models. Lack of access to money movement facilities or facilities that were expensive led to mobile airtime being used as money. This led to the creation of M-PESA.

A mobile based service for payments and money transfer, M-PESA was launched in Kenya in 2007 by Safaricom, a telecom service provider owned by Vodafone. It is an SMS-based money transfer system; it allows individuals to deposit, send, and withdraw funds using their cell phone. M-PESA now reaches approximately 38 % of Kenya's adult population, and is used in other developing countries such as Tanzania, Afghanistan, and South Africa. It combines telecom infrastructure, mobile banking, and micro-payments to enable payments, money transfer, and banking services. Customers can deposit and withdraw money from a network of agents that include airtime resellers and retail outlets acting as banking agents. As the payment system has caught on, it has grown beyond Kenya.

The M-PESA prepaid Safari Card is an international PrePay card that can be pre-loaded with funds, in Kenya Shillings, and can be used to withdraw cash in any currency from over 1.6 million ATMs worldwide, as well as to make purchases at over 28 million VISA branded shops and other merchant outlets worldwide.

M-PESA has been especially successful in reaching low-income Kenyans: new data indicates that the percentage of people living on less than $1.25 a day who use M-PESA rose from less than 20 % in 2008 to 72 % in 2011. By 2013, a staggering 43 % of Kenya's GDP flowed through M-PESA with over 237 million person to person transactions (www.forbes.com). As of 2015, 70 % of adult Kenyan population use M-PESA through its 40,000 agent network and 25 % of Kenya's GNP flows through M-PESA. Safaricom in Kenya now is the repository of the largest proportion of information relating to payments in the country. The Central Bank of Kenya depends on information from the telecom operator to understand the nature of cash flows in the country.

Moreover, M-PESA has also helped financial inclusion. Since, the opening of bank accounts is dependent on Know Your Customer (KYC) norms which are made easier in Kenya due to the national IDs, programs such as M-Shwari are able to aid to the financial inclusion process by providing credit access to the previously unbanked individuals.

In order to open the M-Shwari bank account, the user does not have to visit any bank branch. He/she can do so using their M-PESA enabled phones, clicking on a single link to open a savings bank account and the account is opened instantaneously. This is a complete reduction in the time taken for a customer to open a bank account since only 46 % of the Kenyan population can reach a bank within 10 minutes whereas in the same time, 72 % can get to a mobile money agent who will help them open an M-PESA account. According to a research report by Consulting Group to Assist the Poor (CGAP), FSD Kenya and Central Bank of Kenya, 88 % of M-PESA users had their account opened within 30 minutes and for less than 2 %, the process took more than a day. Hence, this reduced the time taken to open a bank account (through M-PESA) from a few days, including activation, as was the norm in Kenya, to a few minutes (Jack and Suri 2010).

An infrastructure deficiency and a customer need led to a new business model being implemented that adds value and concentrates information with the service provider.

Another example is provided by the October 2007 launch of *In Rainbows*, Radiohead's recent CD where the managers decided not to follow the conventional release process with the record company, EMI, but as an experiment to release the CD on the band's website.

Fans were invited to pay whatever they wished for the tracks, which also offered a collector's box set. In Radiohead's case, this approach is widely considered to have been a success. The band's website registered over 3 million visits during the first 60 days after the release; while about one third chose to pay nothing, the remaining two thirds paid an average of £4. The net revenue to the band thus came in at around £2.67 per album on average—far more than the band's share would have been under their normal business agreement.

Later, *In Rainbows* was taken off the website, licensed to a publisher for sale in the USA, UK, and elsewhere, and released through the regular commercial distribution channels. Even though it had been available for download for over 60 days at low prices (even for free), the CD debuted at number one in both the USA and the UK, and sold over 1.7 million CDs through commercial channels in the subsequent 21 months—56 times more than Radiohead's earlier CDs. More than 100,000 collector box sets also were sold—a new revenue source for the band. Whatever revenue Radiohead might have lost through its initial download experiment was more than compensated for by the far greater publicity the band received. The changed value chain configuration for part of the sale process appears to have made the old business model also more productive in getting sales.

U2 and Apple are collaborating on a new, "interactive format for music", due to launch in 2016. It is supposed to have a new technological scheme which "can't be pirated" and will reimagine the role of album artwork. Media reports suggest that it is a new way to package and sell an album and may let artists bundle visuals, interviews, bonus content, and other items along with the music. Meanwhile, in September 2014, U2's album was distributed free with i-Tunes as a beginning of this process. It generated a large volume of traffic on the i-Tunes store, which had been facing declining traffic. The giveaway lasted until October 2014, after which buyers had and were willing to pay for the music (https://vulcanpost.com/20137).

From a Straight Value-Based, Straight Value Chain Model to a Two-Sided, Value-Based Model with a Completely Different Value Chain Configuration

Bharti Airtel is the largest Indian telecom operator with more than 200 million subscribers in India and more than 350 million subscribers across Asia and Africa. Airtel's Indian expansion was made possible thanks to its large distribution channel and its highly expanded infrastructure, what has become a comparative advantage. Changing a constraint into an asset is a quality the company had since the early days. Infrastructure is not developed in India and costs are high. For that reason, Airtel made the decision to focus on its core business—marketing and customer acquisition—and outsourced most of the other operations, all thought to be part of a telecom company. They thus outsourced the building and maintenance of their telecom network to Ericsson and Nokia, their IT operations to IBM, and the customer service to IBM Daksh, among others.

This strategy had two positive consequences. First, it allowed the contracting companies to work more efficiently because of their better knowledge and infrastructure support. Second, it allowed a significant decrease in costs, which in turn was reflected in their low pricing strategy. The company marketed its SIM cards and recharge coupons through post offices, something that had not been done before. It also distributed its products in retail outlets of gas stations and cooking gas distribution centers thanks to a partnership made with the state-owned Indian Oil. This was referred to as the "matchbox strategy", namely making Airtel recharge cards available wherever matchboxes can be bought.

Moreover, it executed different distribution strategies according to different geographical areas. In urban zones, it started a two-layer model in which a network of small, family-owned businesses supplied retailers directly, while in rural zones, the company created a three-layer distribution model of so-called "super distributors" who supplied rural distributors, the ones who, in turn, served retailers. It is also interesting to point out that in order to keep the costs as low as possible and increase the market entry, the company adopted a high-volume and low-commission incentive structure for its dealers' network, but it also requested from them an exhaustive list of prerequisites in order to be an eligible dealer (www.airtel.in/partnerworld).

Having implemented a large distribution channel, resulting in large sales volume, and outsourcing most of its activities to companies with better knowledge and higher economies of scale had put its pricing strategy in line with their desire to keep prices as low as possible in order to target low-income market. The interesting part from a BMI perspective is that Bharti Airtel changed the value chain configuration and created new players in the cellular phone network and its distribution system. It moved from a straight value-based, straight value chain model to a two-sided, value-based model with a completely different value chain configuration—something that is not easy to pull off.

5.5   Business Model Innovation, the Innovation Ecosystems, and Their Future

A business model concept is only a concept. It is fraught with unknowns and risks. Three types of risks have been identified: business execution (initiative) risks; co-innovation (interdependence) risks; and adoption (integration) risks (Adner 2006). While execution risk is about managerial capability and some environmental factors, interdependence with other players and factors and adoption by other players are key for a BMI to succeed. These constitute the innovation ecosystem or the overall context in which the business model is supposed to work.

Interdependencies exist when a set of activities taken together give an outcome that is different from that of the activities taken in isolation. Interdependencies are created by managers when they: (a) choose a set of organizational actions to satisfy a customer need; (b) design and implement linkages that weave together different activities into a system; and (c) use governance mechanisms to get the different activities within and across a firm to work together. When these activities, linkages, and governance mechanisms span organizational boundaries, then the business model is embedded in a larger ecosystem and successful innovation in the business model would require a good understanding of the larger innovation ecosystem as well.

Like many concepts that become more relevant at various points in time, innovation ecosystems are not new. BMIs take place in a context. More than 100 years ago, when the internal combustion engine started becoming the accepted mode of powering automobiles, for the automobile to take off and become a mass market product, it took the coming together of an entire innovation ecosystem consisting of: (a) roads, petrol/gas stations; (b) an increase in income levels that people could buy cars; (c) mass producers of cars like Ford that paid their workers many times the existing wage rates so that they could afford cars; and (d) the passing of regulation that allowed cars to be driven without having a speed limit of four miles an hour and a person walking in front with a flag warning people that a car was coming. Ford's BMI of mass-producing cars, vertically integrating manufacturing, and paying the workers well over the going rate succeeded because the innovation ecosystem consisting of roads, gas stations, lighting, an increase in income levels, and a change in regulation all came together at the same time. Indeed, Ford could be said to have helped in creating some elements of the ecosystem.

Companies, therefore, increasingly exploit the choice space that is available to consumers to leverage adaptive eco-complexes of relationships rather than go it alone. The business model, therefore, does not exist in isolation—it is part of an ecosystem of firms that work together to provide value. Firms plug into ecosystems and/or create new ecosystems as they invent new business models.

Recent work in the area of business ecosystems suggests that while business model templates and frameworks are adequate to analyze the challenges faced by existing organizations, they may not be ideal when examining the interdependencies of organizations that are emerging in the same innovation ecosystem (Sinfield et al. 2012). A particular example is the ecosystem of electric vehicles, where the value creation includes not only the automobile product market but also electricity services, ICT network service industries, and battery technology industries. Such business model eco systems require innovative collaborative partnerships, which include inter-industry partnerships. In developing countries which are short of space and road networks but have dense population centers with limited physical space in existing urban agglomerations, a key dimension of the success of electric vehicles that will come from the ecosystem is the management of the urban space to provide the required facilities at required distances in the time window for a particular firm to succeed.

Apple provides a good example. It is an instance of a company that is at the center of an innovation eco-complex as an experienced brand; it does not make any of its products, relies on others' content (which is increasingly modular: music, video, photos, and many other applications), and makes money from third-party apps and commission fees. As a platform, it does not manufacture the hardware; it simply designs the hardware and provides the operating system. The effect of the change in the Apple business model is clear. With the iTunes music store, Apple hit 6 billion downloads and a market share of 70 % of the worldwide digital music sales by 2010. The iPhone applications were even more successful with over 1 billion downloads in 2009. Apple is also achieving significant revenues in the new areas: iPod and music-related services contributed to almost 30 % of turnover; the iPhone and related services almost 20 % by 2010.

There is, however, a second dimension of the innovation ecosystem—and that is to do with the customer experience journey that a focal firm provides in collaboration with many other firms. L'Oréal's new mobile app, Makeup Genius, is available on tablets to help young women with a personalized makeup experience by recording the customer's face, and providing options for different makeups. The intention is to achieve particular types of looks, and then help the customer buy from retailers. Makeup Genius is an example of a firm engendering a fundamental change in the customer experience journey that is also changing the value configuration within the innovation ecosystem (Edelman and Singer 2015). The information contained in this part of the innovation ecosystem was earlier not available to any player—including the innovator, L'Oréal.

The Apple business rests both on its role at the center of an innovation ecosystem and on the design of customer experience in a context of constantly shifting choices as new players attempt to exploit the many opportunities that arise from the innovation eco-complex. The L'Oréal business model, in contrast, sits in an innovation ecosystem that does not include any other players of significance that directly impact the customer experience, though L'Oréal now has a greater influence on where it can direct its customers for the purchase because it has a direct connection with the customer experience journey and is able to capture that information in real time.

Firms at the center of such innovation ecosystems are often difficult to dislodge. One could argue that the closer the firm is to the customer experience of the end-customer as a part of its business model, the more difficult it is to dislodge. Furthermore, a key feature of the future is that as information becomes more appropriable by organizations, they will have the opportunity to create new changes in the value configuration. Such changes are likely to be one major source of BMI. This information may be about the customer experience or the flow of goods and services in the channel, or the movement of money associated with the payment for goods and services.

Innovation ecosystems are also often dependent on the ability of some players to shoulder more of the risk at any given point in time. Netafim, a drip irrigation firm, was not able to convince farmers to adopt its drip irrigation technology that enabled farmers to reduce water consumption by fine tuning application to the content, salinity, and fertilization of the soil and to increase productivity by 300–500 %. Adoption finally happened when farmers were offered a free integrated package that included system design and installation, all required hardware, and periodic maintenance, and the payment mechanism by the farmer was indexed to the extra produce that was generated by the use of the technology. This change limited the downside for the farmer. The innovator, Netafim, picked up the risk. For Amazon, in contrast, in its growing years, at a time when it was selling only books and was innovating a new business model, the inventory risk of carrying books was borne by the wholesalers and distributors who invested in stocking books, thus utilizing a member of the earlier ecosystem that it then proceeded to destroy.

Finally, BMI also requires changes within the organization. A process that is vital, therefore, for changing the business models of already existing organizations is that of leading change in the organization. This can be a puzzle. Who is responsible for BMI and alignment with innovation ecosystems? Functional heads will lack authority over the whole organization, but business models will require testing of aspects of and interactions between operations, engineering, marketing, sales, and finance, and BMI may well involve conflicts with some or all of these functions. Indeed, at the Intrapreneurship Conference in Paris in December 2012, the idea of a Chief Business Model Officer was mooted—as a complement to a Chief Technology Officer or a Chief Innovation Officer.[4] Related to all of this are the existing belief systems in the organization that also need to change for BMI.

The challenge with change within the organization at a business-model level becomes even more complicated when one looks at the typical budgeting process of an organization that is investing in new products, processes, markets, or businesses. There is the expectation of a certain rate of return that is required by the management before allocating funds. A CEO, Chief Financial Officer (CFO), or other relevant manager has to budget in a way that is constrained by existing processes and needs to provide predictability of returns. By contrast, a venture capitalist will expect that about 70 % of the investment decisions will fail, about 20 % will provide moderate success, and about 10 % will be the unicorns that help to provide returns to the investors, something that may not be possible within the confines of an established organization's structure and functioning.[5] Such a modus operandi is very hard to achieve in an established organization—which is perhaps why BMIs tend to come from leaner, newer organizations rather than established organizations. The challenge, then, for incumbent firms is to build the processes and systems that enable a Venture Capital (VC)-type of approach in the innovation ecosystem. One may suppose that as the entrepreneurship ecosystem becomes more mature in many countries such as the USA and now increasingly in India, with its set of VCs that operate on a different mode from a typical firm, it will lead to more BMI driven by the different time scale and financial modus operandi of returns.

CEOs of small companies may be ideally suited to the task, especially if they are also owners of the business. However, a real problem with relying upon the CEO to lead change is that they likely rose to their position via the current business model, which is now deeply familiar—even comforting—while potential alternative models will be unfamiliar and may even seem threatening. Thus, although in the best position to lead it, the CEO may actually act in ways that retard business model experimentation and innovation.

Another possible organizational source of BMI could be the general managers of specific businesses in larger firms. But while these managers may have the authority, they are typically rotated from one position to another every two to three years, which may be too little time to formulate the experiments, conduct them, collect the data, analyze the data, develop inferences and interpretations of that data, and then reframe the analysis in ways that are sufficiently persuasive to guide the transformation to a new business model (Burgelman 1983).

Three other major trends are likely to lead to major BMIs. The first is the advent of 3D printing. As the technology advances, factories that are meant to do mass scale manufacturing for consumers will disappear. Instead, we will have factories that enable consumers to become mini factories for the products that they need. The nature of the value chain configuration will change, as will the nature of information capture. The second is the digitization of products and payment systems across the world that will decrease the marginal costs of products—especially information-based products and services—and increase the velocity of money flow. Increase in the velocity of money flow will result in greater instability in financial markets that will mean greater financialization of business. Digitization of products means a decrease in the value of manufacture; it also means an increased value for information capture and use. The third is the roboticization of major chunks of work that are done by humans at home, in the factory, and in schools and universities.

In the end, BMI is, to an extent, circumscribed by managerial beliefs. Every industry is built around long-standing, often implicit beliefs about how to make money. In retail, for example, it is believed that purchasing power and format determine the bottom line. In telecommunications, customer retention and average revenue per user are seen as fundamental.

Success in pharmaceuticals is believed to depend on the time needed to obtain approval from the US Food and Drug Administration. Assets and regulations define returns in oil and gas. In the media industry, hits drive profitability. Brand loyalty is an article of faith in most fast moving consumer goods categories (De Jong and van Dijk 2015). Philips Lighting, for example, questioned the belief that lighting is a replacement business when it developed LED lighting technology. In India, provincial governments are buying LED lights in bulk and giving them to households for free because the reduction in the electricity consumption and the extra revenue from other customers makes up for the investment in buying the LED lights.

All in all, business model innovation will continue to be a hard task and a good understanding and leveraging of the innovation ecosystem within which a BMI takes place would be an important determinant of BMI success.

Notes

1. In the airline industry, one key metric of performance is how much it costs the airline to move one passenger one mile—also called the cost per seat mile.
2. Approximately 700 out of 1650 headcount of naukri.com in 2016 is employed in the salesforce; in addition, naukri uses very little advertising; the rationale is that the category is high involvement and with a dominant market share, "customers" are getting exposed to the brand all the time without the advertising.
3. Personal Notes of the first author based on an assignment with an ICT firm.
4. Personal notes of the first author, December 2012.
5. Deliberations at the IIMA London Alumni Association Event on November 24, "Confluence 2015: The Future of Innovation" Statement by Rajiv Mishra, Softbank.

References

Adner, R. 2006. Matching Your Innovation Strategy to Your Innovation Eco-system. *Harvard Business Review* 84(4): 98–107.

A.T. Kearney—CSCMP Study. 2014. *Supply Chain 2025—Trends & Implications for India*, April.

Burgelman, Robert. 1983. A Process Model of Internal Corporate Venturing in the Diversified Major Firm. *Administrative Science Quarterly* 28(2): 223–244.

Chatterjee, Sayan. 2013. Simple Rules for Designing Business Models. *California Management Review* 55(2): 97–124.

De Jong, Marc, and Menno van Djik. 2015. Disrupting Beliefs: A New Approach to Business Model Innovation. *McKinsey Quarterly*, July.

Edelman, David C., and Marc Singer. 2015. Competing on Customer Journeys. *Harvard Business Review*, November, 70–79.

European Commission DG Research and Innovation. 2014. The Need for Innovation in Business Models: Final Policy Brief.

Gleed, Richard. 2009. Business Model Innovation: Pathways to Success. *IBM Global Services Presentation*.

http://www.swissinfo.ch/eng/cows-for-hire---farmer-milks-global-interest/1015518. Accessed April 28, 2016.

http://business.mapsofindia.com/sectors/manufacturing/hindustan-unilever-ltd.html. Accessed November 9, 2015.

http://www.forbes.com/sites/danielrunde/2015/08/12/m-pesa-and-the-rise-of-the-global-mobile-money-market/#25df3efc23f5. Accessed November 9, 2015.

https://vulcanpost.com/20137/u2-releases-new-album-itunes-free-collaborates-awkwardly-apple/. Accessed October 10, 2015.

INDIA. *Airtel.in.* Accessed October 10, 2015. http://www.airtel.in/partnerworld/Partner_Process_Selection.htm

Indian Railways Lifeline of the Nation. 2015. *Ministry of Railways, Government of India*, February.

Jack, William, and Tavneet Suri. 2010. The Economics of M-PESA, August. http://www.mit.edu/~tavneet/M-PESA.pdf

Johnson, M.W., C.M. Christensen, and H. Kagermann. 2008. Reinventing Your Business Model. *Harvard Business Review* 86(12): 50–59.

Keen, Peter, and Ronald Williams. 2013. Value Architecture for Digital Business: Beyond Business Models. *MIS Quarterly* 37(2): 643–648.

Lambert, Susan. 2015. The Importance of Classification to Business Model Research. *Journal of Business Models* 3(1): 49–61.

Santos, J. 2009. Towards a Theory of Business Model Innovation in Incumbent Firms. *Working Paper*, INSEAD.

Sinfield, J.V., E. Calder, B. McConnell, and S. Colson. 2012. How to Identify New Business Models. *MIT Sloan Management Review* 53(2): 85–90.

Sosna, M., R.N. Trevinyo-Rodríguez, and S.R. Velamuri. 2010. Business Model Innovation through Trial-and-Error Learning—The Naturhouse Case. *Long Range Planning* 43: 383–407.

Stahel, W. 1994. *The Utilisation-Focused Service Economy: Resource Efficiency and Product-Life Extension*. Washington, DC: National Academy Press.

Teece, David. 2010. Business Model, Business Strategy, and Innovation. *Long Range Planning* 43(2–3): 172–194.

Zott, Christoph, and Raphael Amit. 2008. The Fit between Product Market Strategy and Business Model: Implications for Firm Performance. *Strategic Management Journal* 29(1): 1–26.

———. 2010. Designing Your Future Business Model: An Activity System Perspective. *Long Range Planning* 43(2–3): 216–226.

6

Business Model Revolution: Four Cases of the Fastest-Growing, Disruptive Companies of the Twenty-First Century

Robin Chu

6.1 Introduction & Background

George Bernhard Shaw once said, 'the reasonable man adapts himself to the world; the unreasonable one persists in trying to adapt the world to himself. Therefore all progress depends on the unreasonable man' (Shaw 1903). It illustrates how innovation at its core is divided into two main types, namely, incremental (improve the existing) and disruptive (obsoleting the existing).

As a strategy consultant focused on business and pricing model innovation, I have had the privilege to work for a wide variety of companies dealing with similarly versatile business challenges in competitive strategy. One common theme that perpetually and with increasing frequency returns is innovation; whether it is through changing the way of working, developing new products and services or designing new pricing models, innovation is key for the right to exist in the market. What is curious about innovation is that it in essence requires change, leading to the

R. Chu (✉)
Simon-Kucher & Partners, Amsterdam, The Netherlands

© The Author(s) 2017
A. Brem, E. Viardot (eds.), *Revolution of Innovation Management*,
DOI 10.1057/978-1-349-95123-9_6

following juxtaposition: everyone hates change, but everyone loves innovation.

With increased access to information, technology and flexible mobility of people and goods, the pace of innovation seems to be ever increasing with unexpected origins like start-up companies. Entire industries are under pressure due to the persistence of small groups of individuals with disruptive ideas to solve issues that have long been neglected or given up on by large firms. Most of the disruptors' successes are not only dependent on innovating on a product or revenue model; the key underlying reason for their success is the innovative combination of elements to create groundbreaking, new business models.

This chapter aims to conceptualize the mechanics of business model innovation and describes how companies use its elements in order to develop compelling value propositions with successful, disruptive market adoption. In Sect. 6.2, the business model framework is explained and its practical use illustrated with examples. Section three dives deep into four of some of the fastest-growing, disruptive companies of the twenty-first century followed by closing remarks in Sect. 6.4.

6.2   Business Model Framework

Before delving into the four cases of the fastest-growing, disruptive companies of the twenty-first century, this section aims to provide the fundamentals of business models and the business model framework.

The business model framework provides a conceptual overview of how a company creates and captures value. It consists out of three pillars: value creation, value proposition and value capture (see Fig. 6.1). Through this model, we are able to depict clearly how individual companies successfully combine the possibilities within and across the three value pillars.

How a company *creates value* is conditional to its people, assets and partners; it is determined by the extent a company chooses to 'make' (develop products and engage in activities in-house), 'buy' (procure products/services from suppliers) or 'ally' (outsource to and collaborate with strategic partners) (Geyskens et al. 2006).

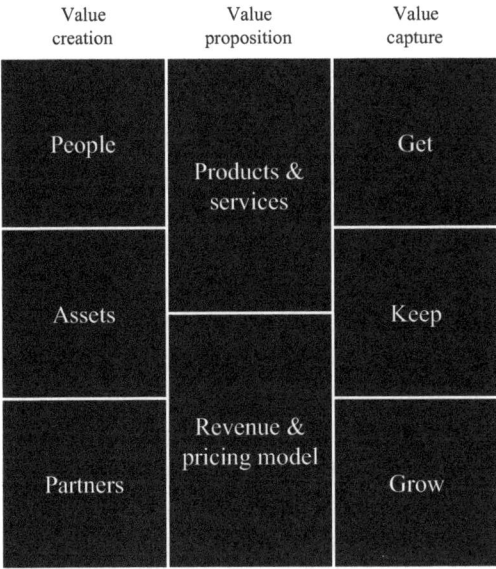

Fig. 6.1 Business model framework (Chu 2015a)

How a company distills its created value in a *value proposition* is derived from products and services the company decides to offer to the market. Benefits of value propositions that meet customer needs are simplified to whether a product or a service makes things 'easier', 'better', 'faster' and/or 'cheaper' (Shingo 1988). Besides product/service benefits, the choice of a distinctive revenue and pricing model—a largely overlooked component of value propositions—can deter or add value due to its ability to differentiate and amplify aforementioned benefits.

How a company *captures value* is determined by how a company 'gets' new customers, 'keeps' existing customers and 'grows' share of wallet. A company may find its core challenge in one or more of the three components depending on its position in the lifecycle and the nature of the industry.

In this section, the business model framework will be further explained and illustrated with examples from various industries.

Value Creation

In essence, there are three main components to develop products and services: people, assets and partners. These three elements constitute the business model framework's first pillar 'value creation' (Fig. 6.2). In essence: What resources does a company use to create its value proposition?

- *People*—employees related to primary activities (e.g. procurement, in- and outbound logistics, manufacturing, marketing and sales, customer service) and secondary activities (e.g. HR, management) (Porter 1985)
- *Assets*—tangible assets (e.g. buildings, machinery, stock) and intangible assets (e.g. brand, intellectual property, goodwill)
- *Partners*—partners can range from suppliers to strategic partners

A company's value proposition can be more or less reliant on each of the components in the value creation pillar of the business model

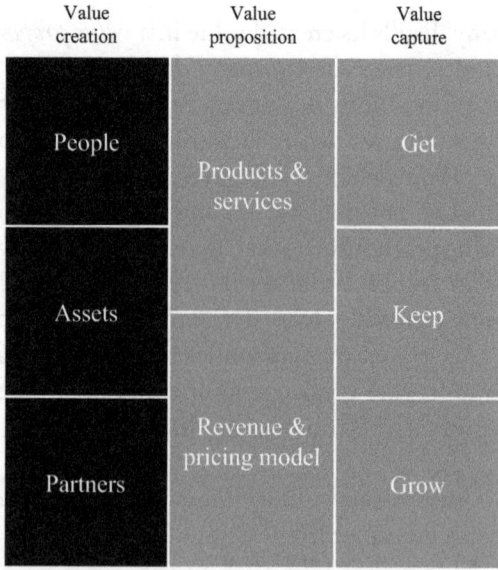

Fig. 6.2   Business model framework pillar 1: value creation (Chu 2015a)

framework. For instance, if we were to depict the reliance of companies on each of the value creation components, we could distinctively show to what extent a company does or does not exploit certain activities in order to create its value proposition.

To illustrate the components, let us take a closer look at the financials of V&D Holding and RFS Holland Holding in Table 6.1.

Both V&D Holding and RFS Holland Holding are mainly active in retail in the Netherlands with a similar size of business in terms of revenue. Due to these similarities in geographical focus, industry and size, we can compare these two companies to illustrate the different ways of developing value propositions through people, assets and partners.

Whereas both firms are active in retail, they conduct their business very differently, which can be traced back in the historic DNA of each firm. V&D Holding, with their 67 retail outlets, typically focused on physical retail (or, in modern business jargon, 'bricks and mortar') and has only recently introduced and focused on their online channel. RFS Holland Holding started out as a mail-order catalog for mattresses but quickly

Table 6.1 V&D Holdings versus RFS Holland Holdings (Dutch Chamber of Commerce 2014)

2014 (€M)	V&D Holding	RFS Holland Holding	Delta V&D versus RFS (%)
Year founded	1887	1952	
Industry	Retail	Retail	
Business model	Bricks & clicks	Pure online	
Revenue	618	498	24
Net income	−42	15	
No. of employees	6324	787	704
Total assets	263	712	
Total fixed assets	157	538	
Tangible fixed assets	130	50	160
Intangible fixed assets	27	128	
Other fixed assets	0.01	360	
Total current assets	105	174	
Stocks	75	41	83
Debtors	22	107	
Other current assets	8	26	

expanded to a wide assortment of products, which are purchasable via their websites (also known as an e-tailer or pure online player).

Concentrating on each of the company's value creation components, we see that V&D has more than seven times the number of employees compared to RFS, 160 percent more tangible fixed assets (e.g. buildings) and holds 85 percent more stock with merely 24 percent more sales. Without knowledge of their go-to-market and channel focus, these numbers may be surprising. However, considering retail outlets need more employees to service customers, more buildings and more stock to ensure that they minimize out-of-stock situations, this data paints a more colorful picture: physical retailers require higher costs to create their value proposition (and are less scalable) than online retailers. In Figs. 6.3, 6.4 and 6.5, the required number of employees, tangible fixed assets and inventories for every million euros revenue is shown for V&D and RFS to depict reliance on value creation components.

Value Proposition

The value proposition pillar of the business model framework consists of two main components: products and services, and the revenue and pricing model. Unlike traditional thinking, a value proposition is not only

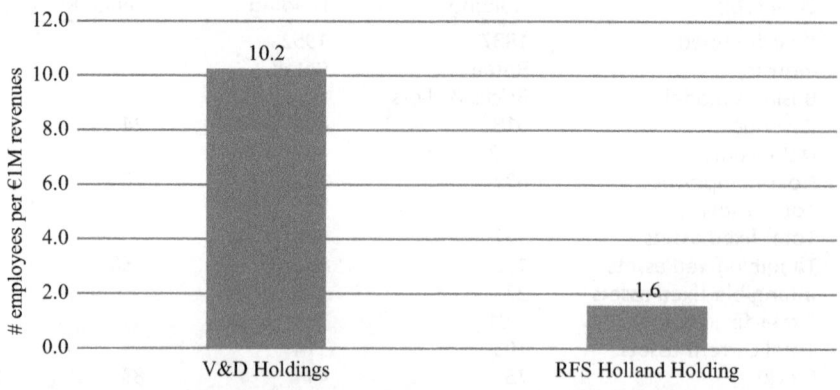

Fig. 6.3 Number of employees required to generate €1 m in revenue (Dutch Chamber of Commerce 2014)

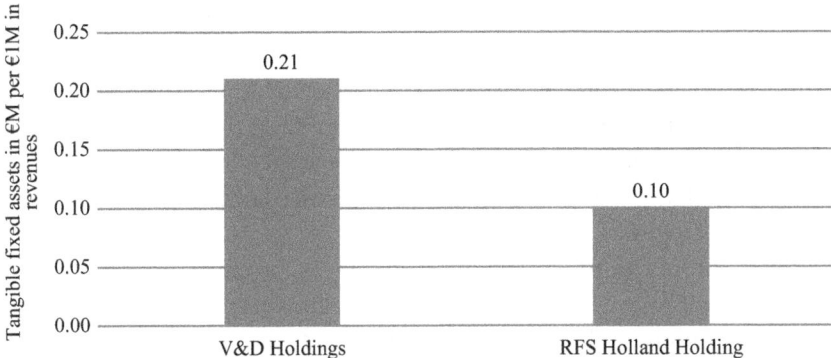

Fig. 6.4 Tangible fixed assets €M required to generate €1 m in revenue (Dutch Chamber of Commerce 2014)

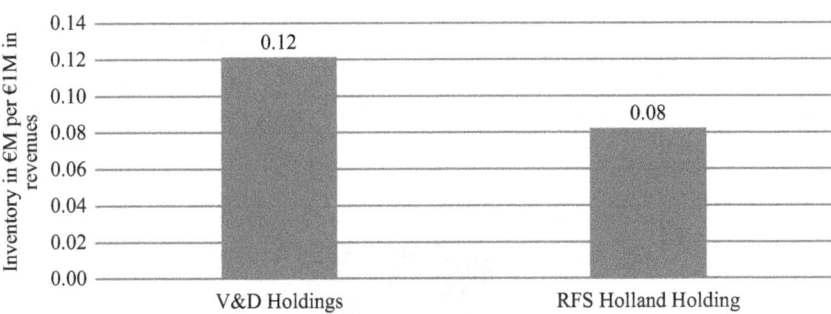

Fig. 6.5 Inventory €M required to generate €1 m in revenue (Dutch Chamber of Commerce 2014)

composed of the perceived value from products and services; the revenue and pricing model play an increasingly key role in how customers perceive value propositions. Each of the two components will be elaborated upon in this section.

Products & Services

Traditionally, many companies tried to achieve competitive advantage through creating 'better' (through R&D and feature/quality enhancement) or 'cheaper' (through cost reduction) products. However, in the age of centralizing the customer, digitalization and servitization, the shift from quality and cost has quickly readjusted to customer experience in the form of 'easier' and 'faster'. The four cases described later in this chapter are examples of how companies have grabbed the opportunities technology has given us to meet customer needs in terms of customer experience (Fig. 6.6).

Value propositions are often described as products or services; for example, a computer or repairing shoes. However, value propositions should be translated into benefits that products and services provide, such as, faster computing power or cheaper shoe repair.

One of the disadvantages of existing models and definitions of 'value propositions' is that the given contents of the value proposition can quickly get confusing, resulting in a complex palette of features and benefits.

To simplify value proposition and benefits, the business model framework lends thought leadership from lean theory (Shingo 1988). Shigeo Shingo once described that there are four purposes of improvement:

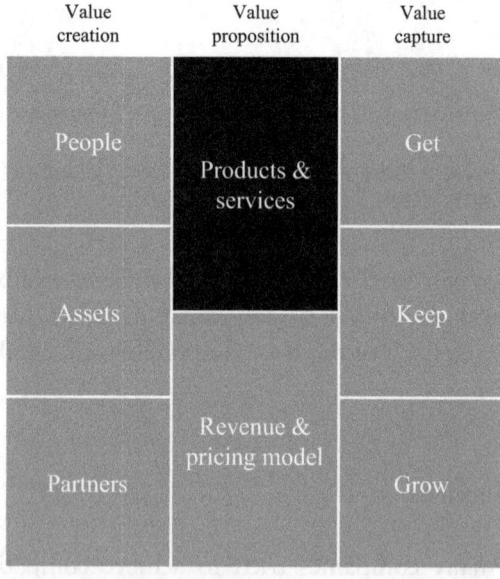

Fig. 6.6 Business model framework pillar 2: value proposition (Chu 2015a)

easier, better, faster and cheaper. Benefits of products and services to customers in the business model framework are condensed to its essence; whether the product/service makes things or is:

- *easier*—a product/service makes things easier (e.g. similar time required, but with less effort; convenience)
- *better*—a product/service is better (e.g. in terms of quality)
- *faster*—a product/service is faster (e.g. less time required)
- *cheaper*—a product/service is cheaper (e.g. lower price or total cost of ownership)

To illustrate, let us apply these value proposition benefits to a fictional example with a bricks and mortar retailer and a pure online retailer. For the fictional retailers, let us assume that they have similar size of business and product assortment.

- Is an online retailer easier?
  Depending on the situation of the customer, one could argue that an online retailer is easier for a customer than a traditional, physical retailer for a number of reasons. Generally speaking, the foremost reason is that a customer who buys via an online channel exerts less physical effort to browse for, find and buy a product (e.g. from the comfort of the customer's home, easier to find the right product, compare alternative products with ease). Winner: online retail.
- Does an online retailer provide better products in terms of quality?
  Concerning the quality of the products, online versus traditional retailers do not necessarily have to differ if they offer the same products. However, one or other retailer offering a wider range of assortment could be perceived as being better. Assuming both retailers are offering a similar range of products: draw.
- Is an online retailer faster?
  Most of us would instinctively say that an online retailer is faster. However, the end-to-end process from browsing, finding, buying and receiving (returning) a product for the online channel is longer than when a customer would physically go to the store. The end-to-end process for an online purchase can take up at least a day before the

customer has actually received the product due to delivery time. Conversely, a purchase at a bricks and mortar could take one to three hours depending on traveling time to the store. For the purposes of this example, let us assume that the bricks and mortar retailer has the product in stock and indeed delivery time for the online player takes at least one day. Winner: bricks and mortar.

- Is an online retailer cheaper?
  In many cases, due to the cost advantages an online retailer has, online retailers are able to offer lower prices than their physical competitors are. However, this is dependent on economies of scale: a physical retail chain could theoretically negotiate better prices with their suppliers provided the retailer is significantly larger than its online competitor is. Contrarily, it is easier for online retailers to grow faster due to the scalability of their business model. Besides the costs of products, online retailers have the burden of including or excluding shipping costs for the customers. Especially for 'smaller basket' purchases,[1] shipping costs can become a threshold for customers to buy. Assuming both retailers in this fictional case are of similar size, mostly attract customers that are looking to impulsively buy low-value products and that the online retailer charges customers for shipping costs⊠winner: bricks and mortar.

Table 6.2 shows the scorecard results for our fictional case. These results allow us to examine the improvement opportunities for online retailers, and bricks and mortar retailers.

Provided that the scoring is done with equal weighting for each benefit category, the bricks and mortar retailer would win in terms of comparative

Table 6.2 Scorecard benefits online versus bricks & mortar

Products & services benefits categories	Online retailer	Bricks & mortar retailer	Importance
Easier	√		?
Better	√	√	?
Faster		√	?
Cheaper		√	?
Total score	2/4	3/4	

benefits. However, for a consumer, the 'easier' category or convenience of online shopping may weigh much more in their decision to shop online or offline. In other words, if weighting is applied to the benefit categories and 'easier' is of much higher importance than the remaining three categories, the online retailer would win in terms of comparative benefits of the value propositions. Moreover, consumers' assessment of how important they perceive benefits can change over time, changing the game for the players.

For the 'easier' category, we see that bricks and mortar retailers have quickly tried to catch up with online retailers by expanding their business model to bricks and clicks (adding an online channel).

Secondly, in the 'better' category, both types of retailers are attempting to provide a wider range of assortment. Online retailers such as Amazon. com collaborate with partners (see the value creation pillar of the business model framework) in order to be able to provide a wider range of products. Conversely, bricks and mortar retailers try to get exclusive partnerships with brands or have partnered up through a shop-in-shop business model (department stores that rent out shop space to brands, in which brands are free to market their products to generate traffic for the entire store).

Thirdly, the 'faster' category is one that has seen a lot of development in the past years. Third-party logistics providers and online retailers alike have jumped into this space by developing extremely fast delivery methods ranging from same day delivery to within-two-hours delivery (e.g. Amazon Prime, Postmasters and Google Express). Besides delivery time, return orders are a particular challenge for online retailers; many consumers buy clothes in a certain [size] and then return and reorder if it does not fit. The premium apparel brand Ralph Lauren has recently introduced interactive mirrors in their flagship store in Manhattan for customers to digitally fit clothes (Nazario 2015). If a start-up would be able to get these mirrors in most of consumers' homes, the 'faster' category would see a major improvement in favor of online retail due to potentially fewer returns and reorders.

Finally, the 'cheaper' category, in which our fictional bricks and mortar retailer won, is one that online retailers have been and still are struggling with (Chao 2015). Shipping costs can range from $4 to $10 per package and, as stated earlier, can become a threshold especially for 'smaller basket' purchases. Amazon.com has been working on a drone delivery system dubbed Amazon Prime Air (Weinberg 2015), which, if successful, may reduce delivery costs dramatically.

Revenue and Pricing Model

Eight out of ten companies underestimate the impact of pricing on profit (Simon-Kucher & Partners 2014); revenue and pricing models are subsequently often overlooked in value propositions. With over 30 years of experience at Simon-Kucher & Partners, we have observed that setting optimal prices, choosing the right pricing model and using pricing tactics are key success factors in the business model framework and can create value in terms of the benefit categories outlined in the preceding section (Fig. 6.7).

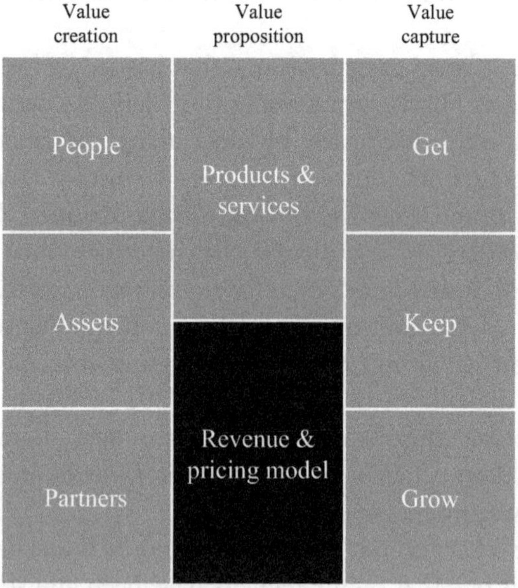

Fig. 6.7 Business model framework pillar 2: revenue and pricing model (Chu 2015a)

In essence, the profitability of every company is determined by a simple formula: 'volume × price − costs'. From our experience, we see that price has the highest impact on profit; with a 1 percent price improvement, we typically see an impact of over 10 percent on profit. Setting the optimal price is therefore crucial for value capture.

Besides setting the optimal price, choosing the right pricing model can add value to the value proposition; a suboptimal pricing model that does not match customers' needs can stifle market adoption. For example, when a tire manufacturer developed new truck tires with significantly lower wear and tear, it was unable to sell in great volumes due to its higher price and due to the economic crisis. However, when the same tire manufacturer moved to a variable pricing model (pay per kilometer), market adoption soared with even higher markups than projected compared to the former pricing model.

Finally, pricing differentiation tactics such as laddering or bundling (see 6.2.2.2.3 for an explanation and examples) can help to capture customer segments with varying levels of willingness to pay.

The three key pricing pitfalls are:

1. under- or overpricing your product or service
2. choosing a pricing model that does not match customers' needs
3. elementary pricing differentiation

Below, ways to circumvent the three pricing pitfalls are illustrated through best practice.

Pricing Pitfall 1: Under- or Overpricing Your Product or Service

Determining the price for a product can be done through three methods: cost-based, competition-oriented or value-based (see Fig. 6.8). Respectively, each of the methods requires a more sophisticated capability in gathering and processing external information.

Cost-based pricing—or cost-plus pricing—has been, and still is, widely used by many manufacturing companies and requires the capability to determine total costs of units sold, volume and investment forecasting

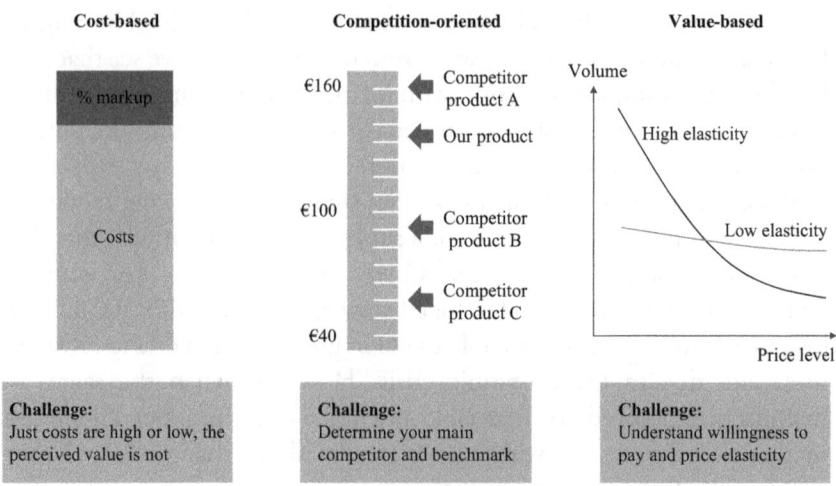

Fig. 6.8 Three types of pricing (Chu 2015e)

capabilities. Based on the costs of goods sold and preceding or forecasted investments (e.g. R&D, marketing, promotion), companies are able to determine total cost per unit sold. By identifying the total cost per unit sold, one can then determine a markup (e.g. 20 percent) to establish the selling price. Fundamentally, there is nothing wrong with cost-based pricing; a company ensures to cover its costs and investments and attains a profit per unit sold. However, a product's price based on cost-plus may not be the profit-optimal price. For example, tap water in the Netherlands typically costs €0.01 per liter. However, 'premium' bottled water (e.g. VOSS) is priced at €6.48 per liter (Unik Wijnhuis 2016). If a bottled water manufacturer priced their products based on costs alone, they would run the risk of underpricing if they had inadequate and insufficient external information.

From cost-based pricing, we move on to *competition-oriented pricing*, which requires competitive intelligence capabilities. If the previously mentioned bottled water manufacturer were to have more information on their competitors' pricing, it could more optimally determine its own products' prices; it could determine which competitor's product is most similar and decide on a lower or higher price compared to that specific competitor. Choosing the competition-oriented pricing method should be paired with the cost-based method, in which the latter is used as a checkpoint. In some cases, companies may conclude their competitive landscape permits them to price their products at, let us say, €1; however, this particular company's total cost per unit may exceed the selling price of €1, leading to a loss per unit sold. This should trigger management into rethinking whether to introduce this product or to delay until they are able to reduce costs or develop a product that permits a higher selling price.

Finally, *value-based pricing* is the pinnacle of determining the optimal price and requires capabilities in gathering specific customer and market intelligence. The main challenge to value-based pricing is to understand thoroughly willingness to pay. For instance, in the automotive industry, there are different types of coating finishes for cars. Besides the variety of colors, the options of metallic or non-metallic coating are a differentiating opportunity for car sellers. Typically, metallic coating costs about €20 based on raw materials. If a car manufacturer decided to use a cost-based pricing method with a seemingly high markup of 50 percent, it would sell metallic coating for €30 per car. However, metallic coatings provide distinct added value for customers with stronger resistance to scratches and a more appealing aesthetic look. From market research, willingness to pay for metallic paints amounted to €770 per car, or a whopping 3750 percent markup (Simon-Kucher & Partners 2014). To determine value-based prices, it is paramount to understand and quantify the benefits to the customer of your value proposition (easier, better, faster). See Table 6.3 for an overview of products with some of the highest markups.

Table 6.3 Ten most overpriced products (adapted by Chu from: Crowe 2010)

Product	Markup (%)
Text messages	6000
Bottled water	4000
Brand name drugs	3000
Movie theater popcorn	1275
Hotel mini bar	400
Coffee	300
Wine	300
Greeting cards	200
Hotel in-room movies	200
Pre-cut vegetables and fruits	40

Value-based pricing or pricing based on willingness to pay is not a new phenomenon, it is one that is more difficult to determine and requires specific organizational capabilities. However, with enhanced access to business customers and consumers alike, the use of value-based pricing is bound to become the dominant method of pricing across industries and the value chain.

Pricing Pitfall 2: Choosing a Pricing Model That Matches Customers' Needs

The choice of pricing model can stifle or accelerate a company's path to achieving success. Oftentimes, pricing models are mixed up with other elements of pricing such as value-based pricing (described in the previous section) and pricing differentiation (explained in the next section).

There are three main pricing model types: pay-to-own, pay-to-use and free-to-use (see Fig. 6.9). Each pricing model type has its own characteristics, advantages and disadvantages.

Pay-to-own is best described as the traditional pricing model in which a customer buys a product and ownership transfers from the producer or retailer to the customer. The advantage of pay-to-own is that the seller captures the monetary value of a product's benefits immediately,

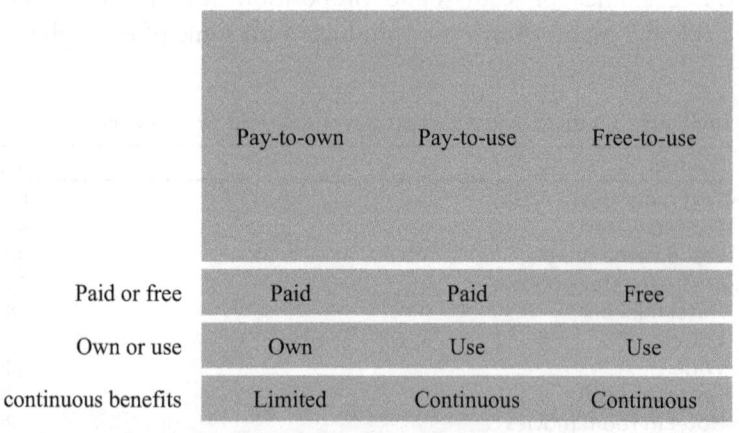

	Pay-to-own	Pay-to-use	Free-to-use
Paid or free	Paid	Paid	Free
Own or use	Own	Use	Use
Limited or continuous benefits	Limited	Continuous	Continuous

Fig. 6.9 Pricing model types (Chu 2015c)

regardless of how much or little a customer is going to utilize of those benefits. For customers, the advantage lies in that they 'own' the benefits of that product, meaning that they can make use of those benefits whenever they want until the product reaches the end of its lifecycle or utility (e.g. product breaks, newer/better versions are introduced). However, the key disadvantage is frequency of buying decisions. Every time a product owned by a customer reaches end of lifecycle, customers come close to their next buying decision and, depending on alternatives in the market, may well choose for a competitor product for their next purchase. Buying decisions are a risk for incumbent companies and an opportunity for competitors to win market share. Finally, the pay-to-own model will have a higher lump-sum price compared to a pay-to-use model, creating a higher threshold to gain customers.

The *pay-to-use* model is becoming increasingly predominant in the market. Often a pay-to-use model can be found in the form of subscriptions (e.g. newspaper, cable TV and telecommunication), lease or rentals (e.g. cars). It intrinsically reduces the number of buying decisions (reducing the risk of losing customers to competitors), lowers entry thresholds (lower payments are spread over a period of time) and subsequently creates customer lock-in. The key characteristic is that a customer pays for use and not for ownership, meaning that the customer pays for the benefits of a product for a certain time (e.g. rent a car for a day). Even though a pay-to-use model can be attractive and even accelerate market penetration, it requires specific organizational capabilities in forecasting, customer service and legal in order for it work effectively.

'If you're not paying, you're not the customer, you're the product' once was said to describe the *free-to-use* model. In some aspects, whoever coined this phrase was and is right. As of the third quarter of 2015, Facebook has surpassed 1.55 billion monthly users (Statista 2015f). To monetize on these users, Facebook shows ads and each ad view or click presents value to a wide array of advertisers; attention is valuable.

Having dived into the three main pricing model types, let us take a closer look at how they are used in practice by looking at the home entertainment media industry (e.g. movies and TV shows on DVD or digital). Figure 6.10 shows US spending on home entertainment media from the 4th quarter of 2014 to the 3rd quarter of 2015. Sales of packaged

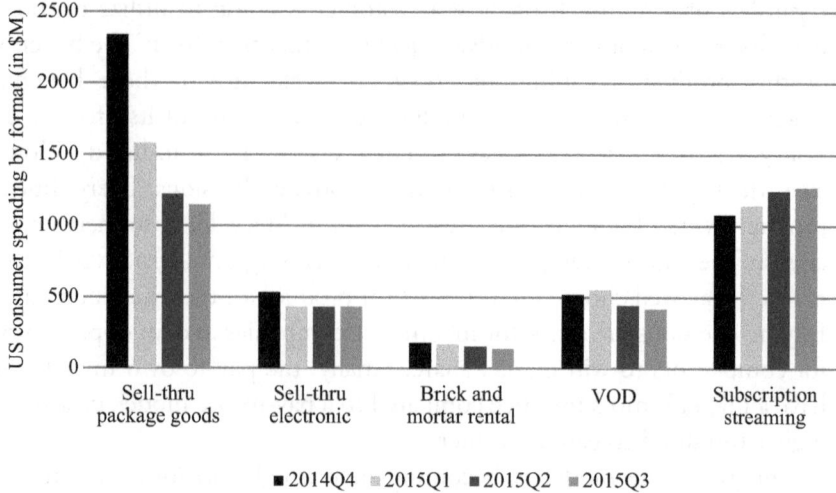

Fig. 6.10 US consumer home entertainment media spending (adapted by Chu from: The Digital Entertainment Group 2015)

and electronic goods (DVDs and digital downloads) show steep drops whereas subscription streaming is growing steadily. Rental sales, whether physical or digital, have seen their peak decades ago and have quickly lost ground to streaming entertainment players such as Netflix.[2]

Pay-to-use is clearly on a path to win in the home entertainment media industry, which leaves us with food for thought whether, or rather when, the first free-to-use player will arise.

Pricing Pitfall 3: Elementary Pricing Differentiation

Elementary pricing differentiation is the third pricing pitfall and is best characterized by companies that do not put time and effort into developing their pricing strategy. For a conceptual depiction of limited pricing differentiation, see Fig. 6.11. One-size-fits-all price (e.g. one product variation, one price) will almost always mean that some customers are excluded due to the fact that the price exceeds their willingness to pay. On the other end of the spectrum, customers with willingness to pay that exceeds the set price are suboptimally monetized. By introducing different

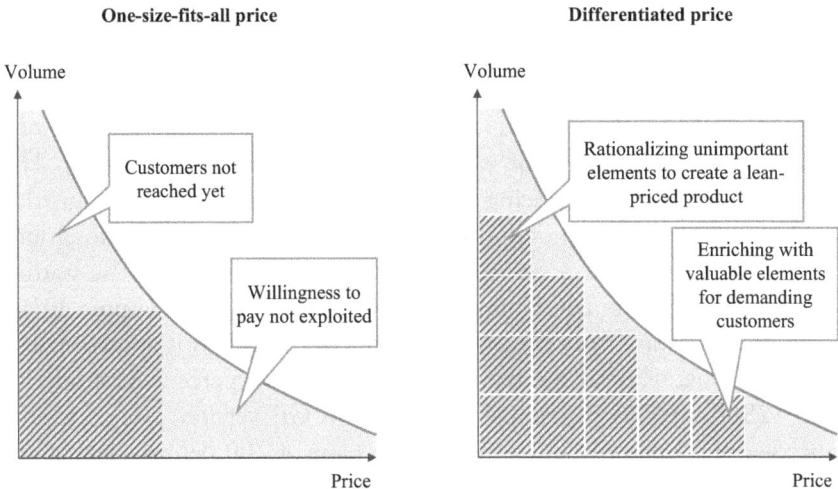

Fig. 6.11 Price laddering and bundling (Chu 2015b)

versions of a product (e.g. more features) or creating different bundles of products (e.g. more volume, additional products or services), a company can better capture value across levels of willingness to pay from different customers.

The idea of having different versions of the same product can be traced back to a movie theater in Chicago in 1967 (Orr 2012). An area manager by the name of David Wallerstein, who would later introduce menu bundling at McDonald's, was trying to determine how he could make more revenue from the concessions stands. What were the options he had? He could have chosen to introduce new products in the assortment, or perhaps even build a new, novel concession stand. However, what this manager chose in the end was a much simpler, more elegant solution.

He decided to experiment with popcorn and introduce a second, larger bag of popcorn. The bag would contain 50 percent more popcorn than the original smaller one, while the price would 'only' be 20 percent higher than the former. The reasoning behind it was that the cost of popcorn was negligible, but customers would be willing to pay extra since they would perceive to be getting more value for money. When the manager later decided to add an even larger bag to the popcorn stand, he was surprised to find out there were still people who chose the extra-large bag of popcorn.

It goes without saying that revenues increased strongly due to the laddering pricing tactic used. It shows that with different versions of a product, different levels of willingness to pay can be captured. This particular technique in pricing is now widely used in variety of industries.

To illustrate with a more present-day example, let us take a closer look at the buildup of prices for Apple's iPhone 6+. We see that the starting price is €799 for the 16GB and €899 for the 64GB version (Apple 2015). The price increase from the 16GB to the 64GB version is approximately 12.5 percent, whereas the memory increase is 300 percent. Considering the 128GB (€999) in comparison to the 16GB version, we get a price increase of 25 percent and a memory increase of 700 percent. By removing the 32GB version of the phone (which Apple used to offer in the past), Apple has made the 64GB even more attractive. Since the additional profits outweigh the costs of additional memory, Apple can generate significant profits by motivating consumers to buy the 64GB instead of the 16GB version.

By using laddering as a pricing technique, Apple taps into the rational side of people's minds. In the iPhone 6+ example, customers perceive better value for money as they go up the ladder. The use of pricing tactics may not always be perceived as fair pricing. Nevertheless, it is safe to say that many consumers will end up buying advanced versions of the product with higher prices, leading to large revenue and profit gains for Apple.

Value Capture

Now that we have looked into the elements of value creation and value proposition, we come to our next challenge: value capture. Without the right commercial, loyalty and growth strategy, companies can have the most valuable products that would suboptimally sell.

Instead of using terms that are often used in theory (marketing, promotion, commercial strategy), the business model framework gets down to brass tacks with three components: how do we 'get' our

Value creation | Value proposition | Value capture

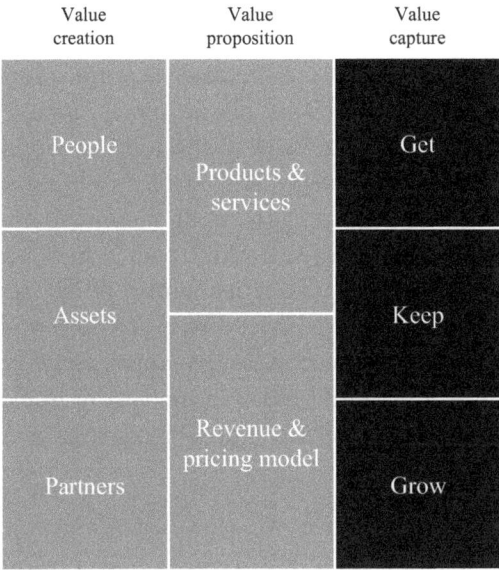

Fig. 6.12 Business model framework pillar 3: value capture (Chu 2015a)

customers, how do we 'keep' our customers and finally, how do we 'grow' our customers (Fig. 6.12).

Various companies and industries experience challenges differently across the three components in value capture. For example, getting new customers may be the prime focus for many start-ups, whereas keeping customers is a key challenge for companies with highly commoditized products (e.g. utility, telecom and base chemicals firms). Growing customers through cross-sell and upsell is a challenge experienced by companies that lack a wide portfolio of products, value-adding services or capabilities to effectively cross-sell and upsell.

Getting New Customers

The traditional method to get new customers requires strong organizational 'hunting' capabilities: lead generation (e.g. cold calling, mass e-mails, attending events such as trade shows, and advertising). Usually, these 'hunting' capabilities come in the form of sales people who generate and nurture leads to conversion.

In the 1950s, Tupperware, the producer of various home and kitchen products but best known for its plastic food containers, devised an interesting strategy to generate sales in the form of Tupperware parties. Brand enthusiasts were encouraged and enabled to become freelance sales representatives for Tupperware with strong commission-based remuneration. In 2013, Tupperware reportedly had a freelance salesforce of approximately three million (The Economist 2013) across the world enabling Tupperware's reach to extend to every nook and cranny in the global market. Traces of the enthusiast-based principles of Tupperware's sales strategy can still be found today in modern technology companies: Google, to date, still uses an invitation-based strategy to launch new products.

Keeping Current Customers

Depending on the industry a company is active in, acquiring new customers is anywhere between 5 and 25 times more expensive than keeping current customers (Gallo 2014). It is therefore unsurprising that many companies focus on customer experience and keeping the customer happy through enhancing their capabilities in customer service. As mentioned before, especially highly commoditized industries experience a severe challenge in keeping their current customers (or, in jargon, reducing churn). Identifying the reasons why customers are leaving the company, can be done through extensive customer surveys, or even through something as simple as adding a question in the call scripts of customer service representatives. However, for highly commoditized industries the key reason for leaving is almost invariably that the competitor has lower prices.

Regardless of level of commoditization, companies can choose more indirect loyalty strategies. Gamification (the application of typical elements of game playing such as point scoring) is a widely used method to create customer lock-in. Many supermarkets (collecting points to get discount on specific products), commercial airliners (Air Miles) and telecom providers (collecting points to use in an online shop) have developed loyalty programs, of which some have a long history. The possibilities to structure such loyalty programs are endless and provide solid grounds for the next revolution.

Growing Existing Customers

Growing one's existing customer base through cross-sell or upsell is the third challenge in value capture and is closely related to how loyal your customers will be. Philips, manufacturer of an interactive home lighting system called Hue, recently introduced a better version of their product. With the introduction of this new product that essentially replaces the old version, Philips actively approached existing customers with a promotion to upgrade (Philips Hue 2015). Another example is Sonos, an American consumer electronics company in home sound systems. Sonos has created a product range (Sonos 2015) that is wide in variety and can be linked with one another to easily create a complete sound ecosystem for consumers' homes. However, technologically speaking, Sonos' products can only be linked to one another; in other words, it is a closed system. Therefore, with every additional product purchased from Sonos, lock-in is increased and the threshold is heightened for customers to switch to a competitor.

The value capture pillar completes the business model framework. With this conceptual framework at hand, the next sections will highlight four of the fastest-growing, disruptive companies of the twenty-first century.

6.3   Four Cases of the Fastest-Growing, Disruptive Companies

Business model innovation, in its most disruptive form, changes the way people live their lives. This section describes the cases of some of the fastest-growing, disruptive companies today.

To illustrate the impact of the four cases to be detailed in this section, some food for thought:

- The world's largest taxi company owns no vehicles
- The fastest-growing music provider was helped by the founder of the most successful (illegal) music-sharing platform
- The most valuable retailer has no inventory
- The world's largest accommodation provider owns no real estate

Respectively, the four cases are Uber, Spotify, Alibaba and Airbnb, each changing different aspects of the way we live our lives.

For each case, a brief growth history is described, followed by highlights of the business model framework (value creation, value proposition and/or value capture) and finalized with what these companies' may hold for us in the future.

Uber

Uber's Growth History

In 2009, Travis Kalanick and Garrett Camp founded Uber, the app that has revolutionized the taxi and personal mobility industry. Uber is currently active in 68 countries and is planning further global expansion (Uber 2015c). Uber's value proposition has hit the traditional taxi industry at its core. On Christmas Eve in 2015, Uber passed the milestone of one billion rides (Kokalitcheva 2015). In December 2015, Uber was valued at $62.5 billion (Austin et al. 2015). Compared to its valuation in August 2013 of $3.8 billion, it is a staggering valuation growth of over 1545 percent in little under 30 months (Austin et al. 2015) (see Fig. 6.13). Comparing Uber's soar in valuation to Nasdaq, Microsoft and Facebook for the same period makes its rise even more apparent (see Fig. 6.14).

The phrase mentioned in the introduction went viral in 2015 ('The world's largest taxi company [Uber], owns no vehicles') and illustrates the impact Uber has on the taxi industry. However, it is inaccurate. Uber's business model resembles two-sided, marketplace business models (such as eBay) rather than taxi companies; its value proposition is highly dependent on their IT capabilities and their revenue model. The reason

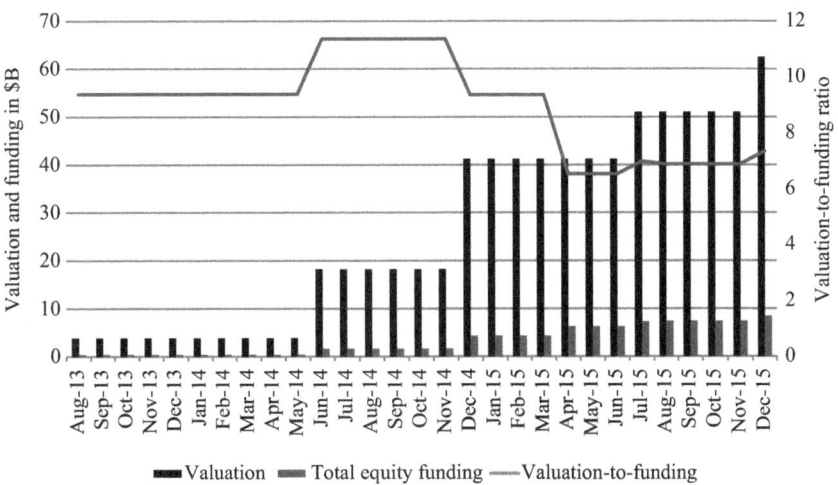

Fig. 6.13 Uber valuation and equity funding (adapted by Chu from: Austin et al. 2015)

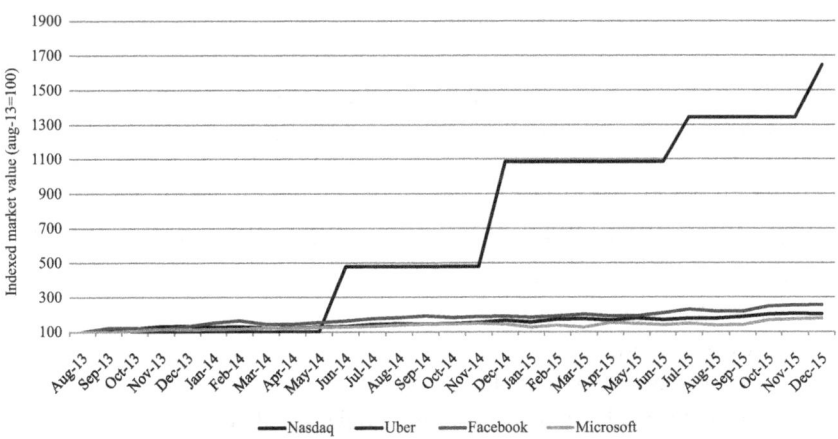

Fig. 6.14 Uber valuation mutation versus Nasdaq, Microsoft and Facebook (data from Yahoo Finance 2015)

why Uber is revolutionizing the market is that it has been able to link online business model benefits (e.g. ease of use, convenience, speed) with the offline experience of taxi services.

Value Proposition

Regarding the value proposition, Uber provides added value to both taxi drivers and consumers alike.

Some of the benefits of the value proposition toward customers are:

- *Easier*: App that allows consumers to hail a cab/car with ease; app linked with credit card to allow automatic payment
- *Better*: Immediate, two-way reviews (user and driver), creating a self-sustaining quality control system
- *Faster*: End-to-end process of ordering a ride is faster; waiting time is reduced due to that users know where the driver is and how long it will take for the driver to arrive
- *Cheaper*: UberPOP allows individuals (non-professionals) to work as a driver with lower fees for consumers

On the other end of the business model, the benefits of the value proposition toward drivers are:

- *Easier*: No more need for searching for customers' location, the app provides the location of the customer and provides directions; finding a ride does not require receiving calls or looking out the window to spot potential customers; the app notifies you of new customer ride requests
- *Better*: Taxi drivers get to rate customers as well as being rated, leading to more pleasant interactions with customers
- *Faster*: Waiting times significantly reduced, since anywhere in a given location, customers can now easily request a ride (as opposed to waiting in a line of other taxis at the airport)
- *Cheaper*: Uber claims it is more beneficial for drivers to work via their app (20 percent commission is incurred by Uber; the remainder is for the driver)

Pricing Model

Besides the benefits of its value proposition to drivers and customers alike, Uber's pricing model deserves some attention. Besides the 20 percent commission fee, Uber uses surge pricing to manage demand (Uber 2015a). Surge pricing occurs when there is high demand and low supply, leading to higher prices, sometimes shockingly so (RT 2016). Obviously, drivers welcome a much higher rate; however, due to Uber's data analytics capability, it can forecast high demand, communicate to drivers (who are incentivized through the high potential number of rides and possibility of surge pricing) and subsequently manage demand.

Get-Keep-Grow

Early adopters were a key growth lever for Uber when it launched its app in San Francisco (GrowthHackers 2015). The tech-savvy San Franciscans are continuously looking for technology to improve their lives and word-of-mouth travels fast among the internet-connected. Uber took to sponsorships in order for word-of-mouth to start snowballing. For example, Uber gave away free rides for people attending various (tech) events.

Concurrently, Uber used, and still uses, an invitation-based growth model in which users are incentivized to invite friends to start using Uber; both the inviter and the invitee are rewarded with money in their Uber accounts to be used for their next ride.

Future of Uber

In my opinion, the real revolution lies not in Uber's current proposition, nor in the controversial UberPOP. Recently, Uber announced it is looking into two new ridesharing services named UberHOP and UberCOMMUTE (Tarantola 2015). Whereas Uber's current proposition is mostly a platform to match up consumers and drivers, UberHOP and UberCOMMUTE aim to tap into the sharing economy where multiple consumers are matched up to share a ride. If these new propositions work as well and easily as Uber's current proposition, drivers will see a steep drop in total trips and, consequently, revenues.

Besides adjacent propositions, what lies ahead of Uber is not only further global expansion; Uber has launched two other propositions under the names of UberCARGO (Uber 2015b) and Operator (Operator

2015). With a similar business model, UberCARGO aims to bring transporters and customers together. Operator, in its turn, aims to digitize 90 percent of commerce that is not digital; it works as a crowd-sourced hotel concierge with its services just a text message away. Uber's disruptive path in creating efficiency in any market that is transportation-related promises a lot more than what we have already seen in the past couple of years.

Spotify

Spotify's Growth History

From 1973 until 1981, music on vinyl dominated the market in terms of revenues (see Fig. 6.15). From the 1980s on, the cassette soon took over as the key choice of format for music but was soon overtaken by compact discs in 1990. With these three media carriers, the music industry boomed with a peak in 1999. Everything changed quickly after that year.

In 1999, Sean Parker founded Napster (Lamont 2013), a peer-to-peer sharing internet service aimed to connect users all over the world. Napster users were able to share digital files with one another. With Napster's success, numerous others arose in the arena, which soon would become

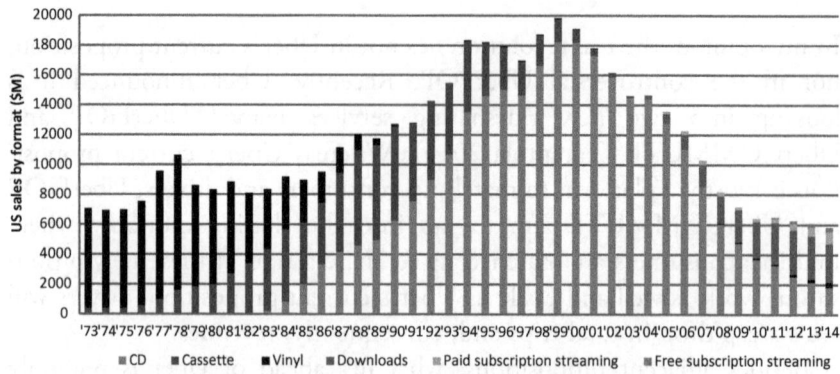

Fig. 6.15 United States music revenues by format (adapted by Chu from: IFPI 2011)

and still is the David to the music's industry's Goliath. Peer-to-peer sharing set in a new age with immense challenges for copyright holders; the challenge of illegal downloads of music, movies and TV shows yet has to be to overcome.

Naturally, Napster's services were attractive to consumers worldwide due to that it was free (but, again, illegal). However, an underemphasized benefit of using Napster was that users could download only the songs that they really wanted instead of having to buy the entire album.

With Napster and its competitors steadily but surely chipping away at CD album sales, Apple jumped in on an opportunity to revolutionize the way we listen to music on the go and introduced iPod and iTunes in 2003 (Apple 2003). From 2003 until 2014, digital downloads have quickly become the dominant revenue generator for the music industry. The music industry as a total still is in a strong downward trend, which raises the question as to why this is happening. One of the reasons is related to the underemphasized benefit of Napster, which, with the introduction of iTunes, becomes much more apparent. In Fig. 6.16, global music volume by format is shown. After 2003, the year iTunes was launched, we see a strong positive change in sales of singles and a perpetuated negative change in full album sales (volume for LPs, MCs, CDs, music video, other and digital albums are full albums). From 2004 to 2014, full albums' volumes show an average year-on-year decline of 10 percent,

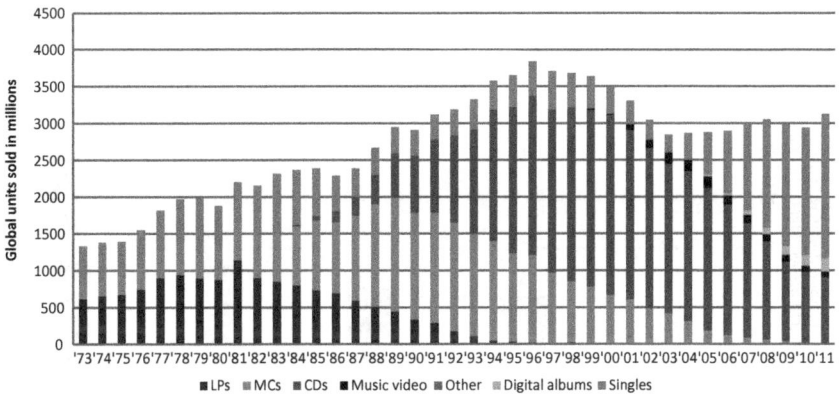

Fig. 6.16 Global volume by format (adapted by Chu from: IFPI 2011)

whereas singles' volumes sold showed year-on-year increases of 28 percent (see Fig. 6.16). With consumers' preference to purchase singles over albums and the rise of digital music stores, singles quickly started to cannibalize full album sales.

Despite the fact that digital downloads have become the dominant format since 2012, we are at the beginning if not amid the next revolution; digital music streaming. In 2006, Daniel Ek and Martin Lorentzon founded Spotify (Sawers 2012), the current market leader in digital music streaming (coincidentally, Napster's founder, Sean Parker, helped Spotify to its success today). The service provides unlimited streaming of music and the ability to easily create playlists, share playlists among friends and discover new music based on your music history (Spotify 2015). Not only is Spotify available for a fixed, monthly subscription fee, it also offers a free, advertised option. Spotify has increased its paying user base from 2011 to 2015 by 700 percent (see Fig. 6.17).

Value Proposition

Diving into the benefits of Spotify to the customer, we can again ask ourselves whether its value proposition is easier, better, faster and/or cheaper.

- *Easier*: Immediate access to large library of music from multiple devices.

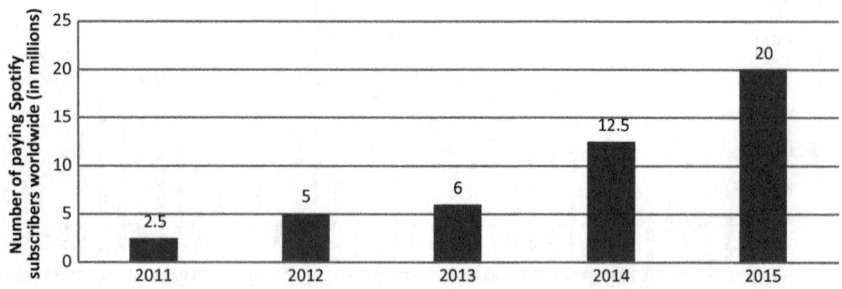

Fig. 6.17 Number of paying Spotify subscribers worldwide (adapted by Chu from: Statista 2015b)

- *Better:* Music quality–wise, there would be little difference between Spotify and digital sales. The quality also heavily depends on the internet connection one has. Concerning the breadth of assortment, Spotify has had and still has incidents with maintaining partnerships with some of the most popular musicians due to royalty fees' disagreements. Despite these challenges, Spotify has a significantly broad portfolio with over 30 million songs available.
- *Faster:* From search to purchase to actual listening to music, Spotify definitely beats its physical competitor. Compared to digital downloads, Spotify is slightly faster (no need to go through a purchase and payment process for each song).
- *Cheaper:* Depending on each consumer's individual music consumption behavior (e.g. digital sales, physical format sales), Spotify can be a cheaper alternative. To illustrate, a single sold through iTunes costs roughly between 69 cents (USD) and 1.29 cents. Spotify's monthly subscription fee would set a consumer back $10. Thus, anyone who used to roughly buy 8–13 digital singles a month would be better off with Spotify's service.

Pricing Model

Besides its paid subscription, Spotify offers a free subscription as well. With almost 55 million additional free users, the music industry is a clear example of business model revolution from buy-to-own (cassettes, CDs, LPs) to pay-to-use (paid streaming subscriptions) to free-to-use (free streaming, YouTube). Free-to-use subscriptions offer free content, but with intermittent advertising (similar to YouTube's revenue model).

Get-Keep-Grow

Not only is Spotify the frontrunner in digital music streaming, it is also leading in partnering as a strategy to get, keep and grow customers. Spotify's long list of partners include Facebook, Uber and, most recently, Starbucks (Prins 2015). The partnership with Starbucks could lead to some interesting loyalty programs in the form of Starbucks reward points for premium Spotify subscribers. In 2011, Spotify in the Netherlands engaged in an exclusive partnership with telecom provider KPN, which included a Spotify premium subscription in their mobile bundles (KPN 2011). For the telecom provider, the inclusion of a streaming service in their subscription bundles worked as a differentiator in their commoditizing industry. Conversely, the partnership ensured yet another growth lever for Spotify's fee business.

Besides partnerships to ensure growth and loyalty of Spotify's customers, Spotify's choice of revenue model plays a part in creating lock-in, the less attractive cousin of loyalty. With every minute of effort invested by users in creating and curating their playlists, the sunk costs in terms of time becomes increasingly higher over time leading to higher barriers to switch to competitors.

Future of Spotify

Spotify is on a tremendous growth trajectory and clearly, with its 20 million current paying users, it still has ample opportunity to scale up on a global level. With large companies such as Apple and Google entering the digital music streaming market, it will be interesting to see in what ways Spotify is going to maintain its first mover advantage.

Netflix, with a similar business model to Spotify but with content in the form of TV shows and movies, has made the transformation from a two-sided business model to becoming a successful producer of original content as well (e.g. critically acclaimed TV shows House of Cards and Orange is the New Black) (Kafka 2015). Perhaps, while we are amid the digital streaming revolution, the next one is already in the making.

Alibaba

Alibaba's Growth History

Alibaba Group was founded in 1999 by Jack Ma, a former English teacher from Hangzhou (China), and started out as an online marketplace enabling small enterprises to compete on a national and global scale (Alibaba

Group 2015a). Through Alibaba.com, companies seeking products are enabled to connect with manufacturers all over the world to source from. However, Alibaba Group today has grown from a Business-to-Business marketplace to a Business-to-Consumer retailing enabler to even Consumer-to-Consumer e-commerce. Besides their dominance in e-commerce, it is very active in acquisitions and developing business models in anything internet-related.

In Fig. 6.18, we see the growth in shoppers through Alibaba Group companies from 2012 to 2015. With a year-on-year growth of 34 percent, Alibaba has been able to grow its user base by more than two times over the course of three years. Moreover, in terms of market penetration, Alibaba is used by 98 percent of active online Chinese shoppers in 2015. Not only is Alibaba able to reach virtually all Chinese online shoppers, it also has grown average revenue per user (ARPU) by 16 percent year-on-year from 2012 until 2014 (see Table 6.4). With the increasing

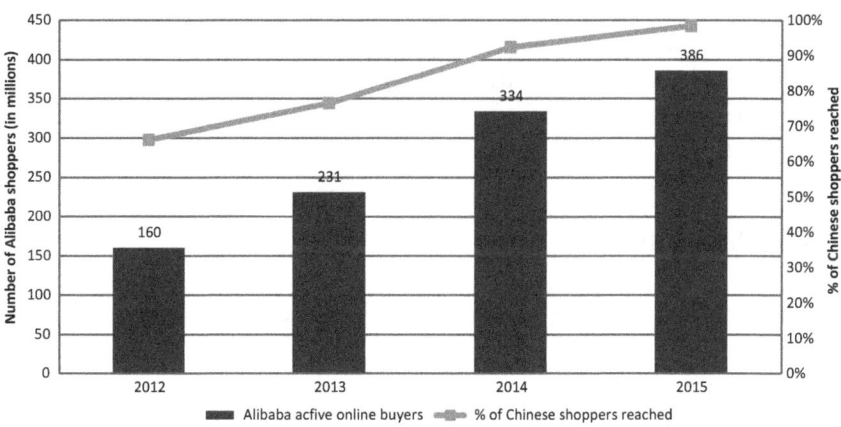

Fig. 6.18 Alibaba Chinese shoppers and percentage of total market (adapted by Chu from: Statista 2015d and Statista 2015e)

Table 6.4 Alibaba revenues, users and average revenue per user (adapted by Chu from: Statista 2015c and Statista 2015d)

	2012	2013	2014	2015	4Y CAGR (%)
Revenue (in ¥M)	20.025	34.517	52.504	76.204	56
Users (in millions)	160	231	334	386	34
ARPU (in ¥)	125	149	157	197	16

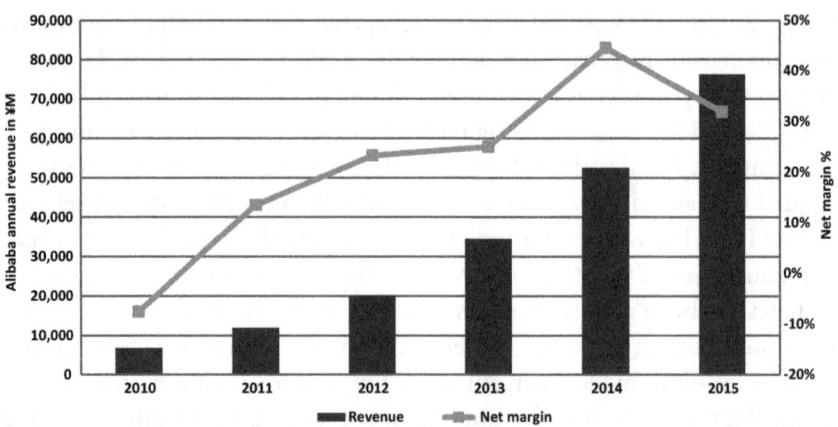

Fig. 6.19 Alibaba annual revenues and net margin (adapted by Chu from: Alibaba Group 2015b)

average revenues from users, Alibaba sales increased by 63 percent year-on-year between 2010 and 2015 (a staggering 1042 percent total increase) and increased net margins from −8 percent in 2010 to 32 percent in 2014 (see Fig. 6.19).

Value Proposition

Defining what the driving benefits are to Alibaba's value proposition is more complicated compared to the previous cases; there are too many value propositions to dive into. Figure 6.20 shows Alibaba's annual revenues by segment. At first sight, China commerce as a segment clearly is the dominant revenue stream for Alibaba with a more than healthy looking growth trajectory. However, a closer look at the growth rates for the remaining three segments shows a different dynamic (see Table 6.5); The 'Other' segment shows a year-on-year growth rate of 96 percent for the past six years.

In six years, annual revenues in the 'Others' segment nearly doubled, but not all organically. A closer view of Alibaba's acquisition activities in 2014 alone shows investments in 14 different companies each active in different end markets in terms of purpose of use and with very different value propositions (see Fig. 6.21). The only thing in common though is

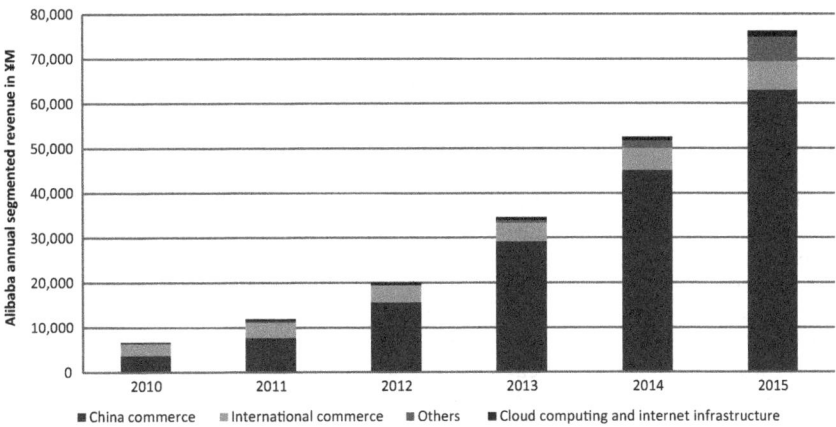

Fig. 6.20   Alibaba segmented annual revenues (adapted by Chu from: Statista 2015c)

Table 6.5   Alibaba revenues CAGR by segment (adapted by Chu from: Statista 2015c)

	China commerce	International commerce	Others	Cloud computing & internet infrastructure
6Y CAGR	76 %	20 %	96 %	55 %

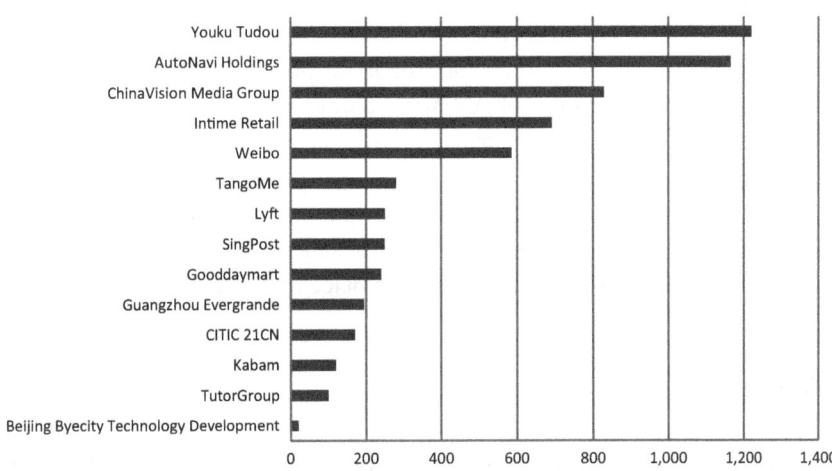

Fig. 6.21   Alibaba group stake value of companies acquired in 2014 (adapted by Chu from: The Economist 2015)

Table 6.6 Some of Alibaba's companies and their western equivalents (adapted by Chu from: Kuo et al. 2014)

Alibaba companies	Products/services	Western equivalent
Alipay	Online payments	PayPal
Aliyun	Cloud services	Amazon web services
Aliyun App Store	Mobile apps	Google play
Aliyun OS	Mobile OS	Android
AutoNavi	Maps and navigation	Google maps
InTime	Retail outlets	JCPenney
Juhuasuan	Group buying	Groupon
Kanbox	Cloud storage	Dropbox
Laiwang	Mobile messaging	WhatsApp
Lyft, Kuaide	Car service, ride sharing	Uber
Taobao	C2C e-commerce	eBay
Taobao Travel	Online travel booking	Orbitz
Tmall	B2C e-commerce	amazon.com
TutorGroup	E-learning	Kaplan
Weibo	Microblogging	Twitter
Xiami	Music streaming	Spotify
Youku Tudou	Streaming video	Netflix
Yu'e Bao	Money-market funds	ING Direct

the internet. Alibaba's vision is that their customers meet, work and live at Alibaba (Alibaba Group 2015c), essentially meaning that Alibaba and its companies would become central to people's lives.

To illustrate the versatility of Alibaba's portfolio of companies, see Table 6.6, in which some of Alibaba's companies are compared to more familiar equivalents, to Western standards. Not only does the list include Uber, Spotify and Netflix, which have been previously discussed in this chapter, it ranges from PayPal to Groupon, from WhatsApp to eBay. Business models of companies that have had paradigm-shifting impacts on the way we live our lives all found a place in Alibaba's portfolio.

Future of Alibaba

Alibaba's wide range of brands with equally versatile value propositions shows how a company is able to combine older and new revolutionary business models. Whether continued success is guaranteed, taking into account the management complexities of a broad portfolio, is something that only time can tell. Nevertheless, the intense growth trajectory of Alibaba that shows no evidence of slowing down anytime soon is impressive to say the least.

Airbnb

Airbnb's Growth History

Airbnb was conceived in 2007 when founders Brian Chesky and Joe Gebbia found themselves unable to afford rent (Crook and Escher 2015). They decided to set up three airbeds to rent out to lodgers (thus the original name of the company, Airbed and Breakfast). After significant struggles to raise funds, Airbnb grew from a start-up into a full-blown global company and a serious threat to the hotel industry. The platform allows private homeowners to rent out their homes as if they were hotel owners.

To illustrate Airbnb's growth and the severity of the threat to the hotel industry, let us take a closer look at the number of rooms available and the number of bookings made. Rooms available in December 2014 jumped up from 300,000 in February to approximately a million, a 233 percent increase in 11 months (Mudallal 2015). In contrast, some of the largest hotel groups reportedly manage slightly under 700,000 rooms (InterContinental Hotels Group, Hilton, Marriot), making Airbnb the largest provider of rooms in the world. Marriot is expecting to surpass the one million mark by the end of 2015. In terms of room-nights, in 2015, 80 million nights were booked via Airbnb, 100 percent up from 2014's approximately 40 million nights (Somerville 2015). For 2016, it is projected that this number could grow to 129 million room-nights (Barclays 2015).

Airbnb's growth in the number of rooms and reservations clearly is a sign that it is able to scale up its business model fast due to the fact that it in essence is not a hotel business model. Airbnb can be better compared to Booking.com (a booking website enabling customers to find the ideal hotel for their planned travel). Both Booking.com and Airbnb create market efficiency and transparency with their two-sided business models.

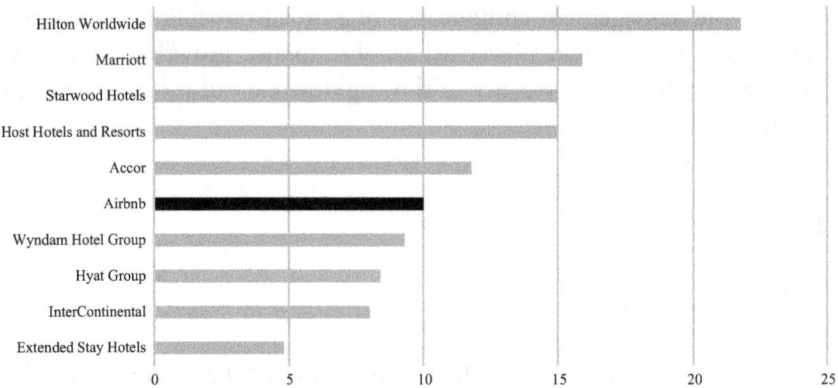

Fig. 6.22 Airbnb and hotel valuations in $B, March 2014 (adapted by Chu from: Rusli et al. 2014)

Comparing valuations across hotels and Airbnb, in 2014, Airbnb was valued between Wyndam Hotel Group and Accor (see Fig. 6.22). However, with its last equity fundraising, Airbnb was valued at $25.5 billion in 2015, surpassing Hilton Worldwide (O'Brien 2015).

Value Proposition

Just like Uber and Spotify, Airbnb's value proposition and its benefits are two-sided. Individual hosts are able to tap into the shared economy by offering their homes for a fee and guests are able to book rooms and apartments in an easy way with lower prices.

To elaborate on the benefits of the value proposition, let us look into the benefits to the hosts and guests:

- *Easier*: Without Airbnb, subletting or lodging your home or a room is a lot more complicated. Challenges that are overcome with Airbnb are, among others, having guests find you and dealing with payment. For guests, the process of booking a room via Airbnb is similar to booking a hotel room via, for instance, Booking.com.
- *Better*: Risks of having issues with guests are minimized by Airbnb's two-way evaluation process, similar to Uber's, which creates a self-

controlled quality assurance system. For guests, the quality of Airbnb rooms is more variable; some Airbnb hosts provide all amenities and facilities like hotels, whereas other hosts provide basic lodging.

• *Faster*: The end-to-end process from potential guests finding the host until payment are faster than without using Airbnb's value proposition. However, comparing Airbnb with Booking.com, the difference is negligible.

• *Cheaper*: Airbnb's average daily rate is lower than the average rate of hotels. Considering fewer amenities and facilities offered, this should not come as a surprise. Besides, hotels have a high-cost structure whereas private homeowners have costs that they would have to make regardless of whether they are or are not able to rent out their homes. To illustrate, on average, Airbnb apartments in selected US cities were 23 percent cheaper and Airbnb rooms 54 percent lower in price (see Fig. 6.23).

Pricing Model

Similar to hotels, Airbnb rooms and apartments are priced per night. Airbnb acts as a platform and marketplace where supply and demand meet. Airbnb's two-sided business models generates revenue from host fees (typically 3 percent of the reservation value, Airbnb 2015b) and from guests fees (6–12 percent of the reservation value, Airbnb 2015a).

Future of Airbnb

Airbnb's ambition is to further expand the portfolio of products and services to their customers to satisfy their traveling needs (Curry 2015). In December 2015, Airbnb trialed a new feature in San Francisco, where it offered host-customized trips to guests. In this trial, Airbnb offered three options: hiking trips, best restaurants and a tour of the city's hotspots.

The host-designed trips would fill the growing need from travelers to be able to experience city trips like locals, instead of using a more generic

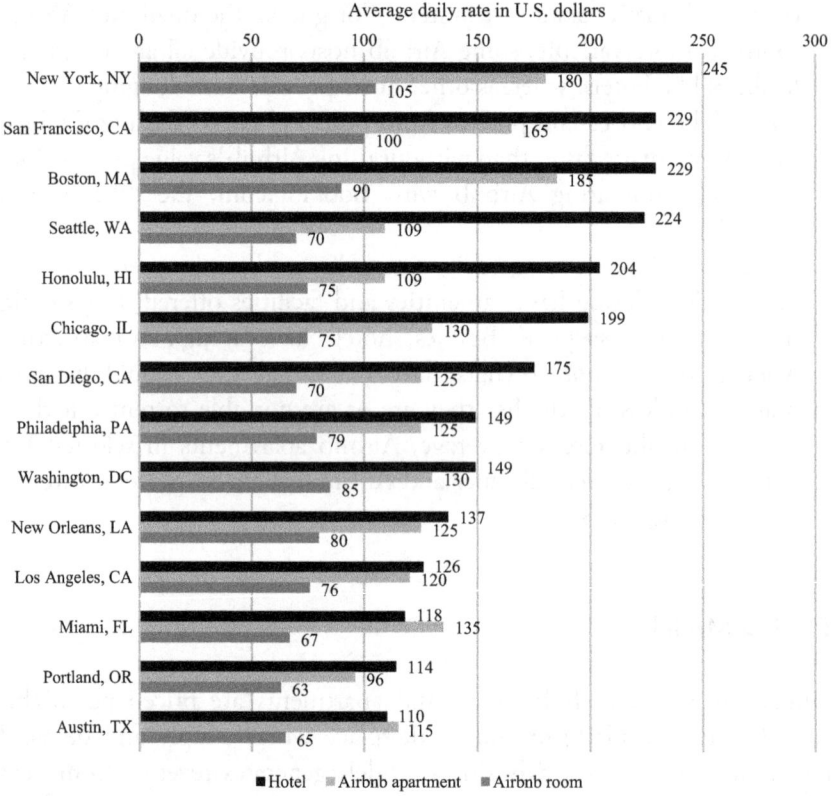

Fig. 6.23 Comparison Airbnb and hotel prices in selected US cities as of June 2013 (adapted by Chu from: Statista 2015)

guidebook or commercial tour guide. In other words, maybe it is time for commercial tour guides and publishers of guidebooks to rethink their value proposition before the next Airbnb disruption starts.

6.4   Closing Remarks

The capability of companies to develop new value propositions through business model innovation is increasingly becoming key for long-term survival in a turbulent and fast-changing environment. Without innovation—or change—competitive advantage is likely to become less and less sustainable in the future. In particular, the threat of extreme scalability of newcomers has the potential to quickly topple current market leaders who might be under the illusion of being in a comfortable, well-defended position. The business model framework helps to pragmatically identify and analyze the areas of high potential improvement. Do not hate change, embrace it like innovation.

Notes

1. An example of a 'small basket' would be if a consumer bought only one tube of toothpaste as opposed to toothpaste and several other products with a higher total monetary value.
2. Lesser known to consumers outside of the United States, Netflix started out with renting out DVDs, which is still does today. Please see the case studies later in this chapter for a detailed picture of Netflix and its business model revolution.

References

Airbnb. 2015a. What are Guest Service Fees? https://www.airbnb.com/help/article/104/what-are-guest-service-fees. Online.

———. 2015b. What are Host Service Fees? https://www.airbnb.com/help/article/63/what-are-host-service-fees. Online.

Alibaba Group. 2015a. Company Overview. http://www.alibabagroup.com/en/about/overview. Online.

———. 2015b. History and Milestones. http://www.alibabagroup.com/en/about/history. Online.

———. 2015c. http://www.alibabagroup.com/en. Online.

Apple. 2003. Apple Launches the iTunes Music Store. https://www.apple.com/pr/library/2003/04/28Apple-Launches-the-iTunes-Music-Store.html. Online.

———. 2015. www.apple.com. Online.

Austin, S., et al. 2015. The Billion Dollar Startup Club. http://graphics.wsj.com/billion-dollar-club/?co=Uber. Online.

Barclays. 2015. Hotels: Is Airbnb a Game-Changer? Print.

Chao, L. 2015. Retailers Struggle Getting E-commerce Goods to Customers, Study Says. http://www.wsj.com/articles/retailers-struggle-getting-e-com merce-goods-to-customers-study-says-1446634802. Online.

Chu, R. 2015a. Business Model Framework. Simon-Kucher & Partners. Print.

———. 2015b. Price Laddering and Bundling. Simon-Kucher & Partners. Print.

———. 2015c. Pricing Model Types. Simon-Kucher & Partners. Print.

———. 2015d. Simon-Kucher Project Content. Simon-Kucher & Partners. Print.

———. 2015e. Three Types of Pricing. Simon-Kucher & Partners. Print.

Crook, J., and A. Escher. 2015. A Brief History of Airbnb. http://techcrunch.com/gallery/a-brief-history-of-airbnb/. Online.

Crowe, A. 2010. 10 Most Overpriced Products You Should Avoid. http://www.dailyfinance.com/2010/09/27/10-most-overpriced-products-you-should-avoid/. Online.

Curry, D. 2015. Airbnb Wants to Book Your Entire Trip in the Future. http://www.digitaltrends.com/mobile/airbnb-handcrafted-trips/. Online.

Dutch Chamber of Commerce. 2014. Company Filings. Data.

Gallo, A. 2014. The Value of Keeping the Right Customers. https://hbr.org/2014/10/the-value-of-keeping-the-right-customers/. Online.

Geyskens, I., et al. 2006. Make, Buy, or Ally: A Transaction Cost Theory Meta-Analysis. *Academy of Management Journal* 49(3), June 1, 519–543. Print.

GrowthHackers. 2015. Uber—What's Fueling Uber's Growth Engine?. https://growthhackers.com/growth-studies/uber. Online.

IFPI. 2011. Recording Industry in Numbers—The Recorded Music Market in 2011. 2012 Edition. Print.

Kafka, P. 2015. Here are the Original Shows Netflix Viewers Say They're Watching. http://recode.net/2015/08/26/here-are-the-original-shows-netflix-viewers-say-theyre-watching/. Online.

Kokalitcheva, K. 2015. Uber Completes 1 Billion Rides. http://fortune.com/2015/12/30/uber-completes-1-billion-rides/. Online.

KPN. 2011. Exclusieve samenwerking KPN en Spotify in Nederland. http://corporate.kpn.com/pers/persberichten/exclusieve-samenwerking-kpn-en-spotify-in-nederland.htm. Online.

Kuo, et al. 2014. All the Western Companies You'd Have to Combine to Get Something Like Alibaba. http://qz.com/206283/all-the-western-companies-youd-have-to-combine-to-get-something-like-alibaba/. Online.

Lamont, T. 2013. Napster: The Day the Music was Set Free. http://www. theguardian.com/music/2013/feb/24/napster-music-free-file-sharing. Online.

Mudallal, Z. 2015. Airbnb Will Soon be Booking More Rooms than the World's Largest Hotel Chains. http://qz.com/329735/airbnb-will-soon-be-booking-more-rooms-than-the-worlds-largest-hotel-chains/. Online.

Nazario, M. 2015. I Tried the New Fitting Room at Ralph Lauren and It Blew My Mind. http://uk.businessinsider.com/ralph-lauren-interactive-mirrors-2015-11?r=US&IR=T. Online.

O'Brien, S.A. 2015. 'Crazy Money'—Airbnb Valued at Over $25 Billion. http://money.cnn.com/2015/06/27/technology/airbnb-funding-valuation-update/. Online.

Operator. 2015. Your Next Shopping Experience Starts with a Text. https://operator.com/. Online.

Orr, G. 2012. Supersized: Why Our Portion Sizes are Ballooning. http://www.independent.co.uk/life-style/food-and-drink/features/supersized-why-our-por tion-sizes-are-ballooning-7852014.html. Online.

Philips Hue. 2015. http://www2.meethue.com/en-us/productdetail/philips-hue-bridge. Online.

Porter, M.E. 1985. *Competitive Advantage*. New York: The Free Press, Chap. 1, 11–15. Print.

Prins, N. 2015. The Spotify-Starbucks Partnership is Digital Co-Branding Genius. http://www.forbes.com/sites/nomiprins/2015/05/19/the-spotify-starbucks-part nership-is-digital-co-branding-genius/. Online.

RT. 2016. $25 a Mile?? Uber 'Surge' Angers NYE Riders. https://www.rt.com/news/327714-uber-surcharge-nye-anger/. Online.

Rusli, E.M., et al. 2014. Airbnb is in Advanced Talks to Raise Funds at a $ Billion Valuation. http://www.wsj.com/articles/SB10001424052702303802 104579451022670668410. Online

Sawers, P. 2012. Spotify: The Spotify so Far. http://thenextweb.com/eu/2011/07/14/spotify-the-story-so-far/#gref. Online.

Shaw, B. 1903. *Man and Superman*. Cambridge, MA: The University Press. Print.

Shingo, S. 1988. *Non-Stock Production: The Shingo System for Continuous Improvement*. Cambridge, MA: Productivity Press. Print.

Simon-Kucher & Partners. 2014. Global Pricing Study 2014. Print.

Somerville, H. 2015. Exclusive: Airbnb to Double Bookings to 80 Million This Year—Investors. http://www.reuters.com/article/us-airbnb-growth-idUSKC N0RS2QK20150928. Online.

Sonos. 2015. http://www.sonos.com/nl-nl?r=1. Online.

Spotify. 2015. http://www.spotify.com. Online.

Statista. 2015a. Comparison between Airbnb and Hotel Prices in Selected United States Cities as of June 2013 (in US Dollars). http://www.statista.com/statistics/314822/comparison-of-airbnb-and-hotel-prices-in-selected-cities-us/. Online.

———. 2015b. Number of Paying Spotify Subscribers Worldwide from July 2010 to March 2016 (in Millions). http://www.statista.com/statistics/244995/number-of-paying-spotify-subscribers/. Online.

———. 2015c. Annual Revenue of Alibaba from 2010 to 2016, by Segment (in Million Yuan). http://www.statista.com/statistics/298839/revenue-of-alibabacom-segment/. Online.

———. 2015d. Cumulative Number of Active Buyers across Alibaba's Online Shopping Properties from 2nd Quarter 2012 to 1st Quarter 2016 (in Millions). http://www.statista.com/statistics/226927/alibaba-cumulative-active-online-buyers-taobao-tmall/. Online.

———. 2015e. Number of Online Shoppers in China from 2006 to 2015 (in Millions). http://www.statista.com/statistics/277391/number-of-online-buyers-in-china/. Online.

———. 2015f. Number of Monthly Active Facebook Users Worldwide as of 1st Quarter 2016 (in Millions). http://www.statista.com/statistics/264810/number-of-monthly-active-facebook-users-worldwide/. Online.

Tarantola, A. 2015. Uber is Looking into Launching Two New Ridesharing Services. http://www.engadget.com/2015/12/08/uber-is-looking-into-launching-two-new-ridesharing-services/. Online.

The Digital Entertainment Group. 2015. http://www.degonline.org/. Online.

The Economist. 2013. It's Complicated. http://www.economist.com/news/business/21590341-management-thinkers-disagree-how-manage-complexity-its-complicated. Online.

The Economist, Dealogic. 2015. China: Selected Companies Recently Acquired by Alibaba Group in 2014, by Value of Stake (in million US dollars). http://www.statista.com/statistics/324128/china-alibaba-selected-acquisitions-by-stake-value/. Online.

Uber. 2015a. Uber Surge Pricing. http://uberestimator.com/uber-surge-pricing. Online.

———. 2015b. UberCARGO: A Reliable Ride for Your Items. https://newsroom.uber.com/hong-kong/en/a-ride-for-your-goods-introducing-ubercargo/. Online.

————. 2015c. https://www.uber.com/. Online.

Unik Wijnhuis. 2016. Voss still Water 500 ml PET. http://www.unikwijnhuis. nl/artikel/voss-water/voss-stil-water-500ml-pet/97/772. Online.

Weinberg, M. 2015. We Just Got Our Best Look Yet at Amazon's Drone-Delivery Program. http://uk.businessinsider.com/new-amazon-prime-air-delivery-drone-2015-11?r=US&IR=T. Online.

Yahoo Finance. 2015. Financial Data. Available: http://finance.yahoo.com/. Online.

7

The Role of Communication as a Dynamic Capability in Business Model Innovation

Nicole Pfeffermann

7.1   Introduction

"Successful companies will be those that transform information into value-creating knowledge, and [. . .] use this knowledge to innovate and capture additional profit" (Davenport et al. 2006: 17). Information and knowledge are two contributors to innovation and change. The ubiquitous availability of information and rapid sharing of knowledge require, however, the ability to reinvent and adapt continuously to environmental dynamism. It is through reinvention and adaptation that companies are able to build up capabilities for creating value; for instance, in effectively launching innovations or interacting with vendors and customers as co-creators in value creation processes. The organizational capability to innovate (innovative capability) has become the impact factor for business growth in the information age.

N. Pfeffermann (✉)
FOM Hamburg, Hamburg, Germany

© The Author(s) 2017   **191**
A. Brem, E. Viardot (eds.), *Revolution of Innovation Management*,
DOI 10.1057/978-1-349-95123-9_7

The convergences of disruptive technologies and changes in consumer demands have led to the necessity of understanding capabilities and new business model design for value creation. For instance, analytical and technological capabilities to alter the value chain through interactions with customers via on-demand service platforms on mobile devices (e.g., UBER, myTaxi). Technology has changed the way value is co-created in terms of engaging with knowledge-empowered participants. This implies open communication to be an integral part of innovation, in particular in the open innovation view, which is understood as ". . .the use of purposive inflows and outflows of knowledge to accelerate internal innovation, and expand the markets for external use of innovation [. . .]" (Chesbrough 2006: 1; see also Vanhaverbeke and Roijakkers 2014). Consequently, communication for innovation plays a crucial role, for instance, in information transmission and knowledge acquisition (Mazzarol 2014).

But is the role of communication only limited to the enabler function in the commercialization of new products or in the diffusion of knowledge and idea dissemination for accelerating (internal) innovation? "While numerous firms experiment with involving a crowd in value creation, few companies turn crowdsourcing projects into thriving platforms with a powerful business model" (Kohler 2015). In the digital age, innovation has shifted from the new product development and open innovation view to the business development and open business model innovation view. A starting point is provided by Vanhaverbeke and Roijakkers (2014), by integrating open innovation initiatives into a firm's strategy and differentiating initiatives according to their strategic role, which implies a shift away from new product development to strategic thinking in open innovation. A key task of managers is "identifying the key strategic drivers that can be leveraged by new (technological) developments with partners rather than start out with the need to open up during a new product development process" (ibid.). From this strategic collaboration perspective, it also draws on the idea that organizations engage with start-ups driven by a win-win situation in order to substantially and continuously create value and new business models, for instance, by openness with the other players in start-up support ecosystems (Weiblen and Chesbrough 2015). Those research results in business model innovation show that communication is key: (1) to manage the quality of the relationship between platform and users for users' perception of being valued by the corporation (see Kohler 2015); and (2) to impart information in a respectful manner between corporations and start-up support systems for benefits that are mutual and reinforcing.

The main question, then, is which *(new)* role communication plays in the context of business model innovation. This chapter aims at making a contribution to this field of interest by providing information on the linkage between the *business model innovation* and *strategic innovation communication* concepts in the digitalized information age.

7.2 Literature Review

Business Model Innovation

A formal model of business model innovation (BMI), related to sponsor-based business models, was presented by Casadesus-Masanell and Zhu in 2013. They define BMI as "the search for new logics of the firm and new ways to create and capture value for its stakeholders [. . .] and as a result, business model innovation often affects the whole enterprise" (e.g., Amit and Zott 2001). Hargadon (2015) describes BMI as a determinant of company survival, which means BMI implies a simultaneous change of company's offerings and scope of new capabilities in order to develop and deliver new offerings. It requires "company leaders to commit to building new capabilities, whether inside the organization or through external partnerships" (Hargadon 2015: 33).

In order to search for new logics of the firm, mainly focusing on value proposition design (see Osterwalder et al. 2014; e.g., Magretta 2002; Zott and Amit 2007, 2008; Casadesus-Masanell and Ricart 2010; Gambardella and McGahan 2010; Markides 2010; Teece 2010), any enterprise has to have the capability of developing and implementing new partial models—distribution model, finance model, communication model—embedded in a complete business model design process. A resulting partial model or a complete business model itself might be innovative and, thus, the possibility of competitive imitation is given (for instance, imitation of an innovative communication model or a standard communication model). Entrants have to decide whether to reveal ideas "by competing through the new business model or, instead, to conceal them by adopting a traditional, established logic of value creation and value capture." (Casadesus-Masanell and Zhu 2013: 465). On the other hand, a company has to decide whether to keep a business model or adopt a new business model. Both innovation and imitation of new business models as well as mixed new business models are part of BMI. Third, BMI is understood as internal strategic activities, which are affected by the institutional environment in which an enterprise operates (Zott and Amit 2007).

Communication

Grunig (1984) is given credit for his early focus on "corporate communication management". Cornelissen (2008) states that corporate communication is "a management function that is responsible for overseeing and coordinating the work done by communication practitioners in different specialist disciplines, such as media, public affairs, and internal communication." (p. 5) It is ". . .a management function that offers a framework for the effective coordination of all internal and external communication with the overall purpose of establishing and maintaining favorable reputations with stakeholder groups upon which the organization is dependent" (ibid.). In addition, concepts describe corporate communication from this *function-oriented* perspective, for instance, integrated marketing communication, which is defined as "a process of analysis, planning, organization, implementation, and monitoring that is oriented toward creating unity from diverse sources of internal and external communication with target groups to convey a consistent impression of the company or the company's reference object" (Bruhn 2006: 17; Bruhn 2008: 15; Bruhn and Ahlers 2014). The objective of managing the process is a "uniform image" leading to a company's credibility (ibid.). This *function-oriented perspective* is also applied by Argenti (2007), van Riel and Fombrun (2008), Belasen (2008), and Belasen and Rufer (2014). In contrast, Hübner (2007) focuses on a *behavioral perspective* that defines corporate communication as a discourse about a company's ongoing negotiation processes with its stakeholders so as to achieve legitimation, for the purpose of bringing peers together "in order to create strategic thinking in an ongoing communicative and collaborative process" (Hübner 2007: 165–166).

Dynamic, changing environments are an important reason for the expanding interest in corporate communication management research: changes such as increasing competition in communication markets, dynamic developments in media consumption, new communication channels, and access to and availability of information transformed into knowledge (Argenti 2007; Donsbach 2006; Töhlke et al. 2001)—all of which affect a company's management of communication pertaining to these new challenges.

In the context of innovation, different communication fields are identified in the body of literature: (1) innovation marketing; (2) diffusion marketing; and (3) innovation communication.

First, "innovation marketing encompasses all market-oriented activities of innovation management—that is, all strategic and operative decisions for marketing new products" (Steinhoff and Trommsdorff 2011). Marketing of innovation includes both the commercialization of radical innovations, technologies, and services (e.g., Mohr et al. 2009; Sandberg 2008; Sowter 2000) and strategic marketing (e.g., Trommsdorff and Steinhoff 2007). Research in marketing, consumer behavior, and psychology encompasses, hence, scientific investigations in marketing as an essential part in the innovation process (Crosby and Johnson 2006). Entrepreneurial marketing is a new research field focusing on market-related activities of new ventures.

Second, "diffusion research seeks to understand the spread of innovations by modeling their entire life cycle from the perspective of communications and consumer interactions" (Peres et al. 2010: 91). Regarding communication, three social influence factors are mentioned to be drivers in innovation diffusion: (1) word-of-mouth communication (e.g., Martilla 1971; Mazzarol 2014); (2) network externalities (e.g., Rohlfs 2001; Tomochi et al. 2005); and (3) social signals (e.g., Van den Bulte and Stremersch 2004; Berger and Heath 2008). These social influence factors, referred to as interdependencies among consumers, "affect various market players with or without their explicit knowledge" (Peres et al. 2010: 91). Current research in this field focuses on the effect of online communities, web services, and complex types of product-services categories in marketing diffusion.

Third, innovation communication is defined as a systematic initiation of communication processes with internal and external stakeholders to support technical, economic, and social novelties through: (1) the interest-led construction, revision, and destruction of socially dependent conceptional patterns and communication resources; and (2) by stimulating (or, though the stimulation of) content-related catalysts for the development, as well as through professional promotion of novelties (Zerfaß 2009; translated into English). In this area, scholars have focused on innovation communication and its impact on the innovation process from idea to launch as a part of corporate communication (e.g., Fink 2009; Zerfaß 2009) and have identified three communication fields: (1) internal communication; (2) external communication; and (3) public relations (innovation journalism: Nordfors 2009). The object of communication is primarily the innovation itself, but in many cases it is also the organization behind the innovation.

Dynamic Capabilities, Business Model Innovation, Strategic Innovation Communication

Generic Understanding of Dynamic Capabilities

In the field of strategy, scholarship on dynamic capability is rapidly growing in interest and impact and focusing on moving forward this field by stimulating conversation within the research community and integrating a multi-disciplinary perspective (see di Stefano et al. 2014) to explain business performance in the long-run (Teece 2014).

To clarify the understanding of dynamic capabilities, this chapter summarizes the latest findings provided by Teece (2014: 328–346; originally presented by Teece et al. 1997):

- An enterprise capability is a set of current or potential activities that utilize the firm's productive resources to make and/or deliver products and services. There are two important classes of capability: ordinary and dynamic.

- Ordinary capabilities involve the performance of administrative, operational, and governance-related functions that are (technically) necessary to accomplish tasks. Ordinary capabilities can be measured against the requirements of specific tasks, such as labor productivity, inventory turns, and time to completion, and can thus be benchmarked internally or externally to industry best practices. Best operational practices are those that increase speed, quality, and efficiency. Ordinary capabilities are considered strong when the firm has achieved best practices and its employee base includes the relevant skilled people and advanced equipment. In short, ordinary capabilities can best be thought of as achieving technical efficiency and "doing things right" in the core business functions of operations, administration, and governance.
- Whereas ordinary capabilities are about doing things right, dynamic capabilities are about doing the right things, at the right time, based on new product (and process) development, unique managerial orchestration processes, a strong and change-oriented organizational culture, and a prescient assessment of the business environment and technological opportunities. Dynamic capabilities involve higher-level activities that can enable an enterprise to direct its ordinary activities toward high-payoff endeavors. This requires managing, or "orchestrating," the firm's resources to address and shape rapidly changing business environments. Resources are potentially productive tangible and intangible assets and people that are semi-permanently attached to a firm. Dynamic capabilities are about adapting, orchestrating, and innovating. They allow the enterprise and its top management to develop conjectures about the evolution of consumer preferences, business problems, and technology; validate and fine-tune them; and then act on them by realigning assets and activities to enable continuous innovation and change.
- Successfully building strong dynamic capabilities allows firms to challenge competitors that are enamored with the resources they currently possess, that ignore (or are ignorant of) changing customer needs, that cherish the status quo, that fail to empower entrepreneurs and change agents, and that prioritize efficiency over innovation. Long-run growth and profitability require the presence of strong dynamic capabilities,

but the reverse is not true. Strong dynamic capabilities can become worthless if they are tied to a poor or badly misjudged strategy, and vice versa. Ultimately, good performance requires strong dynamic capabilities to sense, seize, and transform in conjunction with a good strategy.

- Dynamic capabilities reside, in part, with individual managers and the top management team. But the organization's values, culture, and collective ability to quickly implement a new business model or other changes are also integral to the strength or weakness of the firm's dynamic capabilities. Dynamic capabilities demand both an external (outside the organization) and internal orientation by management. The learning and innovation that undergird transformation (and dynamic capabilities more generally) and contribute to durable competitive advantage often need to be global in scope.

The Linkage to Business Model Innovation and Communication

Managers, entrepreneurs, and innovators cannot just leave it up to a hypothetical market devoid of entrepreneurially managed firms to line up specific assets, develop new ones, and integrate them into a well-functioning innovation, production, and marketing system. The reason is that markets for high-specificity (idiosyncratic) assets generally don't exist, and if they do exist they are invariably "thin." *To overcome this problem, managers collect information, sense opportunities, invest in capabilities, innovate, and transform. They become the instruments that help achieve the shrewd allocation of company resources.* (Teece 2014: 346)

Following this argumentation line, dynamic capabilities are linked to business model innovation in a fundamental way to build up an entrepreneurially managed business. In the role of decision-making communication leaders, managers, entrepreneurs, and innovators, which could also be any employee, continuously interact with their internal and external environment to sense, seize, and transform for achieving congruence with customer needs and with technological and business opportunities, as well as doing the right things for a firm's long-term market success.

Innovation Communication as a Dynamic Managerial Capability

A set of communication activities and their outputs and outcomes are the essential drivers of any business to foster innovation and growth as well as competitive positioning on global digital platforms. This results in the importance of focusing on the orchestration ability of an organization and individual to manage communication activities for innovation on both the strategic-entrepreneurial and the operational-routinized level to address resource markets, communication markets, and sales/consumer markets; a market is defined as an environment for demand-supply interactions, for instance, to acquire or allocate resources or present products and services.

In comparison to the traditional corporate communication view, strategic innovation communication is not an enabler of corporate branding, building of investor relations, and public relations rather than key to an entrepreneurially managed business firm for systematically creating value and providing an open innovation culture, which—aligned to strategy—tend to lead to superior business performance in the long-run (for direct and indirect effects of innovation communication, see Pfeffermann 2014).

In this context, innovation communication can be understood as a dynamic capability, as a conceptual definition as follows:

> *An organizational or individual ability of managing transactional procedures of transmitting information related to:*
> *(1) ideas, business models, concepts, prototypes, practices, etc., or a combination of them, referred to as a cluster, that are perceived as new by a recipient;*
> *(2) context-issue(s) for ideas, business models, concepts, prototypes, practices, etc. or cluster;*
> *(3) the innovative capability;*
> *considering interrelation, time, and openness used to create value by building up and modifying stakeholder's knowledge (schemata), improving management of strategic assets, and intensifying reputation (adapted from Pfeffermann 2014).*

Table 7.1 basically shows that innovation communication accomplishes the criteria of dynamic capabilities.

Table 7.1 Innovation communication as a dynamic capability

Criteria	Dynamic capability by Teece (2014)	Innovation communication capability (Pfeffermann 2014)
Purpose	Achieving congruence with customer needs and with technological and business opportunities	• Perceived as new by a recipient (=perception focus)
Mode of attainability	Build (learning)	• Building up and modifying stakeholder's knowledge (schemata)
Tripartite schema	Sense, seize, and transform	• Transmitting information used to create value by building, modifying, improving, and intensifying (=build, modify, improve, intensify)
Key routines	Signature processes	• Managing transactional procedures of transmitting information related to: (1) Ideas, business models, concepts, prototypes, practices, etc., or a combination of them, referred to as a cluster, that are perceived as new by a recipient; (2) Context-issue(s) for ideas, business models, concepts, prototypes, practices, etc. or cluster; (3) The innovative capability
Managerial emphasis	Entrepreneurial asset orchestration and leadership	• Improving management of strategic assets
Priority	Doing the right things	• Considering interrelation, time, and openness
Imitability	Inimitable	• Used to create value by building up and modifying stakeholder's knowledge (schemata), improving management of strategic assets, and intensifying reputation (=value creation through knowledge, strategic assets, reputation; VRIN resources focus)
Result	Evolutionary fitness (innovation)	• =Innovation focus per se see also Fig. 7.1

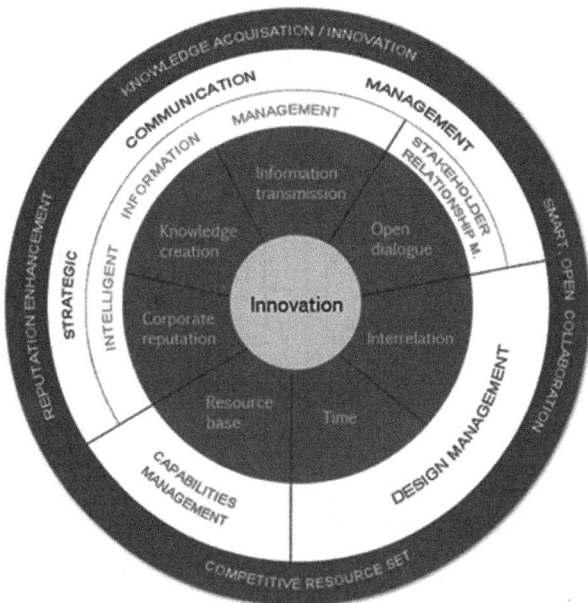

Fig. 7.1 Innovation communication capability related to management

Figure 7.1 illustrates the eight dimensions of the dynamic capability of innovation communication and its five principles of management (see also Pfeffermann 2011, 2014):

7.3 Method & Study Results

The qualitative study in start-up business practice was conducted with international new ventures, so-called born globals (Oxtorp 2014), with the objective to better understand the dynamic managerial capability of innovation communication and in particular how they manage their innovation communication activities linked to their business model.

How was the study designed? Referring to the dynamic capabilities framework, illustrated by Teece in 2014 (Fig. 7.1, p. 334), the qualitative study used an entrepreneurial instrument for standardized data collection and observation in order to provide a basis for comparing results. This

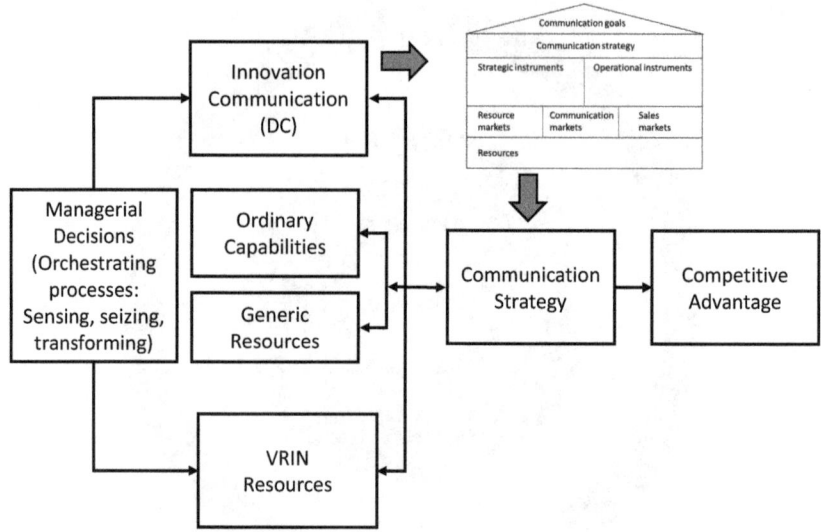

Fig. 7.2 Dynamic capability framework linked to communication (canvas); adapted from Teece 2014

entrepreneurial instrument is derived from the conceptual definition of innovation communication and linked to communication strategy and VRIN resources, as shown in Fig. 7.2.

How were the data collected? Due to the fact that start-ups worldwide, in particular the born globals, use the business model canvas (Osterwalder and Pingeur 2010) and value proposition design (Osterwalder et al. 2014)—both canvas design techniques for designing and developing (new) business models—the communication model canvas was introduced to the participants as a lean entrepreneurial instrument for designing and developing communication activities. It also guaranteed a direct connection to business model innovation.

The elements of a communication plan are shown as fields on a one-page visualization—the communication model canvas, as illustrated in Fig. 7.3: goal, strategy, instruments, markets, and resources. Linked to the business model canvas, this canvas allows businesses:

- to effectively design, develop, and manage communication activities for interacting with key partners and customers (related to channels and relationships described in the business model)

Fig. 7.3 Communication model canvas—entrepreneurial instrument

- to invent, challenge, and reflect a new communication model, as part of an innovative or mixed business model
- to describe and visualize communication plans for managing communication activities in teams resulting in consistency and reputation

How were born globals (cases) selected for this study? Five cases were finally selected for this study (USA/LA, France/Paris, Germany/Berlin and Cologne). The selection criteria of all cases were as follows:

- A start-up business is involved in the business model design process
- A start-up business is managing the process using the *business model canvas* (Osterwalder and Pingeur 2010)
- A start-up business is committed to use the *communication model canvas*

Note: Start-up businesses were interested but they were also afraid of providing the material. That is the reason why this qualitative study describes in general the process, key results, and managerial implications.

How was the research process? In order to compare the results, the procedure was similar:

- Workshop: Understanding the business model canvas/managerial process

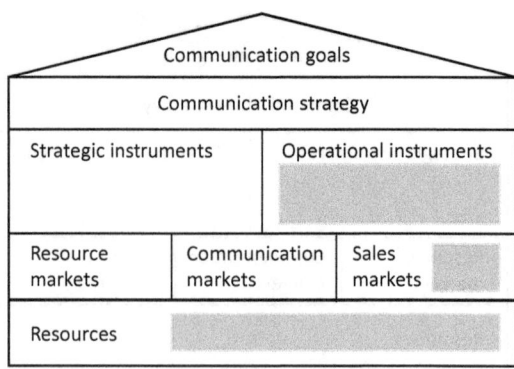

Fig. 7.4 Study results related to communication model canvas

- Workshop: Designing the communication model canvas/managerial process
- Reflective meeting on both processes and in particular on the communication capability

Summary of All Cases

After analyzing the observation material, canvas visualizations, and notes of the reflective meeting, three first main findings can be summarized, illustrated in Fig. 7.4:

- Among the five cases, the participants primarily addressed *sales markets* (customer segments) using standardized *operational media and social media instruments*
- Only one of the participants reflected on the *communication capability* and aimed at building new capabilities for developing the business; other start-up businesses were focused on their technological and analytical skills with the objective to develop a product or service (new product development level), for instance, adapting a new bootstrap framework for a new learning app
- *Communication resources* were not calculated due to the fact that a communication plan was missing; communication was taken for

granted and "doing things right" meant "communication by chance" ("*I saw a conference and took the opportunity to present my new idea*"); the most valuable source were communication experts in public relations (traditional marketing view)

7.4 Conclusion and Outlook

This chapter focuses on communication in business model innovation from a dynamic capability view in strategic management research and, hence, does not provide any review from a communication science/ communication theory perspective. With no doubt, it should be a task on future research agendas for a multi-disciplinary approach including conducting new (triangulative) research studies.

Given the increased communication complexity and innovation dynamics necessitated by the changing environment and increased information and communication technologies, strategic innovation communication emerges as a new communication field. In particular for start-up businesses, the innovation communication capability can theoretically lead to a valuable resource base (VRIN resources) and competitive advantage. Strategic innovation communication might also be an essential value creation and innovation driver for established companies, in particular in the sense of building up an entrepreneurially managed business.

The qualitative study results show, however, that the selected start-up businesses invest in developing a new business model (using the business model canvas), but they do not invest in integrated communication model design or the use of a strategic management and entrepreneurial instrument. As illustrated in Fig. 7.4, only three fields of the communication model canvas were considered by the selected start-up businesses: operational instruments, sales markets, and resources (e.g., social media platforms, such as Facebook, Instagram, Twitter, and LinkedIn).

Managerial implications:

- *Communication management cannot solely focus on sales markets*:

The importance of sales markets is clearly given in order to sell new products and services and to achieve congruence with customer needs and with technological and business opportunities; however, leveraging interactions with stakeholders in different markets, for instance, position new (context-)issues of an innovation in communication markets, can reduce marketing costs and offer new opportunities to address strategic partners and resources, which in turn leads to better business development—"doing the right things"—i.e., a combination of first-order dynamic capabilities and second-order capabilities to positively affect VRIN resources. The results also show that it is focused on generic resources and ordinary processes, for instance, publication of a website using the content-management system "WordPress" and a commonly used bootstrap framework, resulting in the key problem that communication is not linked to communication strategy and communication does not create value, which ends up in imitating communication models in long tails ("copy-cats"), published as "best practices" on blogs and websites for entrepreneurs. If start-ups and investors are interested in increased returns and positive income statements or sustainable business developments, strategic innovation communication, as a dynamic capability on an organizational and individual level, has to become a priority.

- *Fit-for-purpose instruments for strategic innovation communication*:

Public relations has its own instruments (press releases, press conferences, online news room, blogger relations); employee communication has its own instruments (intranet, internal social business networks, magazines, and events); and strategic innovation communication has its own instruments (framing, storytelling, issues management, gamification, co-creation, and multisensory communication). Using the communication model canvas as an entrepreneurial instrument for managing communication activities, managers, entrepreneurs, and innovators focus on the orchestration ability of an organization and individual to manage communication activities for innovation both on the strategic-entrepreneurial and operational-routinized level to address resource markets, communication markets and sales/consumer markets.

* *Integrated innovation communication effectively builds new capabilities*:

Innovation communication should focus on five integrated basic management principles for building a valuable resource base (VRIN resources): (1) strategic communication management; (2) design management; (3) capability management; (4) stakeholder relationship management; and (5) intelligent information management (IT and knowledge management). The importance of building new capabilities in complex systemic environments will be the main task in management of all businesses in the future. "[Liberal art] Skills, not digital or technological ones, will hold the keys to a company's future success" (Perrault 2016). The dynamic capability of innovation communication plays a key role in business model innovation in terms of creating a valuable resource base for business development and competitive advantage. It could be stated that if innovation communication is the fundamental basis of business model innovation, innovation communication belongs to the core of a business. It is suggested that future research could utilize studies to focus on specific archetypes of business models, different business model design processes, and environments linked to innovation communication (using canvas techniques or other data collection processes and instruments).

Add-on material:

7.5 Five Steps for Linking Business Model and Communication Model

Step 1. Design and understand a new business model and value proposition: key partners, customers, key resources and activities, and channels for delivering new offerings

Step 2. Describe a communication model with eight blocks on one page (fields on the communication model canvas): goal, strategy, strategic instruments, operational instruments, resource market, communication market, sales market, and resources.

Step 3.   Invent new instruments which fit to business model and facilitate innovative communication models

Step 4.   Systematically check a communication model by asking questions (critical thinking) to prove the fit to the business model

Step 5.   Leverage this instrument in daily management practice for implementing the new business model and continuously adapt the communication and business model

Requirements: (1) Understanding of how to communicate novelties; (2) communication management basics and instruments from 35 communication fields; and (3) how to use both canvas methods.

Bibliography

Amit R., and C. Zott. 2001. Value Creation in E-business. *Strategic Management Journal* 22(Special Issue), June–July: 493–520.

Argenti, P.A. 2007. *Corporate Communication*, 4th edn. New York, NY: McGraw-Hill.

Belasen, A.T. 2008. *The Theory and Practice of Corporate Communication: A Competing Values Perspective*. Thousand Oaks, CA: Sage.

Belasen, A.T., and R.J. Rufer. 2014. Innovation Communication and Interfunctional Collaboration: A View from the Competing Values Framework for Corporate Communication. In *Strategy and Communication for Innovation*, ed. N. Pfeffermann, T. Minshall, and L. Mortara, 227–240. Berlin: Springer-Verlag.

Berger, J., and C. Heath. 2008. Who Drives Divergence? Identity Signaling, Outgroup Dissimilarity, and the Abandonment of Cultural Tastes. *Journal of Personality and Social Psychology* 95: 593–607.

Bruhn, M., and G.M. Ahlers. 2014. Integrated Communication in the Innovation Process: An Approach to Integrated Innovation Communication. In *Strategy and Communication for Innovation*, ed. N. Pfeffermann, T. Minshall, and L. Mortara, 139–160. Berlin: Springer-Verlag.

Bruhn, M. 2008. Planning Integrated Marketing Communications. In *Communication and Leadership in the 21st Century*, ed. H. Sievert and D. Bell, 13–34. Stuttgart, Germany: Schäffer-Poeschel.

———. 2006. *Integrierte Unternehmens- und Marketingkommunikation. Strategische Plannung und operative Umsetzung*, 4th edn. Stuttgart, Germany: Schäffer-Poeschel.

Casadesus-Masanell, R., and F. Zhu. 2013. Business Model Innovation and Competitive Imitation: The Case of Sponsor-based Business Models. *Strategic Management Journal* 34: 464–482.

Casadesus-Masanell, R., and J.E. Ricart. 2010. From Strategy to Business Models and Onto Tactics. *Long Range Planning* 43: 195–215.

Chesbrough, H.W. 2006. Open Innovation: A New Paradigm for Understanding Industrial Innovation. In *Open innovation: Researching a New Paradigm*, ed. H.W. Chesbrough, J. West, and W. Vanhaverbeke, 1–14. Oxford: Oxford University Press.

Cornelissen, J.P. 2008. *Corporate Communication: A Guide to Theory and Practice*. London: Sage.

Crosby, L.A., and S.L. Johnson. 2006. Customer-centric Innovation. *Marketing Management* 15: 12–13.

Davenport, T.H., M. Leibold, and S. Voelpel (ed). 2006. *Strategic Management in the Innovation Economy: Strategy Approaches and Tools for Dynamic Innovation Capabilities*. Erlangen, Germany: Publicis Corporate Publishing and Wiley-VCH.

Di Stefano, G., M. Peteraf, and G. Verona. 2014. The Organizational Drivetrain: A Road to Integration of Dynamic Capabilities Research. *The Academy of Management Perspectives* 28: 307–327.

Donsbach, W. 2006. The Identity of Communication Research. *Journal of Communication* 56: 437–448.

Fink, S. 2009. Strategische Kommunikation für Technologie und Innovationen—Konzeption und Umsetzung. In *Kommunikation als Erfolgsfaktor im Innovationsmanagement: Strategien im Zeitalter der Open Innovation*, ed. A. Zerfaß and K.M. Möslein, 209–226. Wiesbaden, Germany: Gabler.

Gambardella, A., and A.M. McGahan. 2010. Business Model Innovation: General Purpose Technologies and Their Implications for Industry Structure. *Long Range Planning* 43: 262–271.

Grunig, J.E. 1984. Organizations, Environments, and Models of Public Relations. *Public Relations Research & Educations* 1: 6–29.

Hargadon, A. 2015. How to Discover and Assess Opportunities for Business Model Innovation. *Strategy & Leadership* 43: 33–37.

Hübner, H. 2007. *The Communicating Company: Towards an Alternative Theory of Corporate Communication.* Heidelberg: Physica-Verlag.

Kohler, T. 2015. Crowdsourcing-based Business Models: How to Create and Capture Value. *California Management Review* 57: 63–84.

Magretta, J. 2002. Why Business Models Matter. *Harvard Business Review* 80: 86–93.

Markides, C. 2010. Creativity is Not Enough: How to Create New Market Space through Business Model Innovation. *IMP Perspectives* 2: 73–81.

Martilla, J.A. 1971. Word-Of-Mouth Communication in the Industrial Adoption Process. *Journal of Marketing Research* 8(2): 173–178.

Mazzarol, T. 2014. The Role of Social Capital, Strategic Networking and Word of Mouth Communication in the Commercialization. In *Strategy and Communication for Innovation*, ed. N. Pfeffermann, T. Minshall, and L. Mortara, 173–194. Berlin: Springer Publishing.

Mohr, J., S. Sengupta, and S. Slater. 2009. *Marketing of High-Technology Products and Innovations*, 3rd edn. Upper Saddle River, NJ: Pearson.

Nordfors, D. 2009. Innovation Journalism, Attention Work and the Innovation Economy: A Review of the Innovation Journalism Initiative 2003–2009. *Innovation Journalism* 6: 1–46.

Osterwalder, A., Y. Pingeur, G. Bernarda, A. Smith, and T. Papadakos. 2014. *Value Proposition Design: How to Create Products and Services Customers Want (Strategyzer).* Hoboken, NJ: John Wiley & Sons.

Osterwalder, A., and Y. Pingeur. 2010. *Business Model Generation: A Handbook for Visionaries, Game Changers, and Challengers.* Hoboken, NJ: John Wiley & Sons.

Oxtorp, L.A. 2014. Dynamic Managerial Capability of Technology-based International New Ventures—A Basis for Their Long-term Competitive Advantage. *Journal of International Entrepreneurship* 12: 389–420.

Peres, R., E. Muller, and V. Mahajan. 2010. Innovation Diffusion and New Product Growth Models: A Critical Review and Research Directions. *International Journal of Research in Marketing* 63: 849–855.

Perrault, T. 2016. Digital Companies Need More Liberal Arts Majors. *Harvard Business Review*, Blog. Accessed January 26, 2016. https://hbr.org/2016/01/digital-companies-need-more-liberal-arts-majors?utm_campaign=HBR&utm_source=facebook&utm_medium=social

Pfeffermann, N. 2014. Innovation Communication as an Integrative Management Capability in Digital Ecosystems. In *Strategy and Communication for Innovation*, ed. N. Pfeffermann, T. Minshall, and L. Mortara, 241–270. Berlin: Springer Publishing.

———. 2011. Innovation Communication as a Cross-functional Dynamic Capability: Strategies for Organizations and Networks. In *Strategies and Communications for Innovations*, ed. N. Pfeffermann and M. Hülsmann, 257–292. Berlin: Springer Publishing.

Rohlfs, J.H. 2001. *Bandwagon Effects in High-Technology Industries*. Cambridge, MA: MIT Press.

Sandberg, B. 2008. *Managing and Marketing Radical Innovations*. London: Routledge.

Sowter, C.V. 2000. *Marketing High Technology Services*. Aldershot: Gower.

Teece, D.J., G. Pisano, and A. Shuen. 1997. Dynamic Capabilities and Strategic Management. *Strategic Management Journal* 18: 509–533.

Teece, D.J. 2010. Business Model, Business Strategy, and Innovation. *Long Range Planning* 43: 172–194.

———. 2014. The Foundation of Enterprise Performance: Dynamic and Ordinary Capabilities in an (Economic) Theory of Firms. *The Academy of Management Perspectives* 28: 328–352.

Töhlke, J.M., E.J. Hultink, and H.S.J. Robben. 2001. Launching New Product Features: A Multiple Case Examination. *Journal of Product Innovation Management* 18: 3–14.

Tomochi, M., H. Murata, and M. Kono. 2005. A Consumer-based Model of Competitive Diffusion: The Multiplicative Effects of Global and Local Network Externalities. *Journal of Evolutionary Economics* 15: 273–295.

Trommsdorff, V., and F. Steinhoff. 2007. *Innovationsmarketing*. München: Franz Vahlen.

Steinhoff, F., and V. Trommsdorff. 2011. Innovation Marketing: An Introduction. In *Strategies and Communications for Innovations*, ed. N. Pfeffermann and M. Hülsmann, 105–116. Berlin: Springer Publishing.

van den Bulte, C., and S. Stremersch. 2004. Social Contagion and Income Heterogeneity in New Product Diffusion: A Meta-Analytic Test. *Marketing Science* 23: 530–544.

Van Riel, C., and C. Fombrun. 2008. *Essentials of Corporate Communication. Implementing Practices for Effective Reputation Management*. New York: Taylor and Francis.

Vanhaverbeke, W., and N. Roijakkers. 2014. Enriching Open Innovation Theory and Practice by Strengthening the Relationship with Strategic Thinking. In *Strategy and Communication for Innovation*, ed. N. Pfeffermann, T. Minshall, and L. Mortara, 15–26. Berlin: Springer Publishing.

Weiblen, T., and H.W. Chesbrough. 2015. Engaging with Startups to Enhance Corporate Innovation. *California Management Review* 57: 66–90.

Zerfaß, A. 2009. Kommunikation als konstitutives Element im Innovationsmanagement—Soziologische und kommunikationswissenschaftliche Grundlagen der Open Innovation. In *Kommunikation als Erfolgsfaktor im Innovationsmanagement: Strategien im Zeitalter der Open Innovation*, ed. A. Zerfaß and K.M. Möslein, 23–56. Wiesbaden, Germany: Gabler.

Zott, C., and R. Amit. 2007. Business Model Design and the Performance of Entrepreneurial Firms. *Organization Science* 18: 181–199.

———. 2008. The Fit between Product Market Strategy and Business Model: Implications for Firm Performance. *Strategic Management Journal* 29: 1–26.

8

Innovation in Family Firms: A Review of Prior Studies and a Framework for Future Research

Andrea Urbinati, Simone Franzò, Alfredo De Massis, and Federico Frattini

8.1   Introduction

The aim of this chapter is to provide an overview of the most recent and relevant studies in the growing body of research on innovation in family firms, constituting a ubiquitous form of governance around the world. Moreover, we develop a framework grounded in the search and recombination view of the innovation process with the aim of providing a possible direction to orient future research in this interesting field.

Theoretical and empirical research on innovation in family firms has grown in recent years in response to the significant gap in existing innovation theories and frameworks, that is, their inability to account properly for the effect of different corporate governance systems on innovation processes.

A. Urbinati (✉) • S. Franzò • F. Frattini
Politecnico di Milano, Milan, Italy

A. De Massis
Free University of Bozen-Bolano, Bolzano, Italy

Lancaster University, Lancaster, UK

© The Author(s) 2017   **213**
A. Brem, E. Viardot (eds.), *Revolution of Innovation Management*,
DOI 10.1057/978-1-349-95123-9_8

Corporate governance consists of incentives, monitoring and authority structures as well as norms of accountability that shape the policies and strategies used by firms to create long-term value for stakeholders (Carney 2005). Corporate governance is shown to be highly affected by ownership type and structure, typically examined together. Also generally acknowledged is that innovation is an important determinant of firm performance and long-term value creation (Blundell et al. 1999; Eisenhardt and Schoonhoven 1990; Senyard et al. 2011; Shepherd and Katz 2004; Van Beers et al. 2008; Zahra et al. 1999).

As a consequence, there is now a growing body of literature on how governance and ownership affect innovation. For example, researchers have studied how R&D intensity, an important determinant of innovation, is affected by ownership concentration (Baysinger et al. 1991; Hill and Snell 1989; Lee and O'Neil 2003), the holdings of large shareholders (Hosono et al. 2004), different types of ownership (Munari et al. 2010), the presence of a single large shareholder (Hall and Oriani 2006), and top management share ownership (Czarnitzki and Kraft 2004). Researchers have also examined the relationship between R&D intensity, the composition of the board of directors (Hoskisson et al. 2002) and top management compensation (Cho 1992).

However, empirical research on the link between corporate governance, ownership and innovation is largely focused on a single category of shareholders, namely institutional investors (David et al. 2001; Hoskisson et al. 2002; Zahra 1996), and principally on listed corporations. This literature largely ignores private firms and particularly the much more common family ownership and governance model.

Family ownership of business organizations is ubiquitous around the world and dominant in many countries (Schulze and Geidajlovic 2010; La Porta et al. 1999; Villalonga and Amit 2009). The influence of such firms is significant even in developed economies such as the USA. For example, Astrachan and Shanker (2003) estimate that family firms generate 89 % of total tax returns, 64 % of GDP and employ 62 % of the total workforce in the USA. Anderson and Reeb (2003) show that one third of S&P 500 firms are controlled by the founding family. Family firms make an important contribution to innovation, fostering growth in emerging economies in Asia, South America and beyond. Innovation in family firms also has wider policy implications as an avenue for governments to generate growth from recession.

Nonetheless, research on innovation in family firms is in its infancy (Wright and Kellermanns 2012) and has only recently received growing attention in both the family business and innovation perspective. Consequently, more research is desirable on this important sector of the global economy, especially as family firm innovation processes and outcomes are likely to differ from those in other governance and ownership archetypes due to the influence of family ownership on organizational goals (Chrisman et al. 2012; Zellweger et al. 2010), risk taking (Gómez-Mejía et al. 2007; Zahra 2005) and investment horizons (Lumpkin and Brigham 2011; Zellweger 2007).

The aim of this chapter is to provide an overview of the most recent and relevant studies in literature on innovation in family firms and develop a framework that can orient future research in this intriguing field at the intersection of innovation and family business literature.

8.2 Examples of How Family Firm Governance May Affect Innovation

This chapter is based on the notion that governance characteristics affect how innovation occurs and is managed. Specifically, we focus on a specific and ubiquitous governance form, namely, family firms. Family firms are defined as businesses '[. . .] governed and/or managed with the intention to shape and pursue the vision of the business held by a dominant coalition controlled by members of the same family or a small number of families in a manner that is potentially sustainable across generations of the family or families' (Chua et al. 1999).

In this section, we provide some examples of how family firm governance may affect different facets of the innovation process.

Innovation Development

Models predicting success and failure in product innovation do not consider whether critical success factors differ between family and non-family firms (Ernst 2002; Romano 1990). However, there are strong conceptual reasons to argue that family governance results in distinctive executive compensation, authority structures and monitoring mechanisms (Fama and Jensen 1983; Gedajlovic and Carney 2010; Gedajlovic et al. 2004; Jensen and Meckling 1976) that can create unique efficiency advantages and disadvantages that may significantly modify how the product innovation process is managed and organized.

Furthermore, family involvement in a firm could affect its willingness to engage in open and collaborative innovation (Grimpe and Kaiser 2010; Zhang and Baden-Fuller 2010; Lichtenthaler and Lichtenthaler 2009). Evidence indicates that in their pursuit of socio-emotional wealth, family firms develop strong concerns about the potential loss of control (Gómez-Mejía et al. 2007). Such concerns may complicate collaborative relationships with external partners when open innovation implies a restriction of the firm's control over the technological trajectory of their products (Almirall and Casadesus-Masanell 2010).

Therefore, the propensity to acquire and commercialize knowledge outside the firm's boundaries may well vary between family and non-family firms (Van De Vrande et al. 2009).

Inter-organizational Diffusion

Sociological models of innovation diffusion (Burt 1987; Van den Bulte and Lilien 2001; Robertson et al. 1996) point to information contagion and the bandwagon phenomenon as critical factors affecting innovation diffusion across a population of firms. Social capital theory (Adler and Kwon 2002; Hitt et al. 2002; Lin 2001) suggests that the nature of a family's social interactions and their emotional commitment to the firm may have a strong influence on the underlying mechanisms through which information and technological knowledge is diffused and adopted (Arregle et al. 2007; Sirmon and Hitt 2003).

Intra-organizational Diffusion

Similar arguments apply to the process through which an innovation is adopted in an organization (Damanpour and Gopalakrishnan 2001). There are reasons to think that the unique traits of the family firm's human and internal social capital (Adler and Kwon 2002; Hatch and Dyer 2004), such as higher motivation, cohesiveness and commitment, easier communication and information exchange, and closer relationships between individuals, may affect the modes, approaches and practices with which an innovation is disseminated throughout the organization (Arregle et al. 2007; Gedajlovic and Carney 2010; Habbershon et al. 2003; Sirmon and Hitt 2003; Tagiuri and Davis 1996). Similarly, autonomous motivation (Gagné and Deci 2005; Ryan and Deci 2000), collective orientation (Donaldson 1990; Zahra et al. 2008) and high levels of trust (Mayer et al. 1995; Schoorman et al. 2007) that are said to flourish in family firms are likely to have an impact on the process by which an innovation is adopted within an organization.

Disruptive Innovation

Theories and evidence on disruptive innovation suggest that incumbent firms very often fail to respond to disruptive changes in technology owing to resource dependency and a misperception of their potential value (Jenkins 2010; Christensen 1997). Whether family firms also suffer from the same biases has thus far received limited attention. Family firms are thought to be characterized by a long-term orientation (Dyer 2003; Zellweger 2007), resulting in less pressure for short-term performance (Dunn 1996), which capital markets instead impose on other governance and ownership archetypes (Gómez-Mejía et al. 2001; Zahra 2005). Consequently, family firms may have a greater propensity to invest in potentially disruptive technologies that may take years or even decades to produce tangible returns.

Furthermore, the unique organizational culture arising from the interaction between the family and the business system (Habbershon et al. 2003; Zahra et al. 2004) may positively affect managers' perceptions of resource adequacy (Hoegl et al. 2008) and consequently the way family firms adapt to changes in technology. In the capability-based view (Helfat 2007; Rothaermel and Hess 2007; Teece 2007; Verona and Ravasi 2004; Teece et al. 1997), family involvement in governance and ownership may affect a firm's dynamic capabilities. For example, family firms are less likely to use debt (Le Breton Miller and Miller 2006; Mishra and McConaughy 1999; Steijvers and Voordeckers 2009) or outside equity financing (Wu et al. 2007). Differences in financial structures and the parsimonious preservation of resources (Le Breton Miller and Miller 2006) limit their capacity to invest in potentially disruptive technological opportunities (Teece 2007).

Furthermore, the aversion to follow policies that would reduce the family's control of the firm and thus their socioemotional wealth (Gomez-Mejia et al. 2011; Gómez-Mejía et al. 2007) may reduce their willingness to make such investments. This suggests that family governance and ownership have idiosyncratic effects on how family firms respond to a disruptive change in technology, as recent theoretical studies suggest (for example, Duran et al. 2015).

Exploration vs. Exploitation and Organizational Ambidexterity

Innovation scholars propose several reasons why some firms are more effective innovators than others. Among the most popular models, ambidexterity theory (Jansen et al. 2012; Wilson and Doz 2011; Simsek et al. 2009) argues that a critical aspect is the ability to successfully combine and integrate heterogeneous capabilities (for example, exploration and exploitation, efficiency and adaptability) at the firm level. Extant research suggests that family involvement in ownership and governance may potentially affect the firm's willingness and ability to realize such an ambidextrous organization. For example, family firms are characterized by parsimony (Carney 2005), meaning that the use of family wealth ensures that resources will be used efficiently (Durand and Vargas 2003; Gedajlovic et al. 2004). Furthermore, family managers often act as stewards (Miller et al. 2008), perceiving the firm as an extension of themselves (Carney

2005) and the exploration of opportunities as an important means of corporate and personal growth. Consistently, Gedajlovic et al.'s (2011) study shows that the overlap of ownership and management, which is a common characteristic among family firms (Carney and Gedajlovic 2002), is positively associated with ambidexterity.

Dynamic Interaction Between Innovation and Family Firm Governance

Innovation is a process that often requires firms to acquire new or reconfigure existing competencies (Henderson and Clark 1990), overcome organizational inertia (Tushman and O'Reilly 1996) and reform the top management team (O'Reilly and Tushman 2004). This entails organization-wide change that can affect family involvement and the firm's governance structure. Family involvement can modify (and be influenced by) innovation, which leads us to believe that longitudinal studies are needed on how innovation may alter the nature of family firm governance (and vice versa), since this process is likely to follow idiosyncratic paths.

The examples illustrated above show that there are important theoretical reasons to believe that innovation in family firms follows different paths compared to other governance systems, especially those characterized by the presence of institutional investors and listed corporations, which are currently the main focus of existing innovation research.

This explains why theoretical and empirical research on innovation in family firms has grown exponentially in the last five years. This notwithstanding, our knowledge of the idiosyncratic characteristics of innovation in family firms is still limited and more efforts are needed to overcome the remaining gaps in our understanding. The next section summarizes the main topics addressed in extant research on innovation in family firms, focusing on the most recent and relevant studies published in academic journals.

8.3   A Review of Prior Studies on Innovation in Family Firms

An interesting framework to summarize existing research on innovation in family firms can be found in De Massis et al. (2013), who identify three key steps in technological innovation, namely: (i) innovation input; (ii) innovation activities; and (iii) innovation output.

Existing studies on innovation in family firms can be classified according to these three steps depending on whether they focus on analysing the impact of family governance on the inputs of the innovation process, how innovation takes place and is managed, the results of the innovation process and firm level of innovative performance.

Studies on the Effect of Family Governance on Innovation Input

This category of studies is the most populated and is characterized by findings that are consistent in showing that family firms invest less in R&D than non-family businesses.

According to Block (2012), for example, family ownership is negatively associated with the level of R&D intensity due to less risky and more conservative strategies compared to the strategic practices adopted by non-family firms. However, Block (2012) points out the importance of distinguishing between family ownership and lone founder ownership in family firms. In this case, Block underlines the inappropriateness of classifying these two types of ownership into the same family business category due to their differences in financial performance and growth strategies. In particular, family firms invest not only less in R&D than non-family firms, but also less than lone founder firms. The latter instead are found to be associated with positive levels of R&D investments and productivity despite being hostile to change and following conservative strategies that limit future growth once they turn into family businesses.

Another interesting study is Chrisman and Patel's (2012), showing that the variability of R&D investments in family firms is greater compared to non-family businesses due to differences in the alignment of long- and short-term family goals with their economic goals. However, when family goals and economic goals tend to converge (and this is typically the case when firm performance levels are below the family's aspirations), the variability of R&D investments tends to decrease, despite the long-term orientation of the family business.

In a similar vein, Asaba (2013) shows that family firms tend to invest more than non-family firms in R&D when agency conflicts are reduced but also when the owners' risk preferences and environmental uncertainty are controlled. In this case, the nature of investments, either aggressive or patient, depends not only on the ownership structure, but also on being a family entity and family owners' own priorities and risk preferences.

A recent study by Kotlar et al. (2014a) uses reference point theory to provide a novel and more detailed understanding of the R&D investment decisions of family firms. Based on a longitudinal analysis of data from Spanish manufacturing firms, this paper shows that beyond those related to profitability goals, other reference points are relevant in explaining family firm decisions regarding R&D investments. In particular, the authors argue that family firm managers use reference points related to supplier bargaining power and employ these to infer the external barriers they will face to exert their managerial discretion and, consequently, adjust their R&D investment behaviour. Moreover, the authors find that profitability goals and those related to control follow a sequential logic whereby managers in family firms react more emphatically to an increase in the bargaining power of their suppliers when profitability targets have been achieved.

Similarly, Kotlar et al. (2014a) underline that family involvement has relevant effects on the strategic actions pursued by family firm managers. In particular, the authors point out that family involvement in the business influences the organizational decision-making mechanisms underlying the levels of R&D intensity. The role of family involvement is to positively balance unabsorbed slack resources that exert a negative influence on strategic risk-taking as well as internal performance hazards that positively affect strategic risk taking. In this way, they emphasize that family goals affect strategic and innovation activities, and that factors such as strategic inputs and outputs, competition and feedback information drive the heterogeneity of strategic behaviours in family firms.

Moreover, Sciascia et al. (2014) find that in SMEs the relationship between family ownership and R&D intensity is contingent on the way the family invests its wealth. They show that family ownership is a negative correlate of R&D intensity when family wealth and firm equity overlap is high, implying that the more a family controls firm ownership, the less the SME is inclined to invest in R&D. In this case, family owners are more inclined to protect their socio-emotional wealth. Conversely, if the portion of family wealth invested in the firm is low or firm equity is a small part of total family wealth, cautious behaviours are replaced by a more risk-taking attitude, resulting in higher R&D expenditure.

More recently, Duran et al. (2015) underline that the innovation activity of a family firm is affected by the level of input invested in R&D and innovation. In particular, their meta-analysis suggests that family firms have lower innovation inputs than non-family firms mainly due to their sensitivity to uncertainty and the non-financial desire to retain control. In this case, the strength of non-financial goals and high risk-aversion outclass the financial objectives, and the power position of family firm owners allows them to maintain these preferences.

To summarize, existing research is consistent in finding that family firms invest less in R&D and innovation compared to their non-family counterparts, and this is due to their lower risk-taking propensity and the non-financial desire of family firm owners to retain control. Moreover, the variability of R&D investments in family firms is greater than in non-family businesses and depends on a broad number of contingency factors.

Studies on the Effect of Family Governance on Innovation Activities

Studies on how innovation occurs in family firms and how such activities should be managed in these types of businesses are scarce. This constitutes a serious gap in our understanding, especially in terms of managerial implications and good practices. Innovation managers working in family businesses and policymakers interested in understanding which initiatives are more effective in supporting innovation in family firms are not provided with clear indications and guidelines, since the existing pre-scriptions developed in traditional innovation research do not seem to apply to this particular governance archetype. The few existing studies in this category are reviewed in this section.

Through a multiple case study, De Massis et al. (2015) analyse how and why the anatomy of the product innovation process differs between family and non-family firms. This analysis shows that due to their distinctive characteristics, family businesses differ in their product inno-vation strategies and innovation process organization. For instance, family firms are found to use a functional organization to support the product development process, with high levels of decisional autonomy granted to project leaders. Throughout this process, they rely on a higher number of collaborations with universities and public research centres, while the organizational climate is largely informal and unstructured. Conversely, non-family firms predominantly establish cross-functional teams to carry out these projects, with limited delegation of decisional authority to project leaders and a highly structured and formalized organizational climate. The authors show that the reasons underlying these dissimilarities between family and non-family firms depend on the family firms' resources, authority structures, incentives, orientations and behavioural attitudes.

Kotlar et al. (2013), through an empirical analysis of Spanish manufacturing firms, study whether and why family firms engage more in inbound, open innovation activities compared to their non-family counterparts. The authors find that, independently of the governance archetype characterizing the focal firm, the latter is more likely to acquire technology from external sources through R&D contracting when firm performance falls below the aspiration level. In addition, family firms are found to be more reluctant to acquire external technologies than non-family firms, and the influence of negative aspiration performance gaps becomes less relevant. This effect is attributed to family firm man-agers' attempts to avoid losing control over the trajectory that technolo-gies follow over time. However, this general tendency is mitigated by an important factor, technology protection. Indeed, family firms become more favourable towards inbound open innovation when patents on proprietary technologies increase the managers' perceptions of control over the technology trajectory.

In a recent paper, through a multiple case study involving six small- and medium-sized family firms, De Massis et al. (2016b) investigated the design decisions that fit with family and business approaches to create high-performing, new product development programmes. The empirical analysis suggests that some effective design principles in family firms (concerning team composition, leadership of product development programmes and incentives for project leaders) differ from well-established, customary approaches that can be found in existing product development literature. This research therefore suggests that the particular characteristics of family governance require ad hoc management models for innovation management in family firms.

To summarize, these studies point to the existence of idiosyncratic characteristics of innovation processes in family firms and, as a result, to the need for specific management models for innovation in family businesses. However, there is still much work to be done to identify these good management models and this represents the most promising avenue for research in this field.

Studies on the Effect of Family Governance on Innovation Output

This category of studies comprises a good number of papers, which are however contentious with respect to the effect of family governance on the level of firm innovativeness.

Some scholars find that family governance negatively influences innovativeness. For instance, Chin et al. (2009) show that the tight control characterizing the ownership structure of family firms inhibits their innovativeness. At the same time, Czarnitzki and Kraft (2009) find that companies with broadly distributed capital shares are more innovative, that is, they file more patents compared to companies with other capital structures, such as family firms.

On the other hand, Gudmundson et al. (2003) find that family ownership is positively associated with the ability to introduce new products and services. Similarly, Llach and Nordqvist (2010) suggest that family firms are characterized by greater innovativeness due to their human, social and marketing capital. In a similar vein, Westhead (1997) shows that family firms are able to offer a broader range of product and service innovations than non-family firms in their search for superior competitive advantage.

Other scholars argue that a set of distinctive family firm traits, such as formalization, resource dependence, political resistance, emotional ties to existing assets and a rigid mental model, affect their propensity to respond to discontinuous technological changes (König et al. 2013). In this case, the authors suggest that family governance leads family firms to adopt discontinuous technology later than non-family firms, but at the same time implement the adoption decision more rapidly once taken. In a similar vein, Chrisman et al. (2014b) advance this discussion and explain that the heterogeneity of family business goals (Kotlar and De Massis 2013), governance structures, resources and idiosyncratic situational factors can affect strategic innovation decisions such as the adoption of discontinuous technologies.

Finally, Duran et al.'s (2015) recent meta-analysis suggests that family firms are characterized by a greater ability to transform innovation inputs into innovation outputs. This is due to the non-financial goals of family firms, which are likely to entail high levels of tacit knowledge among employees and the existence of systems and processes capable of efficiently transforming innovation input into innovation output over time.

To conclude, the direction of the impact of family governance on innovation output remains an open question in existing research. However, a very promising avenue for future inquiry is not so much in ascertaining whether family firms are more or less innovative than non-family business, but searching for the management approaches and endogenous factors that enable increasing the innovation output of family firms.

Paradoxical Effects in Innovation in Family Firms

Recently, theoretical and empirical research has pointed to the existence of paradoxical effects characterizing innovation in family firms. In particular, Chrisman et al. (2014a) use ability and willingness as two concepts that enable understanding innovation behaviour in family firms. Ability can be defined as '[. . .] the discretion of the family to direct, allocate, add to, or dispose of a firm's resources' (De Massis et al. 2014: 345). Willingness is instead the '[. . .] favourable disposition of the involved family to engage in distinctive behaviour' (De Massis et al. 2014: 346). These authors argue that family firms are often characterized by a greater ability—in comparison to their non-family counterparts—to pursue innovation due to owning key family assets such as internal and external social capital. This notwithstanding, they do not produce proportionally higher innovation output since they are less willing to innovate, which is a result of their risk aversion and parsimony in deploying existing resources for the achievement of uncertain results, as innovation typically entails.

This paradoxical effect is echoed in a recent meta-analysis on innovation in family firms published by Duran et al. (2015). According to their approach, fostering innovation in family firms requires identifying those management models that allow resolving this innovation paradox.

In a recent paper, De Massis et al. (2015) propose an integrated, contingency perspective on family firm innovation called Family-Driven Innovation (FDI). The authors argue that overcoming the innovation paradox and unleashing the innovation potential in family firms requires consistency between the innovation decisions and approaches that a family firm adopts and the idiosyncratic characteristics of the family firm itself. In particular, FDI is a matter of achieving a good fit among the key drivers of heterogeneity of family firms (mapped along three variables, namely, willingness, ability as discretion and ability as resources) and the factors capturing the heterogeneity of innovation decisions (also mapped along three main variables, namely, locus of innovation search, approaches used to manage the innovation process and type of innovation in which the firm invests). Good strategies and innovation management models in family firms should be designed in a way that ensures a close fit between these dimensions of heterogeneity. Only in so doing will FDI be realized and enable the greater innovation ability of family firms to be translated into superior innovation output.

8.4 A Research Framework for Future Research on Innovation in Family Firms

Based on the results of the analysis summarized in the previous sections, in the remainder of this chapter we develop a research framework designed to address the main gaps in existing knowledge on innovation in family firms and thereby inform future research in the field. The framework adopts a search and recombination conceptualization of the innovation process (Savino et al. 2015) and is accordingly conceived as a set of activities aimed at searching, identifying, integrating and recombining knowledge from different sources to generate and commercialize new products, services or business models.

In particular, the framework focuses on four sources from which family firms can and should draw knowledge resources to foster their innovation process, which are: (i) internal R&D; (ii) tradition and past history; (iii) clients/suppliers/competitors; and (iv) universities/research centres.

The focus on these sources rests on the growing importance that these have acquired in recent years in innovation processes, as shown in existing research.

The framework is intended to inform future research aimed at unearthing the good management models that allow family firms to successfully tap into these resources and use them to innovate successfully. To identify these good management models, the framework adopts a dynamic capabilities perspective (Teece et al. 1997) and thus suggests searching for those identifiable strategic and organizational processes that allow family firms to turn knowledge resources deriving from internal and external sources into successful new products, services and business models. The good management models will therefore be internally consistent sets of dynamic capabilities conducive to superior innovation outputs.

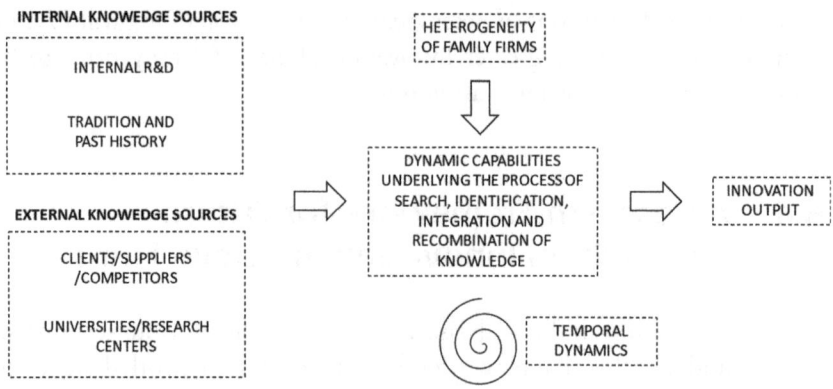

Fig. 8.1 Research framework

Consistent with recent research on family firms (De Massis et al. 2014), this framework argues that dynamic capabilities leading to superior innovation output will be highly dependent on the specific characteristics of family firms and therefore accounting for their heterogeneity.

Figure 8.1 illustrates this framework and a description of each of its building blocks follows thereafter.

Innovation Output

Innovation output is the main dependent variable in the research framework and captures the extent to which the innovation process in a family firm produces higher or lower outcomes (De Massis et al. 2012). As previously explained in this chapter, existing research has long investigated whether family firms are characterized by higher or lower innovation output compared with non-family firms, but the findings of these studies are largely inconsistent.

More importantly, the vast majority of this research aims to understand whether and why innovation output in family firms is superior or inferior to that of non-family businesses, but does not study which dynamic capabilities influence the level of output of the innovation process in family firms. This is instead the aim of our proposed framework, conceptualizing and measuring innovation outputs in family firms along the different dimensions suggested in existing research including: (i) number and quality of patents; (ii) number and quality of new products, services and business models commercialized; (iii) percentage of sales from new products, services and business models commercialized in the last three or five years; and (v) the success rate of innovation projects.

Heterogeneity of Family Firms

An important assumption in most studies on family firm innovation is that family businesses should be conceived as homogeneous entities compared to non-family firms (De Massis et al. 2014). More recently, family business scholars have started to recognize that family firms are instead very heterogeneous and—significantly—should be compared with each other (García-Álvarez and López-Sintas 2001; Melin and Nordqvist 2007; Sharma and Nordqvist 2008; Westhead and Howorth 2007).

Our framework follows this recent trend in family business research and considers heterogeneity as a critical factor to more fully understand innovation in family firms. In particular, heterogeneity is conceived as a factor that influences dynamic capabilities leading to superior innovation outputs in family firms. By following the recent contribution by De Massis et al. (2014), we suggest that willingness and ability are two critical factors to differentiate different types of family firms. The behaviour of a family firm will differ according to the levels of ability and willingness that characterize it.

Therefore, our framework suggests focusing on the measurable factors that affect the willingness and ability of a family firm, such as the strength of family involvement, the types of organizational goals pursued, its age and the number of generations involved. Our assumption is that the dynamic capabilities that influence the output of the innovation process in family firms will vary according to these factors.

Dynamic Capabilities Underlying the Innovation Process

Innovation is the successful implementation of creative ideas for new products, services or business models (Amabile 1988). According to the well-established search and recombination conceptualization (Savino et al. 2015), the innovation process comprises the activities through which a firm searches, identifies, integrates and recombines knowledge from different sources to generate and commercialize new products, services or business models.

To determine the factors that explain why this process leads to higher or lower innovation outputs, we suggest adopting the dynamic capabilities perspective (Teece et al. 1997). The traditional Resource-Based View (RBV) argues that success in innovation stems from scarce, difficult-to-imitate knowledge resources that a firm accesses from different internal and external sources (Wernerfelt 1984). However, more recently, scholars have recognized that resources alone are not sufficient to explain innovation success (Ray et al. 2004). A firm may have access to knowledge pools that could potentially lead to superior innovation output, but may lack the ability to embark on the efforts needed to realize this potential. This notion is captured by the dynamic capabilities framework (Teece et al. 1997), which proposes that success in innovation stems not only from ownership or access to valuable knowledge assets, but from how managers configured these (Cavusgil et al. 2007). We define dynamic capabilities as a set of specific and identifiable strategic and organizational processes through which firms search, identify, integrate and recombine knowledge from different sources to generate and commercialize new products, services and business models (Eisenhardt and Martin 2000).

Through our framework, we aim to unearth the dynamic capabilities through which different types of knowledge resources are transformed into superior innovation output in family firms with different characteristics. The internally consistent sets of dynamic capabilities identified through this analysis will represent the good management models for innovation in family firms. By identifying these, we offer a tangible contribution to current understanding of innovation in family firms and to the quest for practical suggestions that innovation managers working in family firm can follow to increase the competitive advantage of their organizations.

Internal R&D

Investments in internal R&D activities represent the most important source of knowledge resources that foster the innovation process (Chiesa 2001). As previously mentioned, existing research has long studied whether family firms invest more or less in internal R&D compared to non-family businesses (De Massis et al. 2012). The findings of these studies are largely consistent and suggest that a negative relationship exists between family involvement and R&D investments (Block 2012; Chen and Hsu 2009). These findings may be due to the fact that family involvement discourages uncertain and long-term R&D investments, but also because family firm R&D projects tend towards higher productivity and therefore require lower R&D expenditure compared to firms with no family involvement. The latter interpretation seems to be supported by recent research (Duran et al. 2015).

However, with only a few exceptions (see, for example, De Massis et al. 2015), we know very little about how family firms should manage internal R&D projects if wanting to improve their innovation performance. The aim of our framework is to encourage research aimed at identifying the dynamic capabilities that allow family firms to use knowledge generated through internal R&D activities successfully for innovation purposes according to the characteristics of these firms.

Tradition and Past History

Searching for knowledge over time describes the process through which firms 'search for and access knowledge created at different points in the past' to produce innovation outputs (Katila 2002: 995). There are several potential benefits to using temporally distant knowledge, including increased reliability, decreased risk of retaliation and incorrect applications, uniqueness and legitimacy of innovations (Hargadon and Douglas 2001; Nerkar 2003). Temporal search is closely intertwined with the concept of tradition, which refers to the stock of knowledge, competencies, materials, manufacturing processes, signs, values and beliefs pertaining to the firm's past and its territory (Messeni Petruzzelli and Albino 2012).

Tradition can be conceived as a distinct and unique resource, since its sticky and embedded nature renders its imitation more difficult.

Accordingly, scholars have recently pointed to the importance of—for innovative firms and especially family firms—developing appropriate dynamic capabilities that allow firms to leverage tradition and use it for innovation purposes (De Massis et al. 2016a). This would allow them to create and commercialize new products, services and business models, offer new functionalities and meanings, and, by doing so, create and nurture competitive advantage. Through our framework, we suggest that scholars should search for the dynamic capabilities that enable family firms with different characteristics to tap successfully into their tradition and past history.

Clients/Suppliers/Competitors

Accessing knowledge for innovating through collaborating with clients, suppliers and competitors (Laursen and Salter 2006; Pittaway et al. 2004) is essential to the innovation performance of both SMEs and large enterprises (Nieto and Santamaría 2010; Pittaway et al. 2004). Firms search for knowledge beyond their boundaries primarily with the aim of increasing their knowledge base and accessing complementary resources that can be integrated and recombined to produce successful innovations (Classen et al. 2012). There are different ways of tapping into this source of knowledge (Dahlander and Gann 2010; Greer and Lei 2012; West and Bogers 2014). Literature shows that there is strong variation in the impact that collaborating with clients, suppliers and competitors has on innovation output. There are several reasons for this heterogeneity, ranging from the differences in the level of search breadth and depth that characterize the external knowledge sourcing process (Ferreras-Méndez et al. 2015; Laursen and Salter 2006) to the organizational forms—such as informal vs. formal modes of collaborations—through which external knowledge is accessed (Gesing et al. 2015) and the definition of alliance portfolio strategies (Faems et al. 2008). How family firms access external knowledge through different forms of collaboration is thus far a very under-researched topic (Kotlar et al. 2014a). By applying our framework, scholars are encouraged to try to fill this gap by studying the dynamic capabilities that allow family firms with different characteristics to search, identify, integrate and recombine knowledge from clients, suppliers and competitors to innovate successfully.

Universities/Research Centres

A vast body of research highlights the importance of university-industry collaborations to foster knowledge transfer and ultimately enhance innovation outputs and firm competitiveness (Perkmann et al. 2013). Firms engage universities and public research centres via Intellectual Property (IP)–based activities, such as patenting, licencing and spin-outs, as well as through non-IP–based efforts, such as collaborative research, contract research, consulting and informal relationships (Fini et al. 2010). All this notwithstanding, the vast majority of studies have so far adopted the university/public research centre perspective, highlighting the individual and organizational-level benefits of engaging in university–industry collaborations, such as an increase in scientific productivity (Toole and Czarnitzki 2010), a boost in patenting activity (Cirillo et al. 2013) and an improved ability to generate new knowledge (Lavie and Drori 2012). On the other hand, the few studies adopting an industry perspective show that firms engaging universities obtain guidance on technology development (Pertuzé et al. 2010), enhancing their market (Santoro and Betts 2002) and innovative performance (Agrawal 2006). Conversely, literature for the most part remains silent on the management models that allow firms to make the most of knowledge generated in universities and research centres, while how these management models work in family firms constitutes a vast research gap. Our proposed framework aims to fill this gap by encouraging more theoretical and empirical research into the dynamic capabilities that allow family firms to engage universities and research centres successfully for innovation purposes and how these capabilities change depending on the idiosyncratic characteristics of a specific family firm.

Temporal Dynamics

A further interesting notion that our framework captures is the temporal evolution of dynamic capabilities underlying innovation in family firms. This is a critical aspect to be considered in future theoretical and empirical research, as many scholars have emphasized the time-variant nature of family firms and the importance of adopting a temporal perspective to understand family business behaviour (Gagné et al. 2014; Sharma et al. 2014).

To the best of our knowledge, no study has investigated how innovation in family businesses changes and evolves over time. However, an interesting paper by De Massis et al. (2014a) shows that firm proactiveness, which is closely related to innovation, changes over time in family firms following a horizontal-S pattern. This temporal evolution is due to time-variant family dynamics in terms of goal alignment, trust, altruism and interpersonal contract.

Moreover, Kotlar and De Massis (2013) show that goal diversity is more pronounced when an intra-family succession is imminent. Intra-family succession unfreezes the previously stabilized organizational goals, leading individuals to express their goals more fervently and activate social interactions that lead to new stabilizations, similar to the classic description of disruptive change as freezing-transition-unfreezing. Thus, intra-family succession would act as catalyst of revolutionary change and innovation.

These studies point to the importance of adopting a dynamic perspective when studying the dynamic capabilities underlying the search and recombination of knowledge deriving from different internal and external sources, as these capabilities are very likely to change over time in family firms and when some distinct events (such as trans-generational success) occur in these businesses.

8.5   Conclusions

This chapter offers an overview of the most recent theoretical and empirical studies on innovation in family firms. This overview shows that although much has been written on this topic, especially on the impact of family governance on the level of R&D investments and innovativeness of family businesses, an important gap continues to exist in relation to the management models that should be applied in this ubiquitous form of organization.

Starting from this premise, in this chapter we developed a research framework grounded in the search and recombination conceptualization of the innovation process that can ideally inform future research aimed at filling this gap. In particular, we argue that scholars should attempt to identify the dynamic capabilities that allow family firms to search, identify, integrate and recombine knowledge from four different sources (internal R&D, tradition and past history, clients/suppliers/competitors and universities/research centres) for innovation purposes. We also argue that these dynamic capabilities will be strongly dependent on the particular characteristics of each family firm and their development is likely to be time-dependent and affected by some important events that typically occur during the lifecycle of a family business, such as trans-generational succession.

We believe that, through a careful operationalization of this research framework and the empirical studies designed to test it, scholars will be able to strongly improve our understanding of innovation in family firms and in particular unearth a set of good practices and viable approaches that will help family businesses innovate more successfully and, as a result, improve their ability to grow and compete on international markets.

References

Adler, P.S., and S.W. Kwon. 2002. Social Capital: Prospects for a New Concept. *Academy of Management Review* 27(1): 17–40.

Agrawal, A. 2006. Engaging the Inventor: Exploring Licensing Strategies for University Inventions and the Role of Latent Knowledge. *Strategic Management Journal* 27(1): 63–79.

Almirall, E., and R. Casadesus-Masanell. 2010. Open versus Closed Innovation: A Model of Discovery and Divergence. *Academy of Management Review* 35(1): 27–47.

Amabile, T.M. 1988. A Model of Creativity and Innovation in Organizations. *Research in Organizational Behavior* 10: 123–167.

Anderson, R.C., and D.M. Reeb. 2003. Founding-family Ownership and Firm Performance: Evidence from the S&P 500. *The Journal of Finance* 58(3): 1301–1328.

Arregle, J.L., M.A. Hitt, D.G. Sirmon, and P. Very. 2007. The Development of Organizational Social Capital: Attributes of Family Firms. *Journal of Management Studies* 44(1): 73–95.

Asaba, S. 2013. Patient Investment of Family Firms in the Japanese Electric Machinery Industry. *Asia Pacific Journal of Management* 30(3): 697–715.

Astrachan, J.H., and M.C. Shanker. 2003. 'Family Businesses' Contribution to the US Economy: A Closer Look. *Family Business Review* 16(3): 211–219.

Baysinger, B.D., R.D. Kosnik, and T.A. Turk. 1991. Effects of Board and Ownership Structure on Corporate R&D Strategy. *The Academy of Management Journal* 34: 205–214.

Block, J.H. 2012. R&D Investments in Family and Founder Firms: An Agency Perspective. *Journal of Business Venturing* 27(2): 248–265.

Blundell, R., R. Griffiths, and J. Van Reenen. 1999. Market Share, Market Value and Innovation in a Panel of British Manufacturing Firms. *Review of Economic Studies* 66: 529–554.

Burt, R.S. 1987. Social Contagion and Innovation: Cohesion Versus Structural Equivalence. *American Journal of Sociology* 92(6): 1287–1335.

Carney, M. 2005. Corporate Governance and Competitive Advantage in Family-Controlled Firms. *Entrepreneurship Theory and Practice* 29(3): 249–265.

Carney, M., and E. Gedajlovic. 2002. The Coupling of Ownership and Control and the Allocation of Financial Resources: Evidence from Hong Kong. *Journal of Management Studies* 39(1): 123–146.

Cavusgil, E., M.B. Talay, and S.H. Seggie. 2007. Dynamic Capabilities View: Foundations and Research Agenda. *Journal of Marketing Theory and Practice* 15(2): 159–166.

Chen, H.L., and W.T. Hsu. 2009. Family Ownership, Board Independence, and R&D Investment. *Family Business Review* 22(4): 347–362.

Chiesa, V. 2001. *R&D Strategy and Organisation: Managing Technological Change in Dynamic Contexts*. London: Imperial College Press.

Chin, C.L., Y.J. Chen, G. Kleinman, and P. Lee. 2009. Corporate Ownership Structure and Innovation: Evidence from Taiwan's Electronics Industry. *Journal of Accounting Auditing Finance* 24(1): 145–175.

Cho, S. 1992. Agency Costs, Management Stockholding, and Research and Development Expenditures. *Seoul Journal of Economics* 5(2): 127–152.

Chrisman, J.J., J.H. Chua, A. De Massis, F. Frattini, and M. Wright. 2014a. The Ability and Willingness Paradox in Family Firm Innovation. *Journal of Product Innovation Management* 32(3): 310–318.

Chrisman, J.J., J.H. Chua, A.W. Pearson, and T. Barnett. 2012. Family Involvement, Family Influence, and Family-centered Non-economic Goals in Small Firms. *Entrepreneurship Theory and Practice* 36(2): 267–293.

Chrisman, J.J., H. Fang, J. Kotlar, and A. De Massis. 2014b. A Note on Family Influence and the Adoption of Discontinuous Technologies in Family Firms. *Journal of Product Innovation Management* 32(3): 384–388.

Chrisman, J.J., and P.C. Patel. 2012. Variations in R&D Investments of Family and Nonfamily Firms: Behavioral Agency and Myopic Loss Aversion Perspectives. *Academy of Management Journal* 55(4): 976–997.

Christensen, C.M. 1997. *The Innovator's Dilemma: When New Technologies Cause Great Firms to Fail.* Boston, MA: Harvard Business School Press.

Chua, J.H., J.J. Chrisman, and P. Sharma. 1999. Defining the Family Business by Behavior. *Entrepreneurship Theory and Practice* 23(4): 19–39.

Cirillo, B., S. Brusoni, and G. Valentini. 2013. The Rejuvenation of Inventors Through Corporate Spinouts. *Organization Science* 25(6): 1764–1784.

Classen, N., A. van Gils, Y. Bammens, and M. Carree. 2012. Accessing Resources from Innovation Partners: The Search Breadth of Family SMEs. *Journal of Small Business Management* 50(2): 191–215.

Czarnitzki, D., and K. Kraft. 2004. Management Control and Innovative Activity. *Review of Industrial Organization* 24(1): 1–24.

———. 2009. Capital Control, Debt Financing and Innovative Activity. *Journal of Economic Behavior & Organization* 71(2): 372–383.

Dahlander, L., and D.M. Gann. 2010. How Open is Innovation? *Research Policy* 39(6): 699–709.

Damanpour, F., and S. Gopalakrishnan. 2001. The Dynamics of the Adoption of Product and Process Innovations in Organizations. *Journal of Management Studies* 38(1): 45–65.

David, P., M.A. Hitt, and J. Gimeno. 2001. The Influence of Activism by Institutional Investors on R&D. *Academy of Management Journal* 44(1): 144–157.

De Massis, A., A. Di Minin, and F. Frattini. 2015. Family-Driven Innovation: Resolving the Paradox in Family Firms. *California Management Review* 58(1): 5–19.

De Massis, A., F. Frattini, J. Kotlar, A. Messeni Petruzzelli, and M. Wright. 2016a. Innovation Through Tradition: Lessons From Innovative Family Businesses and Directions For Future Research. *Academy of Management Perspectives*, in press. doi: 10.5465/amp.2015.0017.

De Massis, A., F. Frattini, and U. Lichtenthaler. 2012. Research on Technological Innovation in Family Firms: Present Debates and Future Directions. *Family Business Review* 26(1): 10–31.

De Massis, A., F. Frattini, E. Pizzurno, and L. Cassia. 2013. Product Innovation in Family vs Non-Family Firms: An Exploratory Analysis. *Journal of Small Business Management* 51(1): 1–39.

De Massis, A., J. Kotlar, J. Chua, and J.J. Chrisman. 2014. Ability and Willingness as Sufficiency Conditions for Family-oriented Particularistic Behavior: Implications for Theory and Empirical Studies. *Journal of Small Business Management* 52(2): 344–364.

De Massis, A., J. Kotlar, F. Frattini, J.J. Chrisman and M. Nordqvist. (2016b). Family Governance at Work: Organizing for New Product Development in Family SMEs. *Family Business Review*, in press. doi: 10.1177/0894486515622722.

Donaldson, L. 1990. The Ethereal Hand: Organizational Economics and Management Theory. *Academy of Management Review* 15(3): 369–381.

Dunn, B. 1996. Family Enterprises in the UK: A Special Sector? *Family Business Review* 9(2): 139–155.

Duran, P., N. Kammerlander, M. van Essen, and T. Zellweger. 2015. Doing More with Less: Innovation Input and Output in Family Firms. *Academy of Management Journal*, forthcoming.

Durand, R., and V. Vargas. 2003. Ownership, Organization, and Private Firms Efficient Use of Resources. *Strategic Management Journal* 24(7): 667–675.

Dyer, W.G. 2003. The Family: The Missing Variable in Organizational Research. *Entrepreneurship Theory and Practice* 27(4): 401–416.

Eisenhardt, K.M., and J.A. Martin. 2000. Dynamic capabilities: What are they? *Strategic Management Journal* 21(10/11): 1105–1121.

Eisenhardt, K.M., and C.B. Schoonhoven. 1990. Organizational growth: Linking Founding Team, Strategy, Environment, and Growth among US Semiconductor Ventures 1978–1988. *Administrative Science Quarterly* 35(3): 504–529.

Ernst, H. 2002. Success Factors of New Product Development: A Review of the Empirical Literature. *International Journal of Management Reviews* 4(1): 1–40.

Faems, D., M. Janssens, A. Madhok, and B. Van Looy. 2008. Toward an Integrative Perspective on Alliance Governance: Connecting Contract Design, Trust Dynamics, and Contract Application. *Academy of Management Journal* 51(6): 1053–1078.

Fama, E.F., and M.C. Jensen. 1983. Separation of Ownership and Control. *Journal of law and Economics* 26(2): 301–325.

Ferreras-Méndez, J.L., S. Newell, A. Fernández-Mesa, and J. Alegre. 2015. Depth and Breadth of External Knowledge Search and Performance: The Mediating Role of Absorptive Capacity. *Industrial Marketing Management* 47: 86–97.

Fini, R., N. Lacetera, and S. Shane. 2010. Inside or Outside the IP System? Business Creation in Academia. *Research Policy* 39(8): 1060–1069.

Gagné, M., and E.L. Deci. 2005. Self Determination Theory and Work Motivation. *Journal of Organizational Behavior* 26(4): 331–362.

Gagné, M., P. Sharma, and A. De Massis. 2014. The Study of Organizational Behavior in Family Business. *European Journal of Work and Organizational Psychology* 23(5): 643–656.

García-Álvarez, E., and J. López-Sintas. 2001. A Taxonomy of Founders Based on Values: The Root of Family Business Heterogeneity. *Family Business Review* 14(3): 209–230.

Gedajlovic, E., and M. Carney. 2010. Markets, Hierarchies, and Families: Toward a Transaction Cost Theory of the Family Firm. *Entrepreneurship Theory and Practice* 34(6): 1145–1172.

Gedajlovic, E., Q. Cao, and H. Zhang. 2011. Corporate Shareholdings and Organizational Ambidexterity in High-tech SMEs: Evidence from a Transitional Economy. *Journal of Business Venturing* 27(6): 652–665.

Gedajlovic, E., M.H. Lubatkin, and W.S. Schulze. 2004. Crossing the Threshold from Founder Management to Professional Management: A Governance Perspective. *Journal of Management Studies* 41(5): 899–912.

Gesing, J., D. Antons, E.P. Piening, M. Rese, and T.O. Salge. 2015. Joining Forces or Going It Alone? On the Interplay among External Collaboration Partner Types, Interfirm Governance Modes, and Internal R&D. *Journal of Product Innovation Management* 32(3): 424–440.

Gomez-Mejia, L.R., C. Cruz, P. Berrone, and J. De Castro. 2011. The Bind That Ties: Socioemotional Wealth Preservation in Family Firms. *The Academy of Management Annals* 5(1): 653–707.

Gómez-Mejía, L.R., K.T. Haynes, M. Núñez-Nickel, K.J.L. Jacobson, and J. Moyano-Fuentes. 2007. Socioemotional Wealth and Business Risks in Family-controlled Firms: Evidence from Spanish Olive Oil Mills. *Administrative Science Quarterly* 52(1): 106–137.

Gómez-Mejía, L.R., M. Nunez-Nickel, and I. Gutierrez. 2001. The Role of Family Ties in Agency Contracts. *Academy of Management Journal* 44(1): 81–95.

Greer, C.R., and D. Lei. 2012. Collaborative Innovation with Customers: A Review of the Literature and Suggestions for Future Research. *International Journal of Management Reviews* 14(1): 63–84.

Grimpe, C., and U. Kaiser. 2010. Balancing Internal and External Knowledge Acquisition: The Gains and Pains from R&D Outsourcing. *Journal of Management Studies* 47(8): 1483–1509.

Gudmundson, D., C.B. Tower, and E.A. Hartman. 2003. Innovation and Small Business: Culture and Ownership Structure Do Matter. *Journal of Developmental Entrepreneurship* 8(1): 1–17.

Habbershon, T.G., M. Williams, and I.C. MacMillan. 2003. A Unified Systems Perspective of Family Firm Performance. *Journal of Business Venturing* 18: 451–465.

Hall, B.H., and R. Oriani. 2006. Does the Market Value R&D Investment by European Firms? Evidence from a Panel of Manufacturing firms in France, Germany, and Italy. *International Journal of Industrial Organization* 24(5): 971–993.

Hargadon, A.B., and Y. Douglas. 2001. When Innovations Meet Institutions: Edison and the Design of Electric Light. *Administrative Science Quarterly* 46 (3): 476–501.

Hatch, N.W., and J.H. Dyer. 2004. Human Capital and Learning as a Source of sustainable competitive advantage. *Strategic Management Journal* 25(12): 1155–1178.

Helfat, C.E. 2007. *Dynamic Capabilities: Understanding Strategic Change in Organizations.* Malden, MA: Wiley-Blackwell.

Henderson, R., and K.B. Clark. 1990. Architectural Innovation: The Reconfiguration of Existing Product Technologies and the Failure of Established Firms. *Administrative Science Quarterly* 35(1): 9–30.

Hill, C.W., and S.A. Snell. 1989. Effects of Ownership Structure and Control on Corporate Productivity. *Academy of Management Journal* 32(1): 25–46.

Hitt, M.A., R.D. Ireland, S.M. Camp, and D.L. Sexton. 2002. Strategic Entrepreneurship: Integrating Entrepreneurial and Strategic Management

Perspectives. In *Strategic Entrepreneurship: Creating a New Mindset*, ed. M.A. Hitt, R.D. Ireland, S.M. Camp, and D.L. Sexton, 1–16. Oxford, UK: Wiley-Blackwell.

Hoegl, M., M. Gibbert, and D. Mazursky. 2008. Financial Constraints in Innovation Projects: When is Less More? *Research Policy* 37: 1382–1391.

Hoskisson, R.E., M.A. Hitt, R.A. Johnson, and W. Grossman. 2002. Conflicting Voices, the Effects of Institutional Ownership Heterogeneity and Internal Governance on Corporate Innovation Strategies. *Academy of Management Journal* 45(4): 697–716.

Hosono, K., M. Tomiyama, and T. Miyagawa. 2004. Corporate Governance and Research and Development: Evidence from Japan. *Economics of Innovation and New Technology* 13(2): 141–164.

Jansen, J.J.P., Z. Simsek, and Q. Cao. 2012. Ambidexterity and Performance in Multi-unit Contexts: Cross-level Moderating Effects of Structural and Resource Attributes. *Strategic Management Journal* 33(11): 1286–1303.

Jenkins, M. 2010. Technological Discontinuities and Competitive Advantage: A Historical Perspective on Formula 1 Motor Racing 1950–2006. *Journal of Management Studies* 47(5): 884–910.

Jensen, M.C., and W.H. Meckling. 1976. Theory of the Firm: Managerial Behavior, Agency Costs and Ownership Structure. *Journal of Financial Economics* 3(4): 305–360.

Katila, R. 2002. New Product Search Over Time, Past Ideas in Their Prime? *Academy of Management Journal* 45(5): 995–1010.

König, A., N. Kammerlander, and A. Enders. 2013. The Family Innovator's Dilemma: How Family Influence Affects the Adoption of Discontinuous Technologies by Incumbent Firms. *Academy of Management Review* 38(3): 418–441.

Kotlar, J., and A. De Massis. 2013. Goal Setting in Family Firms: Goal Diversity, Social Interactions, and Collective Commitment to Family-Centered Goals. *Entrepreneurship Theory & Practice* 37(6): 1263–1288.

Kotlar, J., A. De Massis, H. Fang, and F. Frattini. 2014b. Strategic Reference Points in Family Firms. *Small Business Economics* 43(3): 597–619.

Kotlar, J., A. De Massis, F. Frattini, M. Bianchi, and H. Fang. 2013. Technology Acquisition in Family and Nonfamily Firms: A Longitudinal Analysis of Spanish Manufacturing Firms. *Journal of Product Innovation Management* 30 (6): 1073–1088.

Kotlar, J., H. Fang, A. De Massis, and F. Frattini. 2014a. Profitability Goals, Control Goals, and the R&D Investment Decisions of Family and

Non-family Firms. *Journal of Product Innovation Management* 31(6): 1128–1145.

La Porta, R., F. Lopez-de-Silanes, A. Shleifer, and R. Vishny. 1999. Corporate Ownership Around the World. *Journal of Finance* 54(2): 471–517.

Laursen, K., and A. Salter. 2006. Open for Innovation: The Role of Openness in Explaining Innovation Performance among U.K. Manufacturing Firms. *Strategic Management Journal* 27(2): 131–150.

Lavie, D., and I. Drori. 2012. Collaborating for Knowledge Creation and Application: The Case of Nanotechnology Research Programs. *Organization Science* 23(3): 704–724.

Le Breton Miller, I., and D. Miller. 2006. Why Do Some Family Businesses Out Compete? Governance, Long Term Orientations, and Sustainable Capability. *Entrepreneurship Theory and Practice* 30(6): 731–746.

Lee, P.M., and H.M. O'Neil. 2003. Ownership Structures and R&D Investments of U.S. and Japanese Firms: Agency and Stewardship Perspectives. *Academy of Management Journal* 46: 212–225.

Lichtenthaler, U., and E. Lichtenthaler. 2009. A Capability-based Framework for Open Innovation: Complementing Absorptive Capacity. *Journal of Management Studies* 46(8): 1315–1338.

Lin, N. 2001. *Social Capital: A Theory of Social Structure and Action*. Cambridge: Cambridge University Press.

Llach, J., and M. Nordqvist. 2010. Innovation in Family and Non-family Businesses: A Resource Perspective. *International Journal of Entrepreneurial Venturing* 2(3/4): 381–399.

Lumpkin, G.T., and K.H. Brigham. 2011. Long-term Orientation and Intertemporal Choice in Family Firms. *Entrepreneurship Theory and Practice* 35(6): 1149–1169.

Mayer, R.C., J.H. Davis, and F.D. Schoorman. 1995. An Integrative Model of Organizational Trust. *Academy of Management Review* 20(3): 709–734.

Melin, L., and M. Nordqvist. 2007. The Reflexive Dynamics of Institutionalization: The Case of the Family Business. *Strategic Organization* 5(3): 321–333.

Messeni Petruzzelli, A., and V. Albino. 2012. *When Tradition Turns into Innovation. How Firms Can Create and Appropriate Value Through Tradition*. Oxford, UK: Chandos Publishing.

Miller, D., I. Le Breton-Miller, and B. Scholnick. 2008. Stewardship vs. Stagnation: An Empirical Comparison of Small Family and Non-Family Businesses. *Journal of Management Studies* 45(1): 51–78.

Mishra, C.S., and D.L. McConaughy. 1999. Founding Family Control and Capital Structure: The Risk of Loss of Control and the Aversion to Debt. *Entrepreneurship Theory and Practice* 23(4): 53–64.

Munari, F., R. Oriani, and R. Sobrero. 2010. The Effects of Owner Identity and External Governance Systems on R&D Investments: A Study of Western European Firms. *Research Policy* 39(8): 1093–1104.

Nerkar, A. 2003. Old is Gold? The Value of Temporal Exploration in the Creation of New Knowledge. *Management Science* 49(2): 211–229.

Nieto, J., and L. Santamaría. 2010. Technological Collaboration: Bridging the Innovation Gap Between Small and Large Firms. *Journal of Small Business Management* 48(1): 44–69.

O'Reilly, C.A., and M.L. Tushman. 2004. The Ambidextrous Organization. *Harvard Business Review* 82(4): 74–81.

Perkmann, M., V. Tartari, M. McKelvey, E. Autio, A. Broström, P. D'Este, and S. Krabel. 2013. Academic Engagement and Commercialisation: A Review of the Literature on University–Industry Relations. *Research Policy* 42(2): 423–442.

Pertuze, J.A., E.S. Calder, E.M. Greitzer, and W.A. Lucas. 2010. Best Practices for Industry-University Collaboration. *MIT Sloan Management Review* 51(4): 83–90.

Pittaway, L., M. Robertson, K. Munir, and D. Denyer. 2004. Networking and Innovation: A Review of the Evidence Networking and Innovation: A Systematic Review of the Evidence. *International Journal of Management Reviews* 5(3): 137–168.

Ray, G., J. Barney, and W. Muhanna. 2004. Capabilities, Business Processes, and Competitive Advantage: Choosing the Dependent Variable in Empirical Tests of the Resource-Based View. *Strategic Management Journal* 25(1): 23–37.

Robertson, M., J. Swan, and S. Newell. 1996. The Role of Networks in the Diffusion of Technological Innovation. *Journal of Management Studies* 33(3): 333–359.

Romano, C.A. 1990. Identifying Factors Which Influence Product Innovation: A Case Study Approach. *Journal of Management Studies* 27(1): 75–95.

Rothaermel, F.T., and A.M. Hess. 2007. Building Dynamic Capabilities: Innovation Driven by Individual-, firm-, and Network-level Effects. *Organization Science* 18(6): 898–921.

Ryan, R.M., and E.L. Deci. 2000. Self-determination Theory and the Facilitation of Intrinsic Motivation, Social Development, and Well-being. *American Psychologist* 55(1): 68–78.

Santoro, M.D., and S.C. Betts. 2002. Making Industry-University Partnerships Work. *Research-Technology Management* 45(3): 42–46.

Savino, T., A. Messeni Petruzzelli, and V. Albino. 2015. Search and Recombination Process to Innovate: A Review of the Empirical Evidence and a Research Agenda. *International Journal of Management Reviews* 00: 1–22.

Schoorman, F.D., R.C. Mayer, and J.H. Davis. 2007. An Integrative Model of Organizational Trust: Past, Present, and Future. *Academy of Management Review* 32(2): 344–354.

Schulze, W.S., and E.R. Geidajlovic. 2010. Guest Editors' Introduction. Whither Family Business? *Journal of Management Studies* 47(2): 191–204.

Sciascia, S., M. Nordqvist, P. Mazzola, and A. De Massis. 2014. Family Ownership and R&D Intensity in Small and Medium-Sized Firms. *Journal of Product Innovation Management* 32(3): 349–360.

Senyard, J.M., P. Davidsson, T. Baker, and P.R. Steffens. 2011. Resource Constraints in Innovation: The Role of Bricolage in New Venture Creation and Firm Development. In *Proceedings of the 8th AGSE International Entrepreneurship Research Exchange*, ed. A. Maritz, 609–622. Melbourne, VIC: Swinburne University of Technology.

Sharma, P., and M. Nordqvist. 2008. A Classification Scheme for Family Firms: From Family Values to Effective Governance to Firm Performance. In *Family Values and Value Creation: How Do Family-owned Businesses Foster Enduring Values*, ed. J. Tapies and J.L. Ward, 71–101. New York, NY: Palgrave Macmillan.

Sharma, P., C. Salvato, and T. Reay. 2014. Temporal Dimensions of Family Enterprise Research. *Family Business Review* 27(1): 10–19.

Shepherd, D.A., and J.A. Katz. 2004. Innovation and Corporate Entrepreneurship. In *Advances in Entrepreneurship, Firm Emergence and Growth*, ed. D.A. Shepherd and J.A. Katz, 1–6. Bingley: Emerald Group Publishing Limited.

Simsek, Z., C. Heavey, J.F. Veiga, and D. Souder. 2009. A Typology for Aligning Organizational Ambidexterity Conceptualizations, Antecedents and Outcomes. *Journal of Management Studies* 46(5): 864–894.

Sirmon, D.G., and M.A. Hitt. 2003. Managing Resources: Linking Unique Resources, Management, and Wealth Creation in Family Firms. *Entrepreneurship Theory and Practice* 27(4): 339–358.

Steijvers, T., and W. Voordeckers. 2009. Private Family Ownership and the Agency Costs of Debt. *Family Business Review* 22(4): 333–346.

Tagiuri, R., and J. Davis. 1996. Bivalent Attributes of the Family Firm. *Family Business Review* 9(2): 199–208.

Teece, D.J. 2007. Explicating Dynamic Capabilities: The Nature and Microfoundations of (Sustainable) Enterprise Performance. *Strategic Management Journal* 28(13): 1319–1350.

Teece, D.J., G. Pisano, and A. Shuen. 1997. Dynamic Capabilities and Strategic Management. *Strategic Management Journal* 18(7): 509–533.

Toole, A.A., and D. Czarnitzki. 2010. Commercializing Science: Is There a University "Brain Drain" from Academic Entrepreneurship? *Management Science* 56(9): 1599–1614.

Tushman, M.A., and C.A. O'Reilly III. 1996. Ambidextrous Organizations: Managing Evolutionary and Revolutionary Change. *California Management Review* 38(4): 7–30.

Van Beers, C.A., R. Ortt Kleinknecht, and V. Verburg. 2008. *Determinants of Innovative Behaviour: A Firm's Internal Practices and Its External Environment.* Houndmills, UK: Palgrave.

Van De Vrande, V., W. Vanhaverbeke, and G. Duysters. 2009. External Technology Sourcing: The Effect of Uncertainty on Governance Mode Choice. *Journal of Business Venturing* 24(1): 62–80.

Van den Bulte, C., and G.L. Lilien. 2001. Medical Innovation Revisited: Social Contagion Versus Marketing Effort. *American Journal of Sociology* 106(5): 1409–1435.

Verona, G., and D. Ravasi. 2004. Unbundling Dynamic Capabilities: An Exploratory Study of Continuous Product Innovation. *Industrial and Corporate Change* 12(3): 577–606.

Villalonga, B., and R. Amit. 2009. How are US Family Firms Controlled? *Review of Financial Studies* 22(8): 3047–3091.

Wernerfelt, B. 1984. A Resource-based View of the Firm. *Strategic Management Journal* 5(2): 171–180.

West, J., and M. Bogers. 2014. Leveraging External Sources of Innovation: A Review of Research on Open Innovation. *Journal of Product Innovation Management* 31(4): 814–831.

Westhead, P. 1997. Ambitions, External Environment and Strategic Factor Differences Between Family and Non-family Companies. *Entrepreneurship & Regional Development* 9: 127–158.

Westhead, P., and C. Howorth. 2007. Types of Private Family Firms: An Exploratory Conceptual and Empirical Analysis. *Entrepreneurship and Regional Development* 19(5): 405–431.

Wilson, K., and Y.L. Doz. 2011. Agile Innovation: A Footprint Balancing Distance and Immersion. *California Management Review* 53(2): 6–26.

Wright, M., and F. Kellermanns. 2012. Family Firms: A Research Agenda and Publication Guide. *Journal of Family Business Strategy* 2(4): 187–198.

Wu, Z., J.H. Chua, and J.J. Chrisman. 2007. Effects of Family Ownership and Management on Small Business Equity Financing. *Journal of Business Venturing* 22: 875–895.

Zahra, S.A. 1996. Governance, Ownership, and Corporate Entrepreneurship, the Moderating Impact of Industry Technological Opportunities. *Academy of Management Journal* 39: 1713–1735.

———. 2005. Entrepreneurial Risk Taking in Family Firms. *Family Business Review* 18(1): 23–40.

Zahra, S.A., J.C. Hayton, D.O. Neubaum, C. Dibrell, and J. Craig. 2008. Culture of Family Commitment and Strategic Flexibility: The Moderating Effect of Stewardship. *Entrepreneurship Theory and Practice* 32(6): 1035–1054.

Zahra, S.A., J.C. Hayton, and C. Salvato. 2004. Entrepreneurship in Family vs. Non-family Firms: A Resource Based Analysis of the Effect of Organizational Culture. *Entrepreneurship Theory and Practice* 28(4): 363–381.

Zahra, S.A., A.P. Nielsen, and W.C. Bogner. 1999. Corporate Entrepreneurship, Knowledge, and Competence Development. *Entrepreneurship Theory and Practice* 23(3): 169–190.

Zellweger, T. 2007. Time Horizon, Costs of Equity Capital, and Generic Investment Strategies of Firms. *Family Business Review* 20(1): 1–15.

Zellweger, T., R.S. Nason, M. Nordqvist, and C. Brush. 2010. Why Do Family Firms Strive for Nonfinancial Goals? An Organizational Identity Perspective. *Entrepreneurship Theory and Practice* 37(2): 229–248.

Zhang, J., and C. Baden-Fuller. 2010. The Influence of Technological Knowledge Base and Organizational Structure on Technological Collaboration. *Journal of Management Studies* 47(4): 679–704.

9

Responsible Research and Innovation Revisited: Aligning Product Development Processes with the Corporate Responsibility Agenda

Fiona Lettice, Helen Rogers, Emad Yaghmaei, and Kulwant S. Pawar

9.1 Introduction

It is well established that society faces some grand challenges ahead that have led to a call for more focus on sustainability and socially responsible business practices (European Commission 2010, 2012; Scherer and Palazzo 2011). It is now widely accepted that human-induced climate change is caused by production and consumption patterns that have emerged to meet society's evolving needs (Unruh 2000; Foxon and

F. Lettice (✉)
University of East Anglia, Norwich, UK

H. Rogers
Technische Hochschule Nürnberg, Nürnberg, Germany

E. Yaghmaei
University of Southern Denmark, Sonderborg, Denmark

K.S. Pawar
Nottingham University Business School, Nottingham, UK

© The Author(s) 2017   **247**
A. Brem, E. Viardot (eds.), *Revolution of Innovation Management*,
DOI 10.1057/978-1-349-95123-9_9

Pearson 2006). There are increasing amounts of legislation to try to encourage more sustainable practices and to reduce carbon dioxide emissions. For example, the 2008 United Kingdom (UK) Climate Change Act (UK Parliament 2008) states that "It is the duty of the Secretary of State to ensure that the net UK carbon account for the year 2050 is at least 80% lower than the 1990 baseline" (p. 1). Other legislation is encouraging manufacturers to take back and recycle their products at the end of their useful lives.

However, legislation for fostering socially responsible business cases and operating more sustainable practices in industry is still in the developmental phase (Scherer et al. 2006). Such regulatory gaps may be reduced when policy makers motivate industrial stakeholders to integrate social and ethical aspects into research and development (R&D) processes. In essence, industry must be encouraged to work with societal actors across the entire research and development process, particularly during product development, to better align the outcomes of R&D with the values, needs, and expectations of society. The integration of societal values and needs into the product development process is recommended from both a social and a technological perspective. From the technological perspective, such integration could help to develop innovative products and services, while from a social perspective such integration provides socially desirable solutions for society (Beckwith and Huang 2005; Patra 2011).

Thus, the question arises of how we may align societal needs and challenges with the outcomes of product development processes, which typically occur within R&D departments. In fact, carrying out product development processes responsibly and sustainably both benefits the company and contributes to making a better society. As such, companies need to integrate social and ethical aspects into their research and development phase. In this regard, the concept of Responsible Research and Innovation (RRI), a phrase and concept coined by the EU as an inclusive approach, highlights the role of societal actors beyond the present notions of strategic corporate social responsibility (CSR) and social innovation (Iatridis and Schroeder 2016).

The term RRI is a concept that has visibility at the highest levels within the EU policy discourse. This policy is predominantly focused on science, with calls for a transformation "from science *in* society to science *with* and *for* society" (Laroche 2011, cited in Owen et al. 2012: 753) and for policy to support "the best science *for* the world rather than the best science *in* the world" (Owen et al. 2012: 753).

The European Commission (2013) defines the term as follows: "RRI is an inclusive approach to Research and Innovation (R&I), to ensure that societal actors work together during the whole research and innovation process. It aims to better align both the process and outcomes of R&I, with the values, needs and expectations of European society. In general terms, RRI implies anticipating and assessing potential implications and societal expectations with regard to research and innovation."

This government push has also been met by consumer pull for organisations to be more responsible in their behaviour and production processes. For example, the organic and Fairtrade markets have gone from being quite niche segments to more mainstream. In addition, many companies have been publicly challenged over using sweatshops and child labour to produce their goods (Burke 2000; Porter and Kramer 2007). In response, the Corporate Social Responsibility (CSR) agenda has become quite well-established in many organisations, with these firms looking to reduce their environmental and carbon footprints, to sell ethically sourced and manufactured products and to become engaged in national or international community projects to alleviate poverty, improve education and reinvest in the natural environment. In many cases, the CSR agenda exerts pressure on firms to pursue a tripartite of economic, environmental and social performance (Sarkis et al. 2010). This need for sustainable development is forcing companies to reconsider their business models and restructure their entire operations (Brammer and Walker 2011; Wu and Pagell 2011). As such, it is very important to closely align sustainable development because of its long-term perspective with the strategic product development processes of the companies. In this regard, green innovation methods could assist with developing products and services that contribute to sustainable development (Salomo et al. 2007). Strategic CSR plans can be applied into organisational practices to extend sustainable developments (Mcwilliams and Siegel 2001), as social innovation strategies could meet the social and ethical needs of various elements of innovation initiatives (Taatila et al. 2006). Furthermore, in order to best anticipate the social and ethical impacts of new products and services, utilising an inclusive approach such as RRI along the various stages of development can assist by examining the relevant aspects of a company's business model right at the outset.

This paper thus views the concept of RRI as an inclusive approach. In essence, the aim here is to define and describe how RRI can work alongside product development processes to improve and develop a company's CSR agenda.

Considering the fact that the mechanisms and activities of NPD processes support sustainable and responsible development, successful NPD requires the harmonisation of RRI agendas at each stage of the process. Scholars have only recently begun to discuss and understand how industry (and in turn companies) can productively work together with societal actors through applying RRI principles. Therefore, this study is timely as it seeks ways of identifying and managing the harmonisation of the NPD and RRI agendas.

This paper will provide an overview of the history and evolution of the topic, from Concurrent Engineering to RRI and how the term RRI has been used in the literature to date. The key contribution of this paper is to extend the use of the term from science and society to the NPD process. This is achieved by outlining the Responsible Research and Innovation tools and techniques that can be used at each stage of an NPD process and by proposing a future agenda for Responsible Research and Innovation for both research and practice.

9.2   Baseline: Existing Theories and Research in RRI

The origins of RRI can be traced as far back as the 1990s. Here for the first time, there was a focus on the need to dispose of an increasing number of products at the end of their useful lives. This led to consideration of not only Design for Assembly, but also Design for Disassembly (Boothroyd and Alting 1992). This was also the key decade for the rise of Concurrent or Simultaneous Engineering (Pennel and Winner 1989; Riedel and Pawar 1991; Lettice et al. 1995). Organisations sought to become better internally integrated to be able to produce high-quality products reliably and at lower cost in ever faster product development cycles. Leading on from an increased internal integration was a shift to consider external integration. How could the supply chain be better managed and integrated? This was also enabled by new computer and IT technologies that allowed for the sharing of more data between an organisation and its suppliers.

From the late 1990s and early 2000s, there was increasing recognition of the need for innovation to ensure survival and growth in an ever more competitive landscape. The attention shifted from the external integration of suppliers to a stronger customer focus. This led to tackling key issues such as how the "voice of the customer" could be integrated into the product development process (Driva et al. 2000) and understanding how organisations could listen more empathically to their customers to better discover their expressed and latent needs (Adiano and Roth 1994; Leonard and Rayport 1997; Narver et al. 2004). Lead user and user-centred design techniques were being developed and more extensively trialled (Franke et al. 2006).

As we move further into the 2010s, the sustainability movement has become more mainstream and there is increasing research on social entrepreneurship and social innovation in response to the need to tackle some of society's big challenges (Lettice and Parekh 2010; Bridgstock et al. 2010). This has been coupled with a social media revolution, opening up opportunities for different business models and approaches to business and new product development (Kenly and Poston 2012).

The Roots of Responsible Research and Innovation

One of the first researchers to use the term "Responsible Innovation" was Tomas Hellstrøm (2003). His argument was that as well as producing benefits, technological innovation also comes with risks and a feeling that these risks are increasingly likely to overshadow the benefits and in many cases the problems caused may be largely irreversible. Hellstrøm (2003) uses one example of agro-food production to show the complex interplay between science, environment and society. There is for example increasing concern over food security, our ability to feed a growing world population, new technologies such as genetically modified organisms, the effects of subsidies or their removal on farming systems and the increased unpredictability of crops caused by increasingly frequent extreme weather conditions.

In recent years, cases involving firms who operate irresponsibly have been widely reported in the media and have centred on environmental and social issues (Federsel 2006). Quite often when safety issues are picked up by regulators, suppliers to pharmaceutical companies are held accountable, and this in turn forces companies to rethink their procurement practices. Recent incidents involving the suppliers of two global pharmaceutical companies, Pfizer and Baxter, illustrate this point. In 2010, Pfizer recalled drugs made by Claris Life Sciences India from the US market after the Food and Drugs Administration (FDA) found contamination in the antibiotic and anti-nausea drug developed by the Indian supplier. Soon after, the facility in Ahmedabad was closed by the FDA. The FDA's investigation of Baxter's Heparin led them to the suppliers of the active ingredient, which had been manufactured in China. At least 10 Chinese companies were involved in the supply chain for contaminated Heparin. Subsequently, the FDA tracked further companies that made or handled products contaminated with Heparin-like substances from Chinese suppliers.

When such cases occur, drugs must be recalled and destroyed, suppliers' facilities are quarantined, the risk of supply disruptions is almost certain, financial liabilities are significant and corporate image issues can be devastating. Responsibility can also be viewed as a liability in which stakeholders are perceived to have actively engaged in causing an injustice and are held responsible for any consequences (Wickert 2014). In the disaster of the factory collapse in Bangladesh in 2013, where five clothes factories located in the Rana Plaza building were destroyed, human rights and labour standards within Bangladeshi sweatshops were heavily criticised. The US, Canadian and European clothing companies and retailers, the owners of sweatshops in Bangladesh and the governmental authorities were all deemed responsible for the conditions. These actors were culpable for the poor environmental conditions and working standards in the Bangladeshi sweatshops because they had not enforced regulations or had denied social responsibilities within their supply chains. Responsible Research and Innovation should, however, extend along a company's entire value chain (Porcari et al. 2015) and all stakeholders should be liable for any of the consequences of "irresponsible research and innovation." These examples and incidents combine to give a "complex array of human needs, economic interests, techno-scientific uncertainties, and political responsibilities" (Hellstrøm 2003: 375) and competing stakeholder priorities. Hellstrøm calls for the need to consider risk and unintended consequences throughout the innovation cycle, using extended peer communities to help with identifying the risks and consequences of proposed new technologies. He advocates the development of a framework for the "preventive foresight and governance of Responsible Innovation" (ibid, p. 382).

Another early paper on the topic was by Guston (2006), who proposed that universities need to be responsible and attach public value to their innovations and "add societal implications components to natural science research and training proposals" (Ibid p. 21). The next wave of literature on Responsible Innovation starts in 2008 with Ishizu et al.'s (2008) focus on the potential societal impacts of nanotechnology. Nanotechnology is widely expected to contribute to progress, future innovation and benefits to society, but it is not without its environmental, health, economic and ethical impacts. They call for responsible R&D for parties involved in nanotechnology development, which means being aware of and responding to society's needs and concerns surrounding the new technologies. They also call for collaboration around standard-setting, to help reduce any risks.

Owen et al. (2009) also recognise that we are entering an era where there is a "growing awareness of the need to innovate, but to innovate responsibly" (Ibid, p. 6902). They state the importance of government-led regulation, which has been instrumental in improving air and water quality and reducing exposure to contaminants such as pesticides and heavy metals, but also identify that this process is slow and lags innovative developments. This is a concern as once products are released, it is very hard to retract them, even when risks have been identified. The authors call for better foresight and tools including horizon scanning and risk governance mechanisms such as insurance to complement regulatory mechanisms. Their key message is for much stronger risk management around the upstream development of new technologies and innovations to promote responsible and sustainable development in a proactive way (Owen and Goldberg 2010).

Another widely circulated definition of RRI has been presented by von Schomberg (2011a) as:

> Responsible Research and Innovation is a transparent, interactive process by which societal actors and innovators become mutually responsive to each other with a view to the (ethical) acceptability, sustainability and societal desirability of the innovation process and its marketable products (in order to allow a proper embedding of scientific and technological advances in our society).

In other words, von Schomberg's definition suggests that key RRI actors should work together on a set of moral values to harmonise the business and RRI agendas. A recent report from a group of experts in the EC identified different indicators to evaluate the impacts of RRI initiatives and to assess their performance in relation to social responsibility goals (European Commission 2015). Additionally, Oftedal (2014: 2) argues that "philosophy of science (should be) a central feature of RRI, not least because openness, transparency, and a broader involvement in research and innovation will require methods, assumptions, and values in research to be explicit, understood, and discussed."

To summarise, while the extant RRI literature generally tends to focus on the development of practices associated with science and its engagement with society, there are some emergent studies that seek to align this RRI agenda with business initiatives (Lettice et al. 2013; Flipse et al. 2013; Yaghmaei 2015). In line with this, we take the broad guidelines developed by those researching and writing about RRI, but rather than continue to focus on the development of theory, we instead shift the focus onto product development processes within organisations, where we believe RRI practices are equally important.

9.3   Research Approach

For this research, we have carried out an extensive literature review on RRI to trace the development of the concept and its meaning. From this, we concluded that the term has been used mainly for science and for those scientists involved in emerging technologies and discoveries such as nano-technologies, pharmaceutical drug discovery and development, geoengineering, information and communication technologies, and security technologies (Von Schomberg 2011b). We have then used this as a basis to argue for the concept to be extended into the product development process across multiple sectors and organisations, not just universities and high-technology R&D laboratories. What follows is the presentation of a framework to apply the principles of RRI to the new product development process. This conceptual work requires empirical testing, which we acknowledge in the conclusions and agenda for future research on this emergent topic.

9.4   Responsible Research and Innovation in the New Product Development Process: Initial Findings

There are many different ways of conceptualising the product development process. For the purposes of this paper, we will use Cooper's (1990) widely adopted, Stage Gate Process. He identifies that after an initial (0) discovery stage, there is (1) a scoping stage, (2) a build-the-business-case stage, (3) a development stage, (4) a testing and validation stage and then (5) a launch stage. For an organisation to be more responsible, we consider some of the mechanisms that can be used or activities that can be completed to ensure that a more responsible approach is taken. Checklists to ensure that these happen can be built into the Stage Gate Process.

Discovery Stage

The discovery stage is where activities are focused on identifying opportunities and generating new product ideas. This stage is the best opportunity for organisations to consider how they can develop responsible innovations. Just as within the scientific domain, this stage is ideal for engaging the public, customers, suppliers and a broad range of external stakeholders. This can be achieved by using traditional market research techniques, such as surveys and focus groups. However, more organisations are starting to experiment with new technology-enabled methods such as "Enterprise 2.0" or "Crowdsourcing" (Howe 2006), also sometimes referred to as "interactive value creation" (Reichwald and Piller 2009). An example of such an approach can be found in the pharmaceutical industry, where an independent web platform links large pharmaceutical MNEs with external individuals who offer corresponding problem solutions for a fee. The business scenario is quite simple: the enterprise is looking for a solution to a problem which cannot be solved by the internal R&D department; it presents the problem with a description on an independent organisation's web platform and offers a reward (remuneration) to the person solving the problem best within a specified time span.

Some organisations are using formal strategies to promote more external engagement, and this has been termed open innovation (Chesbrough 2006; West et al. 2014). A famous example is Proctor and Gamble's Connect and Develop programme (www.pg.com/connect_develop) where they have increased the number of innovations sourced from outside their organisation to over 50%. There has also been a growth in the number of websites that connect organisations with inventors, such as Innocentive (www.innocentive.com) and Ninesigma (www.ninesigma.com).

There has been some debate over whether or not such crowdsourcing techniques work and whether users or non-experts can develop better new product ideas than experts or professionals. Nonetheless, many companies have been experimenting with these approaches, including Dell, Threadless (t-shirts), Apache/Linux, Muji and 3M. In a study on baby products, Poetz and Schreier (2012) found that users generally came up with better solutions that met customer needs, although these proposed solutions may be slightly less feasible. They conclude that depending on the complexity of knowledge needed, which will depend on the industry sector or product category, users can be a good source of new ideas for the NPD pipeline. However, it is important that organisations using this approach frame the problem well, provide appropriate incentives, have the means and the right people to filter and select a wide range of ideas, and carefully manage any intellectual property issues. User-centred approaches such as human-centred design, human-driven design, and participatory design (Niemelä et al. 2014) help to activate stakeholder engagement in research and innovation activities (Porcari et al. 2015).

Sets of tools that can help to frame the problem are now emerging (Lettice and Parekh 2010). These include aspects such as changing the lens, scenario planning and scanning the periphery. Additionally, informal social media tools are being adopted at this stage of the process. Kenly and Poston (2012) found that companies are using social media and Web 2.0 tools to generate new product ideas and requirements at lower cost. They are also using the tools to monitor social networks for customer needs and to gauge the market's perception of brand. But a significant proportion of companies surveyed reported that they lack the internal expertise or best practices required to use these techniques.

At this stage, ideas can be sought from a wide range of stakeholders and tested to see if they are responsible or whether there are too many risks to pursue. By framing good problems that are focused around social responsibility, the pursuit of more Responsible Innovation can be realised. Although social media and Web 2.0 tools are being used, there is a need for more research to see how these tools can be better designed to gather and process product ideas and to identify and share best practice as it emerges.

Scoping Stage

The scoping stage is an assessment of the technical merits of a product and its potential market. Increasingly, as companies put CSR policies into practice, an ethical assessment of the product is also required at this stage.

This typically entails a detailed risk assessment of the societal and environmental impacts and corresponding risks of the product under development. Although there will be many uncertainties, making risks difficult to quantify, by paying attention to these aspects, Responsible Innovation will be easier to achieve. It is especially helpful if focus group opinion can be obtained at this early stage. However, these additional requirements will add costs.

Build the Business Case Stage

This is the feasibility stage to ensure that the project has a good product definition, a strong justification and a plan for delivery. Here, the focus is typically on the technical, market and financial feasibility of the product. For Responsible Innovation, the ethical and environmental feasibility of the product and associated manufacturing and consumption processes should also be considered. Increasingly, more organisations are relying on sourcing raw materials and components from external sources, often from obscure locations. As argued earlier, sometimes the inappropriate and unethical actions of suppliers can seriously damage the image and reputation of large multinational enterprises. Therefore, organisations have to move beyond their legal, environmental and social obligations, as stipulated by CSR directives and guidelines. There are many examples where suppliers, in their desire to increase profit margins, exhibit socially irresponsible behaviours, such as employing child labour, exploiting employees, putting consumers at risk, poisoning the environment and violating regulatory laws.

At this stage, different business models can be considered. For example, there are increasing trends towards product service systems (Baines et al. 2007). For example, Du Pont have shifted from selling floor coverings to providing total servicing to customers including installation, tailored maintenance, take back and recycling. This is coupled with another similar concept: collaborative consumption. New technology enables consumers to form peer communities to share, barter, lend, trade, rent and swap products to enable more sustainable and responsible consumption patterns.

Development Stage

The development stage is when the actual design and development of the product occurs. Raw materials should be sourced appropriately. They should be created in safe facilities by workers who are well-treated and paid suitable wages to work legal hours. Care needs to be taken not to use child labour and prison workers. Cases such as IKEA in Eastern Europe and Apple in China have shown that it is not always straightforward for organisations to achieve these standards throughout their supply chains. The suppliers also need to respect the environment in the manufacture of the products, using materials from sustainable sources and implementing effective pollution and emissions measures and controls.

Testing and Validation Stage

Here the entire project is examined, including the product itself, the manufacturing processes, customer acceptance and the economics of the project. Care should be taken to incorporate the holistic issues covered in the earlier stages of the NPD process.

Moreover, this stage requires ensuring that the product lives up to the claims being made. The product needs to be reliable, maintainable and safe to ensure that customers will not be injured by defective products. High-profile examples of using lead paint for toys from third-party suppliers, e.g. Mattel (www.nytimes.com/2007/08/02/business/02toy.html) and others (http://www.telegraph.co.uk/news/worldnews/asia/china/8944028/One-third-of-Chinese-toys-contain-heavy-metals.html), have shown that this is not always achieved throughout the supply chain. In addition, organisations need to ensure that they are not violating patent, trademark or copyright laws. For some industrial sectors, ensuring that there is no animal testing or experimentation might also be important.

As well as the typical technical and marketing requirements testing, there need to be processes to ensure ethical and environmental standards are met. Waste reduction, recycling and reuse options need to be monitored and improved and detailed life cycle analyses performed to safeguard that the products meet standards at all stages of the lifecycle.

Launch Stage

This stage is the full commercialisation of the product, the beginning of full production and commercial launch. Global consumers are increasingly expressing that they want brands to do well while doing good and prefer to buy from organisations that are supporting good causes than to buy from those that are not (Edelman 2012). In the fashion sector, Marks and Spencer, H&M and Uniqlo provide opportunities for their customers to recycle and donate old clothes to charity, which promotes environmental sustainability and supports people living in poverty. Innocent drinks have launched the Big Knit to support older people during the colder winter months. Supporters of the brand and the cause knit woolly hats for the smoothie bottles and 25p from every hatted bottle sold goes to Age UK, which raised over £1m in 2012 (www.innocentdrinks.co.uk/bigknit). These are examples of encouraging responsible consumerism.

In addition, organisations should make sure that when their products are launched, sufficient information is available to consumers to allow them to make informed decisions and hence purchases. Much eco-labelling is voluntary, but some global and local standards have emerged, such as the Fairtrade label, the Forest Stewardship Council (FSC) for wood-based products from sustainably managed forests and the Marine Stewardship Council (MSC) for sustainable fishing. The European Commission introduced the EU Eco Label in 1992 as a badge to show that organisations adhere to high standards of environmental performance and quality. The take-up of the labelling is mixed, and the proliferation of labels can be confusing, but with time they should help with the move towards more sustainable and responsible consumption of RRI.

Collectively, we find that a common feature of successful NPD while the company progresses through its stages is the fulfilment of mechanisms and activities of each stage. Effective NPD enables more robust product development processes, which in turn result in better end products and

Table 9.1 Mechanisms and activities for each stage of the NPD process

Stage	Mechanisms and Activities
0 Discovery	• Engage a broad range of stakeholders including: surveys, focus groups, crowdsourcing, open innovation, social media, Web 2.0, online forums, etc. • Monitor trends, gather and process product ideas, identify and share best practice
1 Scoping	• Carry out risk assessment in terms of all major aspects such as market, technical (inc. cyber risk), ethical, societal and environmental impacts and risks of product ideas
2 Build the business case	• Ethical and environmental feasibility: extend beyond CSR and into supply chain and supply networks, taking into account supply chain complexity • Product service systems and collaborative consumption
3 Development	• Raw materials from safe facilities and not using child and/or prison labourers • Sustainability factors: sustainable sources, effective pollution and emissions measures and controls throughout the supply chain
4 Testing and validation	• Product/service needs to be reliable, maintainable and safe • Legal factors: not violating patent, trademark or copyright laws • Life cycle factors: detailed life cycle analyses and ensuring waste reduction, recycling and reuse options monitored and improved
5 Launch	• Finishing touches—explore and encourage key aspects to build an ongoing customer relationship, e.g. through information on responsible consumerism, eco-labelling, country of origin, etc.

services. The various mechanisms and activities for each developmental stage are summarised in Table 9.1.

The biggest opportunities to influence RRI lie in the earlier stages of the innovation cycle, which is illustrated graphically in Fig. 9.1. In the later stages, assessments can be made to check that the highest standards are being met. Labelling can also help consumers to identify and then purchase the products of RRI processes. Well-known examples of this are dolphin-friendly labels on tuna cans, Fairtrade coffee, water usage levels during manufacturing, eco textile labelling and associated country of origin information.

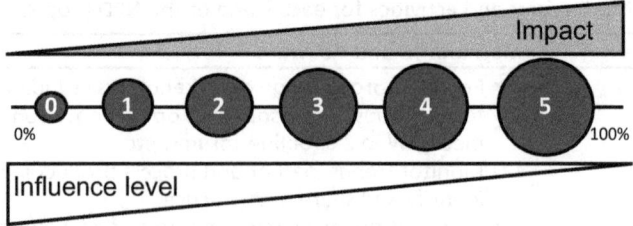

Fig. 9.1   The relative impact and influence by stage of NPD process

9.5   Conclusion and Revised Agenda for Future Research and Practice

The focus thus far has been on RRI for science and particularly around the development of genomics, nanotechnologies, geo-engineering, synthetic biology and ICTs (Owen et al. 2012). There has been a call for more public or civic engagement in the upstream science phases, to help foresee unintended consequences or risks and to reduce public misunderstanding of these new technologies. There has also been a call for more risk management techniques and mechanisms to identify and better mitigate these risks. This does not aim to replace government-led regulation, but instead helps to shorten the lag between the ever-faster development of new technologies and the slower speed at which government regulation can be enacted.

In this paper, we identified some ways in which mechanisms and activities can be introduced at key stages in the new product development process to move towards more Responsible Research and Innovation.

At each stage of the product development process, there are opportunities for companies to consider aspects of Responsible Research and Innovation. As well as focusing internally, the company needs to take into consideration consumers and the corresponding supply chain activities needed to transform traditional innovation practices to RRI practices. Companies need to manage RRI activities at each stage along the new product development process by addressing the main dimensions of RRI, including: RRI awareness, RRI implementation and RRI assessment (Yaghmaei 2015).

New technologies will inevitably enable more solutions towards Responsible Research and Innovation. But with all new innovation, a risk assessment is required with wide stakeholder involvement to ensure that risks and unintended consequences are identified and mitigated. Reflecting RRI into NPD processes still needs to be enriched in many ways. There has been some progress in applying RRI instruments within the nanotechnology industry (e.g. Malsch et al. 2012) but these are so far limited. For future NPD research and innovation projects, as highlighted throughout this paper, responsible research and innovation practices play a vital role. In fact, it is important to emphasize that inclusion of an RRI agenda into NPD processes is in many ways inevitable and companies need to try to embed responsible practices as a matter of routine. Many of the tools, techniques and approaches outlined in this paper are not new. However, their use in an integrated way across the product development process is to be encouraged. Organisations are experimenting with different techniques and some will be more or less suitable depending on the specific product and sector of application. A better understanding of which tools to use and when is therefore needed as a matter of some urgency.

In line with our findings and reflections on RRI and NPD, we propose the following research agenda:

1. Undertake an ongoing literature review of developments in RRI during NPD

   - reflect on lessons learnt from CSR—bring in RRI principles to organisational processes
   - broaden the scope to encompass relevant elements of associated areas such as green innovation, bottom of the pyramid approaches, the circular economy, social entrepreneurship and the role of open innovation in addressing societal challenges
   - develop a structured and thorough classification, highlighting current state of the art themes and dominant research streams
   - ensure that the potential influence of public policy changes and developments is taken into account (e.g. EU directives)
   - this could form a data repository that could be made available via a wiki-style website that will then be able to grow outside of a specific project

2. Gain practical insights through primary research

- identify and target experts from both industry and academia to gauge RRI readiness for NPD
- both survey (via a large scale online questionnaires) and in-depth interviews with a global reach should be undertaken
- questions should be based on eliciting information on key activities for each stage of the NPD process (as listed in Table 9.1)
- analyse from the perspective of empirically based comparative studies on an international basis
- identify the key activities and performance measures for RRI and NPD

3. Develop an RRI for NPD maturity assessment tool

- incorporate technology risk assessment and ethical reflexivity and harmonise both the RRI and business agendas
- in this way—provided multiple industry sectors have participated—a rich picture of the differing requirements by sector is likely to emerge
- this tool would provide the foundations for more informed decision making, given multiple stakeholder perspectives obtained from steps 1 and 2

4. Develop strategies for future planning and implementation

- determine how this assessment tool could be further developed and implemented in a variety of contexts (depending on company size, experience, stakeholder reach, etc.)
- will this lead to the need to develop new tools or add functionality to existing tools and techniques?
- consider how such an assessment tool could incorporate self-learning, using inputs from the data repository/wiki site proposed in step 1.

In summary, we call for extending Responsible Research and Innovation thinking and practices beyond universities and high-technology industries to all sectors that are innovating and are involved in developing new products and services (for both public and private sector organisations). This is an extension of the corporate social responsibility agenda with the aim of more fully embracing RRI concepts at all stages of the new product development process.

Acknowledgements This book chapter was originally published as a conference paper: Lettice F, Pawar P, and Rogers H. 2013. Responsible Innovation: What Challenges Does it Pose for the New Product Development Process? *19th International Concurrent Enterprising (ICE) Conference*, The Hague, 24–26 June.

Furthermore, part of the work presented in this chapter received funding from the European Community's Seventh Framework Programme (FP7/2007–2013) under grant agreement n° 609817 (Responsible-Industry; www.responsible-industry.eu).

References

Adiano, C., and A.V. Roth. 1994. Beyond the House of Quality: Dynamic QFD. *Benchmarking for Quality Management and Technology* 1(1): 25–37.

Baines, T., H. Lightfoot, S. Evans, A. Neely, R. Greenough, J. Peppard, R. Roy, E. Shehab, A. Braganza, A. Tiwari, et al. 2007. State-of-the-Art in Product Service Systems. *Proceedings of IMechE Part B: Engineering Manufacture* 221: 1–10.

Beckwith, J., and F. Huang. 2005. Should We Make A Fuss? A Case for Social Responsibility in Science. *Nature Biotechnology* 23(12): 1479–1480.

Boothroyd, G., and L. Alting. 1992. Design for Assembly and Disassembly. *CIRP Annals—Manufacturing Technology* 41(2): 625–636.

Brammer, S., and H. Walker. 2011. Sustainable Procurement in the Public Sector: An International Comparative Study. *International Journal of Operations and Production Management* 31(4): 452–476.

Bridgstock, R., F. Lettice, O. Ozbilgin, and A. Tatli. 2010. Diversity Management for Innovation in Social Enterprises in the UK. *Entrepreneurship and Regional Development* 22(6): 557–574.

Burke, J. 2000. Child Labor Scandal hits Adidas. *The Observer*. Accessed February, 2015. http://www.guardian.co.uk/uk/2000/nov/19/jasonburke.theobserver

Chesbrough, H. 2006. Open Innovation: A New Paradigm for Understanding Industrial Innovation. In *Open Innovation: Researching a New Paradigm*, ed. H. Chesbrough, W. Vanhaverbeke, and J. West, 1–12. Oxford: Oxford University Press.

Cooper, R.G. 1990. Stage-Gate Systems: A New Tool for Managing New Products. *Business Horizons* 33(3): 44–54.

Driva, H., K.S. Pawar, and U. Menon. 2000. Measuring Product Development Performance in Manufacturing Organisations. *International Journal of Production Economics* 63: 147–159.

Edelman. 2012. Edelman's Fifth Good Purpose Study. *www.purpose.edelman.com*. Accessed February 2015.

European Commission. 2010. COM (2010) 2020: Europe 2020—A Strategy for Smart, Sustainable and Inclusive Growth. http://ec.europa.eu/eu2020/

———. 2012. *Investing in Research and Innovation for Grand Challenges*. Brussels: European Commission, DG Research http://ec.europa.eu/research/erab/pdf/erab-study-grand-challanges-2012_en.pdf

———. 2013. *Options for Strengthening Responsible Research and Innovation*. Luxembourg: Publications Office of the European Union.

———. 2015. Indicators for Promoting and Monitoring Responsible Research and Innovation. *DG for Research and Innovation*. doi:10.2777/9742.

Federsel, H.J. 2006. In Search of Sustainability: Process R&D in Light of Current Pharmaceutical Industry Challenges. *Drug Discovery Today* 11 (21/22): 966–974.

Flipse, S.M., M.C.A. Van der Sanden, and P. Osseweijer. 2013. Improving Industrial R&D Practices with Social and Ethical Aspects: Aligning Key Performance Indicators with Social and Ethical Aspects in Food Technology R&D. *Technological Forecasting & Social Change*. doi:10.1016/j.techfore.2013.08.009.

Foxon, T.J., and P J. Pearson. 2006. Policy Processes for Low Carbon Innovations in the UK: Successes, Failures and Lessons. University of Cambridge, Department of Land Economy, Environmental Economy and Policy Research, *Discussion Paper Series*, November.

Franke, N., E. von Hippel, and M. Schreier. 2006. Finding Commercially Attractive User Innovations: A Test of Lead-User Theory. *Journal of Product Innovation Management* 23(4): 301–315.

Guston, D. H. 2006. Responsible Knowledge-Based Innovation. *Society*, May–June, 19–21.

Hellstrøm, T. 2003. Systemic Innovation and Risk: Technology Assessment and the Challenge of Responsible Innovation. *Technology in Society* 25: 369–384.

Howe, J. 2006. The Rise of Crowdsourcing. *Wired No. 14*, June.

Iatridis, K., and D. Schroeder. 2016. Responsible Research and Innovation. The Case for Corporate Responsibility Tools. *Springer*. doi:10.1007/978-3-319-21693-5.

Ishizu, S., M. Sekiya, K. Ishibashi, Y. Negami, and M. Ata. 2008. Toward the Responsible Innovation with the Nanotechnology in Japan: Our Scope. *Journal of Nanopart Research* 10: 229–254.

Kenly, A., and B. Poston. 2012. Social Media and Product Innovation: Early Adopters Reaping Benefits Amidst Challenge and Uncertainty. *Kalypso White Paper*.

Leonard, D., and J.F. Rayport. 1997. Spark Innovation through Empathic Design. *Harvard Business Review*, November–December, 102–113.

Lettice, F., and M. Parekh. 2010. The Social Innovation Process: Themes, Challenges and Implications for Practice. *International Journal of Technology Management* 51(1/2): 139–158.

Lettice, F., P. Pawar, and H. Rogers. 2013. Responsible Innovation: What Challenges Does it Pose for the New Product Development Process? In *19th International Concurrent Enterprising (ICE) Conference*, The Hague, 24–26 June

Lettice, F., P. Smart, and S. Evans. 1995. A Workbook-Based Methodology for Implementing Concurrent Engineering. *International Journal of Industrial Ergonomics* 16(4–6): 339–351.

Malsch, I., A. Grinbaum, V. Bontems, and A. M. Fruelund Anderson. 2012. Communicating Nanoethics. Accessed October 21, 2015. http://ethicschool.nl/_files/Communicatingnanoethicsreportfinal.pdf

Mcwilliams, A., and D. Siegel. 2001. Corporate Social Responsibility: A Theory of the Firm Perspective. *Academy of Management Review* 26(1): 117–127.

Narver, J.C., S.F. Slater, and D.L. MacLachlan. 2004. Responsive and Proactive Market Orientation and New-Product Success. *Journal of Product Innovation Management* 21(5): 334–347.

Niemelä, M., V. Ikonen, J. Leikas, K. Kantola, M. Kulju, A. Tammela, and M. Ylikauppila. 2014. Human-Driven Design: A Human- Driven Approach to the Design of Technology. In *ICT and Society. 11th IFIP TC 9 International Conference on Human Choice and Computers, HCC11 2014*, Turku, 30 July–1 August 2014, ed. Kai Kimppa, Diane Whitehouse, Tiina Kuusela, and Jackie Phahlamohlaka, 78–91. Springer Berlin Heidelberg.

Oftedal, G. 2014. The Role of Philosophy of Science in Responsible Research and Innovation (RRI): The Case of Nanomedicine. *Life Sciences, Society and Policy* 10(1): 1–12.

Owen, R., and N. Goldberg. 2010. Responsible Innovation: A Pilot Study with the UK Engineering and Physical Sciences Research Council. *Risk Analysis* 30 (11): 1699–1707.

Owen, R., D. Baxter, T. Maynard, and M. Depledge. 2009. Beyond Regulation: Risk Pricing and Responsible Innovation. *Environmental Science and Technology* 43: 6902–6906.

Owen, R., P. Macnaghten, and J. Stilgoe. 2012. Responsible Research and Innovation: From Science in Society to Science for Society, With Society. *Science and Public Policy* 39: 751–760.

Patra, D. 2011. Responsible Development of Nanoscience and Nanotechnology: Contextualizing Socio-technical Integration into the Nanofabrication Laboratories in the USA. *NanoEthics* 5(2): 143–157.

Pennel, J.P., and R.I. Winner. 1989. Concurrent Engineering: Practices and Prospects. Institute for Defense Analyses. In *IEEE Global Telecommunications Conference and Exhibition Part 1*, November 27–30, 647–655.

Poetz, M.K., and M. Schreier. 2012. The Value of Crowdsourcing: Can Users Really Compete with Professionals in Generating New Product Ideas? *Journal of Product Innovation Management* 29(2): 245–256.

Porcari, A., E. Borsella, E. Mantovani. 2015. A Framework for Implementing Responsible Research and Innovation in ICT for an Ageing Society. Published under the Responsible-Industry Project as Deliverable D2.4 for Work Package 2 (WP2). In The Science in Society (SiS) Area (Grant Agreement 609817).

Porter, M.E., and M.R. Kramer. 2007. Strategy and Society. The Link between Competitive Advantage and Corporate Social Responsibility. *Harvard Business Review*: 85, 136–137.

Reichwald, R., and F. Piller. 2009. *Interaktive Wertschöpfung. Open Innovation, Individualisierung und neue Formen der Arbeitsteilung*. Wiesbaden: Gabler.

Riedel, J., and K.S. Pawar. 1991. The Strategic Choice of Simultaneous vs. Sequential Engineering for the Introduction of New Products. *International Journal of Technology Management* 6(3/4): 321–334.

Salomo, S., J. Weise, and H.G. Gemuenden. 2007. NPD Planning Activities and Innovation Performance: The Mediating Role of Process Management and the Moderating Effect of Product Innovativeness. *Product Innovation Management* 24: 285–302.

Sarkis, J., P. Gonzalez-Torre, and B. Adenso-Diaz. 2010. Stakeholder Pressure and the Adoption of Environmental Practices: The Mediating Effect of Training. *Journal of Operations Management* 28(2): 163–176.

Scherer, A., and G. Palazzo. 2011. The New Political Role of Business in a Globalized World: A Review of a New Perspective on CSR and Its Implications for the Firm, Governance, and Democracy. *Journal of Management Studies* 48: 899–931.

Scherer, A., G. Palazzo, and D. Baumann. 2006. Global Rules and Private Actors: Towards a New Role of the Transnational Corporation in Global Governance. *Business Ethics Quarterly* 16: 505–532.

Taatila, V.P., J. Soumala, R. Siltala, and S. Keshinen. 2006. Framework to Study the Social Innovation Networks. *European Journal of Innovation Management* 9(3): 312–326.

UK Parliament. 2008. *Climate Change Act 2008*. London: The Stationery Office.

Unruh, G.C. 2000. Understanding Carbon Lock-in. *Energy Policy* 28: 817–830.

von Schomberg, R. (2011a). Prospects for Technology Assessment in a Framework of Responsible Research and Innovation. In *Technikfolgen abschatzen lehren: Bildungspotenziale transdisziplinarer Methode*, ed. M. Dusseldorp and R. Beecroft, 39–61, Wiesbaden: Springer VS.

———., ed. 2011b. *Towards Responsible Research and Innovation in the Information and Communication Technologies and Security Technologies Fields*. Luxembourg: Publications Office of the European Union. http://ec.europa.eu/research/science-society/document_library/pdf_06/.mep-rapport-2011_en.pdf

West, J., A. Salter, W. Vanhaverbekec, and H. Chesbrough. 2014. Open Innovation: The Next Decade. *Research Policy* 43(5): 805–811.

Wickert, C. 2014. Political Corporate Social Responsibility in Small- and Medium-Sized Enterprises: A Conceptual Framework. *Business & Society* 55 (6): 1–33. doi:10.1177/0007650314537021.

Wu, Z., and M. Pagell. 2011. Balancing Priorities: Decision-Making in Sustainable Supply Chain Management. *Journal of Operations Management* 29(6): 577–590.

Yaghmaei, E. 2015. Addressing Responsible Research and Innovation to Industry—Introduction of a Conceptual Framework. *SIGCAS Computers and Society, ACM Digital Library* 45(3): 294–300.

Index

Note: Page numbers with "n" denote notes.